THE WTO CASE LAW OF 2002
THE AMERICAN LAW INSTITUTE
REPORTERS' STUDIES

This book is the second in a series of annual volumes that will be utilized in the development of an American Law Institute (ALI) project on World Trade Organisation Law. The volumes undertake yearly analysis of the case law from the adjudicating bodies of the WTO. The Reporters' Studies for 2002 cover a wide range of WTO law ranging from classic trade in goods issues to intellectual property protection. Each of the cases is jointly evaluated by an economist and a lawyer, both well-known experts in the field of trade law and international economics. The Reporters critically review the jurisprudence of WTO adjudicating bodies and evaluate whether the ruling "makes sense" from an economic as well as a legal point of view, and, if not, whether the problem lies in the interpretation of the law or the law itself. The Studies do not always cover all issues discussed in a case, but they seek to discuss both the procedural and the substantive issues that form, in the reporters' view, the core of the dispute.

HENRIK HORN is Professor of International Economics at the Institute for International Economic Studies, Stockholm University. He is a member of the Editorial Board of the World Trade Review and is a member of the Centre of Economic Policy Research. He has previously worked for the Economic Research and Analysis Division of the World Trade Organization, and has been a judge in the Swedish Market Court (supreme court for competition law).

PETROS C. MAVROIDIS is Edwin B. Parker Professor of Law at Columbia Law School, Professor at the University of Neuchâtel, and a member of the Centre for Economic Policy Research. He was previously Chair of Competition Law, EUI, Florence, and a member of the Legal Affairs Division of the World Trade Organization.

THE WTO CASE LAW OF 2002

The American Law Institute
Reporters' Studies

Edited by

HENRIK HORN

AND

PETROS C. MAVROIDIS

CAMBRIDGE
UNIVERSITY PRESS

CAMBRIDGE UNIVERSITY PRESS

Cambridge, New York, Melbourne, Madrid, Cape Town, Singapore, São Paulo

Cambridge University Press

The Edinburgh Building, Cambridge, CB2 2RU, UK

PUBLISHED IN THE UNITED STATES OF AMERICA BY CAMBRIDGE UNIVERSITY PRESS,

NEW YORK

www.cambridge.org

Information on this title: www.cambridge.org/9780521834223

First published 2005

Printed in the United Kingdom at the University Press, Cambridge

A catalogue record for this book is available from the British Library

ISBN 0 521 83422 8 hardback

CONTENTS

FOREWORD

This is the second volume in the American Law Institute's effort to contribute to the development of the law of world trade.

In 2004 we published The WTO Case Law of 2001, analyses by distinguished economists and law professors of the decisions rendered by the adjudicating bodies of the WTO in 2001. This book contains analyses of the 2002 decisions. As with the earlier year's work, the draft chapters were analyzed at a meeting of all the Reporters in October 2003. They were then further reviewed and criticized by an international group of experts on the law and economics of the world trading system at a two-day invitational conference in February 2004.

We expect to generate and publish one additional set of studies, discussing the WTO decisions of 2003. Our plan is then to attempt to draft general principles of the law of trade. We believe that we can author principles that will contribute to international discussion and assist the development of a sophisticated and coherent body of law in this growing field.

The analyses in the book are the work of the participating Reporters and not of The American Law Institute. We are grateful to the Reporters and to those who have supplied constructive criticism of earlier drafts. We are also grateful for financial support from Jan Wallander's and Tom Hedelius' Research Foundation, Svenska Handelsbanken, Stockholm, and from the Milton and Miriam Handler Foundation.

Lance Liebman
Director
The American Law Institute

A note on the American Law Institute

The American Law Institute was founded in 1923 and is based in Philadelphia. The Institute, through a careful and deliberative process, drafts and then publishes various restatements of the law, model codes, and other proposals for legal reform "to promote the clarification and simplification of the law and its better adaptation to social needs, to secure the better administration of justice, and to encourage and carry on scholarly and scientific legal work." Its membership consists of judges, practicing lawyers, and legal scholars from all areas of the United States as well as some foreign countries, selected on the basis of professional achievement and demonstrated interest in the improvement of the law. The Institute's incorporators included Chief Justice and former President William Howard Taft, future Chief Justice Charles Evans Hughes, and former Secretary of State Elihu Root. Judges Benjamin N. Cardozo and Learned Hand were among its early leaders.

The Institute's restatements, model codes, and legal studies are used as references by the entire legal profession.

The American Law Institute http://www.ali.org

AMERICAN LAW INSTITUTE REPORTERS

KYLE BAGWELL is Professor of Economics, Columbia University.

GENE M. GROSSMAN is Jacob Viner Professor of International Economics, Princeton University.

HENRIK HORN is Professor of International Economics, Institute for International Economic Studies, Stockholm University.

ROBERT HOWSE is Professor of Law, University of Michigan Law School.

PETROS C. MAVROIDIS is Professor of Law, Columbia Law School and University of Neuchâtel.

DAMIEN J. NEVEN is Professor of Economics, Graduate Institute for International Studies, University of Geneva.

ROBERT W. STAIGER is Professor of Economics, University of Wisconsin.

ALAN O. SYKES is Frank and Bernice Greenberg Professor of Law, University of Chicago Law School.

JOSEPH H. H. WEILER is Professor of Law and Jean Monnet Chair, New York University School of Law.

Introduction

HENRIK HORN AND PETROS C. MAVROIDIS

1 The project

This is the second in the series of Reporters' Studies emanating from the American Law Institute (ALI) project *Principles of Trade Law: The World Trade Organization* (WTO). The aim of the project is to provide systematic analysis of WTO law based in both Economics and Law. Such an interdisciplinary approach is in our view necessitated by the fact that the WTO Agreement has inherently economic objectives, which is not to deny that it may have other objectives as well.

A fundamental methodological problem facing the project is the lack of a "manual" for how to perform a joint economic and legal analysis of the WTO contract; there is no field, "The Economics of Trade Law," that can be relied upon for the purpose of the project. The relevant specialized fields, such as International Trade Law and International Economics, instead differ widely, both in terms of aims and in terms of method, and lawyers and economists are typically too specialized in their respective fields to be able to undertake a legal-*cum*-economic analysis of the law by themselves. Instead, such an analysis requires the joint efforts of economists and lawyers. The main idea behind this project is to develop such collaboration.

The project undertakes yearly analysis of the case law from the adjudicating bodies of the WTO. The intention is each year to analyze all disputes that in the previous year came to an administrative end, either because they were not appealed or because they went through both the panel and the Appellate Body (AB) stages, even though time constraints may prevent us from covering each and every dispute that falls into this category. Each dispute is evaluated jointly by an economist and a lawyer. The general task is to evaluate whether the ruling "makes sense" from an economic as well as legal point of view, and if not, whether the problem lies in the legal text or in the interpretation thereof.

The teams of lawyers and economists will not always cover all issues discussed in a case; they will however seek to discuss both the procedural and the substantive issues that they see as forming the "core" of the dispute.

The Reporters' Studies are initially scrutinized in a meeting of all of the Reporters. After revisions resulting from that meeting, the Studies are next presented and discussed in a meeting with an external advisory group, comprising both lawyers and economists. The final versions, as published in this volume, have been subjected to still another round of revisions derived from the advisory meeting. But despite these collective efforts, each pair of authors remains solely responsible for the Studies it has authored.

The analysis of the WTO case law will serve two purposes. First, given the central role of the Dispute Settlement system in the WTO (and the lack of accountability of its adjudicating bodies seen by some observers), it is of vital importance that the system is constantly and carefully scrutinized. Our yearly independent analysis of the emerging case law will, it is hoped, contribute toward this end.

The other purpose of this work is to serve as a stepping-stone toward an analysis of the core provisions of the WTO contract. Depending on the progress made over the next few years and our views on the quality of the primary and secondary WTO law, our work will eventually take the form of an articulated set of Principles of WTO Law.

In this second year the project focused on the case law of the year 2002. The Reporters' Studies have been drafted by the following persons, who have been appointed Reporters for the project by the ALI:

Kyle Bagwell, Kevin J. Lancaster Professor of Economics, Columbia University, USA.

Gene M. Grossman, Jacob Viner Professor of International Economics, Princeton University, USA.

Henrik Horn, Professor of International Economics, Institute for International Economic Studies, Stockholm University, Sweden.

Robert L. Howse, Alene and Allan F. Smith Professor of Law, University of Michigan Law School, USA.

Petros C. Mavroidis, Professor of Law, University of Neuchâtel, Switzerland, and Edwin B. Parker Professor of Law, Columbia Law School, Columbia University, USA.

Damien J. Neven, Professor of Economics, Graduate Institute for International Studies, University of Geneva, Switzerland.

Alan O. Sykes, Frank and Bernice Greenberg Professor of Law, University of Chicago Law School, USA.

Joseph H. H. Weiler, Joseph Straus Professor of Law and Jean Monnet Chair, New York University School of Law, USA.

As mentioned above, the Reporters' Studies in the volume have been presented to an external advisory group. We have thus benefited from very helpful discussions with the following participants on February 5 and 6, 2004, in Philadelphia.

José E. Alvarez, Columbia University Law School, New York, NY, USA.

Richard E. Baldwin, Department of Economics, Graduate Institute of International Studies, Geneva, Switzerland.

Steve Charnovitz, George Washington University Law School, Washington, D.C., USA.

Susan G. Esserman, Steptoe & Johnson, Washington, D.C., USA.

Wilfred Ethier, Department of Economics, University of Pennsylvania, Philadelphia, PA, USA.

Bernard Hoekman, Research Manager, International Trade Group, The World Bank, Washington, D.C., USA.

Gary N. Horlick, Wilmer Cutler Pickering Hale and Dorr, Washington, D.C., USA.

Andreas F. Lowenfeld, New York University School of Law, New York, NY, USA.

Mitsuo Matsushita, Department of Law, Seikei University, Tokyo, Japan.

Patrick Messerlin, Institut d'Etudes Politiques, Paris, France.

Håkan Nordström, National Board of Trade, Stockholm, Sweden.

Donald Regan, University of Michigan Law School, Ann Arbor, MI, USA.

Joel P. Trachtman, The Fletcher School, Tufts University, Medford, MA, USA.

Jasper Wauters, Legal Affairs Officer, Rules Division, World Trade Organization, Geneva, Switzerland.

David A. Wirth, Director of International Programs, Boston College Law School, Newton, MA, USA.

Diane P. Wood, U.S. Court of Appeals, 7th Circuit, Chicago, IL, USA.

Claire Wright, Thomas Jefferson School of Law, San Diego, CA, USA.

Before turning to the Reporters' Studies, we want to emphasize that this project would not have been possible without the help and support of many individuals and institutions. We would in particular like to express our gratitude to The American Law Institute. Its director, Professor Lance

Liebman, has been extremely helpful in taking the project to where it is today. We have also benefited greatly from the support of Michael Traynor, the President of the ALI, as well as from the very efficient administrative aid provided by Elena Cappella and Michael Greenwald, Deputy Directors of the ALI, as well as by other ALI staff members. We are also extremely grateful for financial support from the Jan Wallander's and Tom Hedelius' Research Foundation, Svenska Handelsbanken, Stockholm, and the Milton and Miriam Handler Foundation.

2   The Reporters' Studies on the WTO Case Law of 2002

We briefly summarize the Studies in the order of their appearance in this volume.

Bagwell and Mavroidis, discussing *US – Section 129*, essentially agree with the outcome reached by the Panel. In this case Canada challenged the legality of the US retroactive system for antidumping and countervailing duty collection, without raising the general question of the time-function of remedies in the WTO system. In the authors' view the Panel rightly dismissed the challenge of Canada. Bagwell and Mavroidis do, however, question the allocation of burden of proof by the Panel, arguing that it imposed an unreasonably high burden by requiring Canada to demonstrate not only that the US legislation in question did not cover the subject matter of the dispute but also that there was no other US legislation dealing with the issue either. The authors also criticize the drafting of the Panel's report, noting a discrepancy between the formulation of Canada's claims in the factual part and that in the legal findings section of the report.

The *US – FSC* arbitral award is examined by Howse and Neven. The EC won the original case, arguing that the United States FSC statute amounts to an export subsidy. Faced with subsequent noncompliance by the United States, the EC then requested authorization from the WTO to impose countermeasures. The Arbitrators authorized the EC to do so up to the value of the total subsidy by the United States (an amount in the neighborhood of 4 billion dollars), the single highest retaliation ever authorized by a GATT/WTO panel. Howse and Neven question the consistency of the recommended remedy with the applicable law and also highlight the resulting impracticalities in the event of sequential legal challenges against the FSC. In the economic analysis of their Study, borrowing from the property rather than the liability rule, the authors argue that a property rule approach to countermeasures does not sit comfortably with established principles of international law. But the paper also highlights an attraction of such an approach, that it may allow for efficient breach even when there is a large number of parties. However, the implementation of a property rule approach to counter-measures may be difficult in practice. For instance, the distribution of rents among victims may raise some difficult issues.

Grossman and Mavroidis discuss the AB report on *US – Corrosion-Resistant German Steel*. In this case, the question before the AB was to what extent the *de minimis* thresholds that were explicitly stated and applied in the context of an original countervailing investigation are also legally relevant in the context of a sunset review where no such explicit reference is made. The authors concur with the AB findings about the nonapplicability of *de minimis* thresholds in such situations and develop additional arguments to support its ruling. They also concur with the AB findings on evidentiary standards during reviews. Both of their conclusions are predicated on their understanding of the function of, or the objectives pursued by, the *SCM Agreement* as currently drafted. They do, however, point to two unsatisfactory aspects of the wording of Article 21.3 of the *SCM Agreement*: the level of permissible countervailing duties when the level of subsidization changes over time is unclear, as are the evidentiary standards that might lead to noncontinuation of counter-vailing duties in a situation in which the originally injured domestic industry no longer has an interest in the matter.

The *US – Non-Recurring Subsidies* dispute, analyzed by Grossman and Mavroidis, concerns an issue the authors dealt with in the previous volume: to what extent non-recurring subsidies are exhausted if subsi-dized assets are sold through arm's length transactions. Although the AB has now substantially deviated from its earlier decision by accepting that arm's length operations do not necessarily exhaust the effect of subsidies previously paid, the AB still falls short of establishing a reasonable stand-ard to be applied in all similar future cases. The reason for the continu-ing disagreement of the authors with the AB, the change in case law notwithstanding, is the AB's securing failure to understand the economic concept of a sunk cost, when insisting that the sales price at which a privatization takes place is relevant to the determination of a continuing benefit from a subsidy. The United States was correct, in the AB's view, when it argued that the price at which a profit-maximizing enterprise acquires an asset will not affect its subsequent production and pricing decisions. That such an enterprise will wish to "recoup a market return on its investment" is simply irrelevant to its subsequent business decisions.

Howse and Neven reflect on the report on *Canada – Aircraft*, a long-standing litigation between Canada and Brazil over subsidization of sales of commuter jets by both countries. The Panel dealt with Brazil's specific challenges to certain transactions in which federal and provincial entities provided financing assistance in connection with the sale of Bombardier aircraft. In the view of the authors, the Panel for the most part applied existing jurisprudence dealing with export subsidies to the factual record. The authors focus on the Panel's application of a "private investor principle," and question whether the conditions under which subsidies that were granted by the export development and industrial policy agencies were more favorable than the conditions that were available from alternative private sources. However, they find it impossible to evaluate the Panel's comparison between the conditions available in the market and those granted by the agencies, since vital factual information concerning the transactions in question were removed from the panel report for reasons of commercial confidentiality. It is striking, they note, that the Panel paid significant attention to the distinction between programs that leave some discretion to the authorities to grant possibly unlawful subsidies and programs that instruct the authorities to do so. The authors thus question the effectiveness of a legal framework that imposes on an institution behavioral norms that contradict its "raison d'être." In their view, this raises the broader question of whether the constraints imposed by the SCM agreement are reasonable, and the authors here make extensive references to the economic literature supporting the use of subsidies under specific circumstances.

In their analysis of the AB's determination in the *US – Line Pipe* dispute, Grossman and Mavroidis argue that the text of the *Agreement on Safeguards* (SGA) suffers from two serious deficiencies: First, Article 4.2b of the SGA calls for a causality test that is economically incoherent, since imports cannot be a cause of injury inasmuch as they are endogenously determined along with the domestic injury. The causality test for a safeguard measure can therefore never be met, and it is consequently not operational. Second, the Agreement fails to make explicit the objectives of the safeguard provisions. With an incoherent text and an absence of clear objectives, it is impossible for the adjudicator to determine when the conditions for a safeguard measure have been satisfied and what is the permissible extent of such a measure. In the *Line Pipe* dispute, Korea claimed that the US had not properly attributed injury to its various causes and that its safeguard measures exceeded in scope what is permitted under the treaty. The AB ruled against the United States essentially on procedural grounds. Grossman and Mavroidis find it difficult to disagree with the AB ruling in view of the causality analysis contained in the USITC investigatory report. However, when the AB embraced the non-attribution requirement in Article 4.2b of the SGA, it lent operational significance to an incoherent requirement. Grossman and Mavroidis thus find the AB ruling flawed in this respect. The AB could instead have ruled that the legal text lacks an internally consistent interpretation and could therefore have refrained from ruling in the particular dispute, instead calling for the WTO Members to address the shortcomings of the text through legislative action. Alternatively, the AB could have interpreted the text imaginatively so as to render it internally consistent and operational. The authors recommend that the latter approach should have been taken, albeit in a cautious manner.

Bagwell and Sykes discuss the AB report on *Chile – Price Band*. In this case, Argentina challenged the legality of a Chilean regime for determining import prices. The dispute also involved safeguard measures, but the Panel ruling on these was not appealed and the authors concentrate instead on the price band issue. They conclude that both from an economic and from a legal perspective, the case could have gone either way. Economically, in order to determine its effects, the authors argue, one would have to wait and see what would be the level of duties that Chile would choose to apply to the goods in question once it had done away with the Price Band system. In their view, the system as it has operated has had some trade-liberalizing features, since Chile *de facto* has not always applied the maximum MFN rate as it was entitled to do under the WTO. Legally, the authors see good arguments to support Chile's practice ever since it amended the original Price Band system and started applying it in a manner that ensured that the MFN duty "ceiling" would not be exceeded. On the other hand, they also see merit in the Argentine claim that due to the convoluted "esoteric" calculations that led to the final imposition, trading partners had no *ex ante* certainty as to the transaction costs for exports to the Chilean market.

Bagwell and Sykes also discuss the panel report on *India – Auto*. In this case, India was called to defend two of its programs, the so-called "indigenization" and "trade balancing" requirements. India's practices were challenged as running afoul of provisions of the WTO *Agreement on Trade-Related Investment Measures* (TRIMs), among other legal provisions, in practice constituting local content requirements. While the authors believe the case does touch on broader legal issues of systemic importance, they consider that it breaks little new ground in any of these matters. The authors agree with the legal reasoning of the Panel. The indigenization and trade balancing requirements are clear violations of GATT 1994 and TRIMs in the absence of a valid defense. India's purported justification for them – a balance of payments justification under Article XVIII of GATT 1994 – had been found insufficient in the earlier proceeding regarding its import licensing system. Viewed from a general economic perspective, the contested types of schemes do essentially amount to local content requirements which may be attractive to an importing country government when market power is present. The authors suggest that the conditions in place in *India – Auto* may indeed have been such as to make the contested scheme desirable from an Indian point of view, shifting profit from foreign automobile manufacturers to domestic input suppliers. However, there are strong reasons to suggest that local content requirements are harmful to trading partners, and the authors therefore conclude that the WTO rules that restrict the application of these schemes rest on a firm economic foundation.

Howse and Neven discuss the *US – Havana Club* report. At issue was a requirement of US law imposed on foreigners in the area of intellectual property protection. In the dispute, the Appellate Body reversed the Panel's findings. In the AB's view, the *Havana Club* legislation constituted a hurdle to the recognition of trademark rights that was imposed on some foreign nationals, but not on US nationals. The AB did recognize that there were serious obstacles faced also by US nationals in a given situation, but there still remained a hypothetical possibility that these might be overcome in a given case, resulting in better treatment of US nationals due to the *Havana Club* legislation. The AB ruling is, in the authors' eyes, a relatively straightforward application of the spirit and letter of the GATT *Section 337* panel ruling. With respect to original owners of trademarks attempting to assert their rights in the United States, the AB found that if there were "two separate owners who acquired rights, either at common law or based on registration, in two separate United States trademarks before the Cuban confiscation occurred" and these trademarks were the same or similar to a Cuban trademark used in connection with a business that was confiscated, and one owner was American and the other Cuban, only the Cuban national would be affected by the regime in the *Havana Club* legislation.

Horn and Mavroidis examine the *US – Lumber* dispute concerning the preliminary determination of countervailing duties by the United States on the importation of Canadian softwood lumber. The authors concentrate on whether the United States had adequately showed that Canadian stumpage programs – the contracts between the government and private harvesters of standing timber – subsidize downstream lumber producers, and that CVDs therefore were justified. Horn and Mavroidis find serious problems with the benchmarks proposed in the dispute. First, the private sector, no-subsidy benchmark imposed by the *SCM Agreement* does not take into consideration whether a divergence between this benchmark and actual government policy reflects the pursuit of legitimate government policies. Second, and in contrast to the views of the Panel, Horn and Mavroidis agree with the United States that it is not reasonable to interpret the private sector benchmark as referring to prices in the domestic market, when domestic prices are significantly affected by subsidization. Third, Horn and Mavroidis also see severe practical difficulties in using a foreign sector benchmark, as proposed by the United States. Like the Panel, they believe that the United States did not adequately prove the existence of subsidization. Their general conclusion is that this may in fact be impossible in cases involving such widespread and complex interventions as those at stake in *US – Lumber*.

In the final Study, Horn and Weiler discuss the *EC – Sardines* dispute. The dispute is noteworthy in that it is the first dispute in which a Technical Barriers to Trade (TBT) issue was fully discussed. The dispute centers on the role that international standards are called to play in the TBT system, and the institutional possibilities for Members to deviate from these standards. Horn and Weiler focus on two related aspects of the AB report. The first is the method of interpretation, exemplified in this decision with its rhetorical emphasis on "textual" interpretation, as opposed to a more contextual interpretation where the provisions of the TBT are evaluated in the light of its function in the WTO Agreement. The second theme is the question of how to allocate the burden of proof in the context of Art. 2.4 TBT. The Panel claimed it falls on the WTO Member that deviates from the international standard to establish that the standard at hand is inefficient or inappropriate to fulfill its legitimate regulatory objectives. The AB instead put the burden on the complainant. But at the same time the AB stipulated an extremely low evidentiary requirement for discharging this burden. The consequence was to underscore the importance of international standards for the purpose of implementing the TBT, without discussing whether these standards have the necessary legitimacy, which the authors put into question. The authors conclude that it helps neither the legitimacy of the AB nor the legitimacy of the WTO as a whole to decide issues such as the relevance of consensus decision making, the cultural integrity of a language, or the presumptions on burden of proof without any meaningful analysis or even indication of an awareness of the deeper policy issues and consequences that are at stake.

As in the previous year's volume, we will make a bold attempt to summarize the outcome of this year's Studies. We have classified the findings of each Study in terms of its acceptance of the rationale and of the outcome of the report discussed. The following classification is our summary judgment of the merits of the reports discussed in this volume. The reader is better served by actually reading the full report for every dispute. This is our summary evaluation:

	Rationale	Outcome
US – Section 129	partly satisfactory	correct
US – FSC	partly satisfactory	correct
US – Corrosion-Resistant Steel	satisfactory	correct
US – Non-Recurring Subsidies	unsatisfactory	correct
Canada – Aircraft	satisfactory	partly wrong
US – Line Pipe	unsatisfactory	correct
Chile – Price Band	satisfactory	correct
India – Auto	satisfactory	correct
US – Havana Club	partly satisfactory	partly wrong
US – Lumber	partly satisfactory	correct
EC – Sardines	unsatisfactory	correct

As can be seen, there is a high degree of acceptance of the outcomes in these disputes; only in two instances would the authors definitely have preferred to see a completely different verdict. But at the same time the Reporters found methodological deficiencies in seven out of eleven reviewed disputes, and in three of them the reasoning was clearly unsatisfactory. This picture closely resembles the one that emerged last year.

Finally, we should be mindful of the fact that it is much easier to criticize selected weaknesses in a dispute report than to construct a solid report. We should also not attribute to the adjudicating bodies problems that really stem from logical errors in the agreements. The basic aim of these Studies is not merely to criticize, but to contribute toward the creation of a body of thought that might ease the difficult work of the WTO adjudicating bodies in the future.

2

United States – Section 129(c)(1) of the Uruguay Round Agreements Act (WTO Doc. WT/DS22/R of 15 July 2002): Beating Around (The) Bush

BY

KYLE BAGWELL*

Columbia University and NBER

AND

PETROS C. MAVROIDIS*

Columbia Law School, University of Neuchâtel and CEPR

1 The Factual And Legal Issues

In this dispute, Canada attacks Section 129(c)(1) of the US trade legislation as a result of the entry into force of the Uruguay Round Agreements [Uruguay Round Agreements Act (URAA), hereinafter "Section 129"] which provides that a new antidumping or countervailing duty determination made by the Department of Commerce (DOC) or the International Trade Commission (ITC) to bring a previous antidumping, countervailing duty or injury determination into conformity with an adverse WTO panel or Appellate Body report applies only to imports that enter the United States on or after the date that the United States Trade Representative (USTR) directs implementation of the new determination.

Section 129 reads:

> EFFECTS OF DETERMINATIONS. – Determinations concerning title VII of the Tariff Act of 1930 that are implemented under this section shall apply with respect to unliquidated entries of the subject merchandise

* We would like to thank all ALI reporters to this project and especially Jasper-Martijn Wauters for their many very valuable comments on previous drafts of this study.

(as defined in section 771 of that Act) that are entered, or withdrawn from warehouse, for consumption on or after –

(A) in the case of a determination by the Commission under subsection (a)(4), the date on which the Trade Representative directs the administering authority under subsection (a)(6) to revoke an order pursuant to that determination, and

(B) in the case of a determination by the administering authority under subsection (b)(2), the date on which the Trade Representative directs the administering authority under subsection (b)(4) to implement that determination.

Canada claims that Section 129 implies that imports that entered the United States **prior to** that date, and that are subject to an order imposing potential liability for the payment of antidumping or countervailing duties, remain subject to future administrative review determinations and definitive duty assessment without regard to the new determination made by the Department of Commerce or the ITC and any consequent revocation or amendment of the original order.

Canada refers to imports of this kind as **prior unliquidated entries**. Such imports entered the United States prior to the date on which the USTR directs implementation of a new determination pursuant to Section 129(a)(6) and Section 129(b)(4) and remain unliquidated (that is, the definitive duty, if any, to be levied on the imports remains undetermined) on that date.

Canada makes two categories of claims: **first**, Canada claims that Section 129 as such, that is, the legislative text independently of any application, violates the WTO Agreement; **second**, Canada claims that Section 129, independently of any application, has the effect of violating the WTO Agreement. Canada claims that both categories of claims establish a violation of the same legal provisions in the WTO contract for the same grounds. The legal provisions are:

(a) Article VI:2, VI:3 and VI:6(a) of the GATT 1994;

(b) Articles 1, 9.3, 11.1 and 18.1 of the WTO Agreement on Antidumping ("AD Agreement");

(c) Articles 10, 19.4, 21.1 and 32.1 of the WTO Agreement on Subsidies and Countervailing Measures ("SCM Agreement");

(d) Canada further submits that, in view of the fact that Section 129 is inconsistent, in its view, with the aforementioned provisions of the AD Agreement, the SCM Agreement and the GATT 1994, Section 129 is also inconsistent with Article 18.4 of the AD Agreement,

Article 32.5 of the SCM Agreement and Article XVI:4 of the WTO
Agreement, because these provisions require that a Member's laws be
in conformity with its WTO obligations as of the entry into force of
the WTO Agreement.

The legal grounds are reproduced in §§ 6.31 and 6.32 of the report.[1] We
quote:

> 6.31 First of all, Canada asserts that section 129(c)(1) "requires", or has the
> effect of "requiring", the Department of Commerce:
>
>> to *conduct administrative reviews* with respect to "prior unliquid-
>> ated entries" after the implementation date pursuant to an anti-
>> dumping or countervailing duty order found by the DSB to be
>> WTO-inconsistent;
>
>> to *make administrative review determinations regarding dumping or
>> subsidization* with respect to "prior unliquidated entries" after the
>> implementation date pursuant to an antidumping or countervail-
>> ing duty order found by the DSB to be WTO-inconsistent;
>
>> to *assess definitive antidumping or countervailing duties* with respect
>> to "prior unliquidated entries" after the implementation date pur-
>> suant to an antidumping or countervailing duty order found by the
>> DSB to be WTO-inconsistent; and
>
>> to *retain cash deposits* in respect of "prior unliquidated entries"
>> after the implementation date at a level found by the DSB to be
>> WTO-inconsistent.
>
> 6.32 Canada alleges, furthermore, that section 129(c)(1), by "precluding"
> particular actions, infringes the WTO provisions identified by Canada.
> Specifically, Canada asserts that section 129(c)(1) "precludes", or has the
> effect of "precluding", the Department of Commerce from:
>
>> *making administrative review determinations regarding dumping or subsidi-
>> zation* with respect to "prior unliquidated entries" after the implementa-
>> tion date in a manner that is consistent with an adverse DSB ruling;
>
>> *assessing definitive antidumping or countervailing duties* with respect to
>> "prior unliquidated entries" after the implementation date in a manner
>> that is consistent with an adverse DSB ruling; and

---

[1] Unless otherwise indicated, every time we refer to particular paragraphs throughout this
report, we refer to paragraphs of the panel report WTO Doc. WT/DS221.

refunding, after the implementation date, *cash deposits* collected on "prior unliquidated entries" pursuant to an antidumping or countervailing duty order found by the DSB to be WTO-inconsistent.

(emphasis in the original).

2   The Panel's Evaluation

2.1   *The order of examining the various claims*

The Panel first explained that it would entertain Canada's claims under Art. 18.4 AD and 32.5 SCM only if Canada had first successfully established a violation with respect to its other claims. In the Panel's view this way of proceeding was legitimized by the fact that, in Canada's view, Arts. 18.4 AD and 32.5 SCM respectively are *ipso facto* violated in case the other violations have been established. It goes without saying that were the Panel to find that Canada did not establish violation with respect to the other claims, its claims under Arts. 18.4 AD and 32.5 SCM would fall.

2.2   *Section 129 as such requires WTO-inconsistent behavior*

2.2.1   The legal benchmark to establish a violation

The Panel lays out its legal benchmark to establish that Section 129 as such amounts to a violation of the WTO Agreement in § 6.22 of the report in the following terms:

> It is clear to us that a Member may challenge, and a WTO panel rule against, a statutory provision of another Member "as such" (for example, section 129(c)(1)), provided the statutory provision "mandates" the Member either to take action which is inconsistent with its WTO obligations or not take action which is required by its WTO obligations.

Then the Panel, following the standing rules in WTO law for allocation of burden of proof (the complainant carries the initial burden of proof), goes on to hold that (§ 6.23):

> . . . it will be clear that Canada's principal claims will be sustained only if Canada succeeds in establishing that section 129(c)(1) mandates the United States to take action which is inconsistent with the WTO provisions which form the basis for those claims or mandates the United States not to take action which is required by those WTO provisions. In other words, for Canada to discharge its burden with respect to its principal claims, it must demonstrate both of two elements: *first*, that section 129(c)(1) mandates

that the United States take or not take the action identified by Canada, and *second* that this mandated behaviour is inconsistent with the WTO provisions that it has invoked.

(emphasis in the original).

The Panel notes, however, that it is not going to examine Section 129 in clinical isolation from the potentially relevant other US legal framework. To this effect, the Panel, as other panels did before, singles out the Statement of Administrative Action (SAA) which is included in the URAA. In the Panel's view, the SAA is relevant for the interpretation of Section 129, a point to which Canada itself has not objected. We quote from §§ 6.36 (Canada's understanding of the relationship between the SAA and Section 129 – a point not challenged by the US) and 6.38 (the Panel's understanding of the relationship):

> The SAA sets forth the authoritative interpretation of the URAA and the US Administration's obligations in implementing the URAA, as agreed between the US Administration and the US Congress. Congress approved the SAA in section 101 of the URAA and provided, in section 102 of the URAA, that "[t]he statement of administrative action approved by the Congress under section 101(a) shall be regarded as an authoritative expression by the United States concerning the interpretation and application of the Uruguay Round Agreements and this Act in any judicial proceeding in which a question arises concerning such interpretation or application".
>
> . . .
>
> Accordingly, in our examination of section 129(c)(1), we must be mindful of the legal status of the SAA in US law and take account of its content. This said, two caveats should be noted. *First*, it should be remembered that section 129(c)(1) is to be interpreted in the light of the SAA, and not the other way round. *Second*, it should be recalled that, even though the SAA is intended to shed light on the meaning of the various provisions of the URAA, the statements contained in the SAA may, themselves, be open to interpretation.
>
> (emphasis in the original).

The SAA is reflected in § 6.40 of the report. We quote:

> Consistent with the principle that GATT panel recommendations apply only prospectively, subsection 129(c)(1) provides that where determinations by the ITC or Commerce are implemented under subsections (a) or (b), such determinations have prospective effect only. That is, they apply to unliquidated entries of merchandise entered, or withdrawn from warehouse, for consumption on or after the date on which the Trade Representative

directs implementation. Thus, relief available under subsection 129(c)(1) is distinguishable from relief available in an action brought before a court or a NAFTA binational panel, where, depending on the circumstances of the case, retroactive relief may be available. Under 129(c)(1), if implementation of a WTO report should result in the revocation of an antidumping or countervailing duty order, entries made prior to the date of Trade Representative's direction would remain subject to potential duty liability.

Having established the context for the interpretation of Section 129 as well as the legal benchmark for establishing a violation, the Panel turned to examine Canada's claims.

2.2.2   What does Section 129 actually do?

It is clear from the text of Section 129 that it applies to AD and countervailing (CVD) duties perceived by the competent US authorities (§ 6.48). Probably the best way to explain what Section 129 actually does is through an example. But before we do that, we should first spend some time understanding how the US system for calculation of dumping margins operates in practice.

The US is one of the few countries that practice the so-called **retrospective duty assessment mechanism**. Most other WTO Members, including Canada and the European Community, use the **prospective duty assessment mechanism**. Under the former, the investigating authority determines the amount of the duty at the end of the investigation period. Such determination, however, serves only as a provisional basis for the collection of cash deposits. Assume for example, that the US conclude their investigation on 1.1.2001 and find that the dumping margin for imports of good X from country Y is 30%. Any importer of good X from country Y will be required to make a cash deposit of 30% for imports occurring on or after 1.1.2001.

The final duty liability is only determined at the end of each year following imposition of the measure and after calculations based on data for the past twelve months. So on 1.1.2002 in our example, the US will recalculate the dumping margin for good X from country Y based on data from transactions occurring from 1.1.2001–1.1.2002. If the duty is higher than originally calculated, the investigating authority will request additional duties to be paid. If it is lower, the investigating authority will release the part of the deposits that was not due.

At the same time, this newly calculated duty rate will constitute the estimated rate on the basis of which provisional duties in the form of cash deposits will be imposed. And so on, and so forth.

By contrast, the duty rate will, in the context of the prospective duty assessment mechanism, be calculated at the end of the period of investigation and will be applied to all future imports (although the possibility exists for interested parties to demonstrate that the actual dumping margin was less and hence be reimbursed). Final liability, however, is determined before imports enter the country, leaving aside the possibility of reimbursement or judicial review which are institutional mechanisms quite different from the actual duty assessment.

Canada's argument is that the final liability in the retrospective duty assessment mechanism will only be determined after the imports have entered the country. To go back to our hypothetical: assume that a WTO panel finds on 1.1.2002 that the US had wrongfully calculated the dumping margin and that actually, following a new correct calculation, the US should have ended up with a smaller figure. Imports between 1.1.2001 and 1.1.2002 *for which no final determination has been made*, will still have to be burdened by the 30% dumping margin because of Section 129.

In Canada's view, this is not an issue for WTO Members which apply the prospective duty assessment mechanism, since such Members apply duties only following a final determination and there is no *uncertainty* as to the duty that will be finally paid.

It stems from the above that effectively Canada is not arguing that Section 129 is a barrier towards providing retrospective remedies. Rather, Canada's argument is much more narrow: the point is that in Canada's view even a prospective remedy recommended by the WTO would oblige a country which follows the retrospective duty assessment mechanism to apply the new WTO-consistent methodology to all transactions that took place in the previous year *because no final determination has been made with respect to such transactions*. The same, by inference, would not be the case when a country applies a prospective duty assessment mechanism, since a prospective WTO remedy will be applicable only to future transactions because all past transactions have benefited from a final determination.

Canada in other words attacks the idiosyncrasy of the US system whereby no final determination has been made for past transactions until the end of each year *without putting into question* the issue of whether the WTO allows for retrospective remedies or not.

We should make it clear that Section 129 does not impose a time span within which the USTR must act, and Canada has made no claims to this effect. Canada's claims are that Section 129, while providing a WTO-consistent solution for all imports of good X from country Y as of the date when the USTR direction has been issued, does not provide a WTO-consistent solution for all entries prior to the date of issuance of the USTR direction (that is, the **prior unliquidated entries**). In Canada's view, the WTO-consistent solution would be, for example, for the US to apply to all imports which took place during the year leading to the end of the reasonable period of time within which the US must bring its laws into compliance with its WTO obligations, the rate found by the WTO adjudicating body to be the appropriate one.

The US respond that Section 129 has nothing to do with prior unliquidated entries and that their treatment will be decided in the context of a separate (but not identified in the US submissions) proceeding (§ 6.42).

2.2.3   Does Section 129 apply to prior unliquidated entries?

The Panel, examining the wording of Section 129 in light of its context (SAA), concluded that Section 129 simply does not apply to prior unliquidated entries, the treatment of which is unaffected by the scope of Section 129 (§§ 6.53 and 6.55) . From there on it was all downhill: having established that Section 129 does not deal with the factual issue identified in Canada's submission, the Panel naturally concluded that Canada did not observe its burden of proof and consequently did not establish a violation of the WTO Agreement.

2.2.4   Concluding remarks

It follows from the discussion under 2.2.3 that the Panel rejected Canada's claims that Section 129 requires from US domestic authorities WTO-inconsistent behavior.

2.3   *Section 129 precludes or has the effect of precluding WTO-consistent behavior*

2.3.1   The legal benchmark to establish a violation

Unsurprisingly, the Panel adopts the same legal benchmark as when examining the first category of claims, with one notable difference: in this context, the Panel makes it clear that all its findings are provisional and will become final only after examining Canada's claims under the explicit wording of SAA. The Panel of course interpreted Section 129 in the context of the SAA after the first category of claims as well; it did not, however, make the distinction between provisional and final findings in that context. The Panel explained the different approach in § 6.58 of its report in the following terms:

> We will first examine the arguments of the parties relating to section 129(c)(1) as enacted. After that, we will consider the parties' arguments concerning relevant portions of the SAA. We wish to be clear that we assess these arguments separately for convenience of analysis only. As we have noted, section 129(c)(1) must be read together with the SAA. Accordingly, we will not reach any conclusions regarding Canada's assertions that section 129(c)(1) has the effect of requiring and precluding certain actions until after we have taken into account relevant parts of the SAA. Our conclusions regarding the assertions in question will, as a result, be based on section 129(c)(1) as interpreted by the SAA, rather than on section 129(c)(1) read in isolation. Moreover, before reaching any conclusions regarding Canada's assertions, we will also address the application of section 129(c)(1) to date.

Implicit in this statement is that the fact that Canada, with respect to this category of claims, argued that Section 129 not only precludes but further *has the effect of* precluding WTO-consistent behavior justifies the current approach. The Panel examined Canada's claims with respect to methodology and revocation cases, as argued by the complaining party. We take each claim in turn.

2.3.2   Section 129 and methodology cases

Canada's claims with respect to methodology cases are discussed in §§ 6.67–6.81. In § 6.67, the Panel explains its understanding of the term **methodology cases** in pertinent, self-explanatory terms:

> Methodology cases are cases in which the section 129 determination does not result in the revocation of the original antidumping or countervailing duty order, but instead results in a new margin of dumping or a new countervailable subsidy rate. Such an outcome may be due, for instance, to the application of a new, WTO-consistent methodology or a new, WTO-consistent interpretation of US antidumping or countervailing duty laws.

The Panel, applying the same logic as with respect to the first category of cases, concludes that Section 129 does not deal with prior unliquidated entries that qualify as methodology cases (§ 6.68 of the report). This, in the Panel's view, means that the US competent authority (the Department of Commerce, DOC) is not required to continue to perceive the same amount of duties independently of changes as a result to the new, applicable methodology (§ 6.69 of the report); on the other hand, it does not automatically follow that because Section 129 does not deal with prior unliquidated entries, the DOC is precluded from applying to such transactions the treatment it applies to transactions post-direction by the USTR (§ 6.72 of the report).

The Panel finds support in its argument when it examines Canada's arguments that the US *intended* to permit temporary retention of extensive cash deposits through Section 129. In the Panel's view, the exact opposite seems to have been the intention of the US Congress: to ensure compliance with WTO rulings affecting transactions that are not what Canada terms prior unliquidated entry. As a result, no US court would, in the Panel's view, interpret Section 129 as suggested by Canada (§ 6.76 of the report).

The Panel finds further support in its line of reasoning when interpreting Section 129 in the light of the SAA (§§ 99–114). The Panel notes that there is no judicial interpretation of Section 129 which contradicts its understanding and that the only administrative interpretation available is simply irrelevant for the purposes of the present dispute (§§ 6.115 and 6.118 respectively).

2.3.3   Section 129 and revocation cases

The Panel then moves to examine the revocation cases (§§ 6.82–6.92). The Panel first defines revocation cases in the following manner (§ 6.82):

> Revocation cases are cases in which the section 129 determination results in the revocation of the original antidumping or countervailing duty order. An antidumping or countervailing duty order would be revoked if a section 129 determination established that there was no dumping, no subsidization or no injury. Pursuant to section 129(c)(1), the revocation of a WTO-inconsistent antidumping or countervailing duty order would apply to all entries that take place on or after the implementation date. We are led to understand that, in practice, this would mean that, as of the implementation date, cash deposits would no longer be required on new entries.

In Canada's view, Section 129 precludes or has the effect of precluding the US from applying the same standard to prior unliquidated entries. The Panel dismisses Canada's claims in the following manner (§§ 6.83–6.84):

> As we see it, since, pursuant to section 129(c)(1), a section 129 determination of this type would not be applicable to "prior unliquidated entries", that determination, as such, would not have an impact on "prior unliquidated entries". In other words, we think it can be inferred from the fact that

a revocation of an antidumping or countervailing duty order would apply only with respect to post-implementation entries that the Department of Commerce would *not* be required, because of section 129(c)(1), to refund cash deposits previously collected on "prior unliquidated entries" on the basis of the WTO-inconsistent antidumping or countervailing duty order, to decline to conduct administrative reviews for such entries, to decline to make determinations regarding dumping or subsidization with respect such entries on the basis of the WTO-inconsistent antidumping or countervailing duty order or to decline to assess definitive antidumping or countervailing duties with respect to such entries on the basis of the WTO-inconsistent antidumping or countervailing duty order.

Conversely, we think it can *not* be inferred from the mere fact that a revocation is inapplicable to "prior unliquidated entries" that the Department of Commerce would be required to retain cash deposits collected on such entries on the basis of the WTO-inconsistent antidumping or countervailing duty order or would be precluded from refunding such cash deposits. Nor does it follow from the fact that a revocation does not apply to "prior unliquidated entries" that the Department of Commerce would be required to conduct administrative reviews for such entries. Nor does the non-application of a revocation to "prior unliquidated entries" necessarily imply that the Department of Commerce would be required to make administrative review determinations regarding dumping or subsidization and assess definitive antidumping or countervailing duties with respect to "prior unliquidated entries" on the basis of the WTO-inconsistent antidumping or countervailing duty order, or would be precluded from making such determinations and assessing definitive duties with respect to such entries in a manner consistent with WTO requirements.

Canada, in its effort to persuade the Panel, offered a counterfactual: in the absence of Section 129, the US would be obliged to revoke all transactions, that is prior unliquidated entries as well. The Panel dismissed this argument and offered a very narrow construction of the counterfactual (§ 6.88):

> Indeed, if there were no section 129(c)(1) and a provision like section 129(c)(1) was subsequently enacted, the consequence of this would be that section 129 determinations would not apply to "prior unliquidated entries". As we have said, this would mean that the Department of Commerce would then not be required, as a matter of US law, to return cash deposits collected on such entries based on the WTO-inconsistent antidumping or countervailing duty order, to decline to hold administrative reviews for such entries and to decline to assess duties with

respect to such entries on the basis of the WTO-inconsistent order. Moreover, as we have also observed, it would not follow from the fact that a revocation would then be inapplicable to "prior unliquidated entries" that the Department of Commerce could not return cash deposits collected on "prior unliquidated entries" could not decline to hold administrative reviews with respect to such entries and could not decline to assess duties with respect to such entries.

2.3.4 Concluding remarks

The Panel hence concluded that Canada did not establish a *prima facie* case that the US Section 129 was WTO-inconsistent and consequently, rejected Canada's claims in this respect as well. The Panel thus also rejected Canada's claims under Arts. 18.4 AB and 32.5 SCM.

3 Evaluation

3.1 Mandatory vs. discretionary legislation

The WTO case law on the legal benchmark to be applied by adjudicating bodies when entertaining claims that a legislation as such is WTO-inconsistent is not a monument of clarity. For years, adjudicating bodies repeated the statement that, unless the complainant shows that the (any) legislation mandates WTO-inconsistent behavior, it cannot successfully absolve its burden of proof. Then came the panel report on *United States – Sections 301–310 of the Trade Act of 1974* (WTO Doc. WT/DS152/R of 22 December 1999) which held that some provisions of WTO treaties may give rise to state responsibility to ensure that even legislation that has discretionary elements does not give rise to a threat or serious likelihood of a WTO violation:

> Article 23 may prohibit legislation with certain discretionary elements and therefore the very fact of having in the legislation such discretion could, in effect, preclude WTO consistency
>
> (§ 7.54 of the report, op. cit).

Hence, the distinction between discretionary and mandatory legislation is not, in this panel's view, as such determinative of state responsibility. State responsibility ultimately flows from the particular nature of the treaty provisions at issue, and must be interpreted accordingly.

Subsequently, the Appellate Body report on *United States – Antidumping Act of 1916* (WTO Doc. WT/DS136&162/AB/R of 28 August 2000 at

§§ 89–91) approves in a footnote the finding of the *Section* 301 panel that some kinds of discretionary legislation might give rise to treaty violations in certain circumstances. It further held that only discretion vested in the executive branch of the government matters for the purposes of this distinction. In the case at hand, the US Department of Justice enjoyed some discretion to initiate or not criminal proceedings. In the words of the Appellate Body, however, such discretion was not

> of such a nature or of such a breadth as to transform the 1916 Act into discretionary legislation, as this term has been understood for purposes of distinguishing between mandatory and discretionary legislation.

The issue took another twist in the Appellate Body report on *United States – Section 211 Omnibus Appropriations Act of 1998* (WTO Doc. WT/DS 176/AB/R of 2 January 2002). There the Appellate Body faced the argument by the EC that the US legislation, the discretionary character of which was acknowledged in the panel report, was imposing an "extra hurdle" on foreign nationals in violation of the national treatment obligation protected under the TRIPs Agreement. It reacted in the following manner and reversed the panel's findings that the legislation at hand, because discretionary, could not be scrutinized by a WTO adjudicating body. We quote from §§ 256, 259–260 and 267–269:

> That "extra hurdle" is this. United States nationals who are successors-in-interest must go successfully only through the OFAC procedure. In the circumstances addressed by Section 211, they are not subject to the constraints imposed by Section 211(a)(2). In contrast, non-United States successors-in-interest not only must go successfully through the OFAC procedure, but also find themselves additionally exposed to the "extra hurdle" of an additional proceeding under Section 211(a)(2). In sum, United States nationals face only one proceeding, while non-United States nationals face two. It is on this basis that the European Communities claims on appeal that Section 211(a)(2), as it relates to successors-in-interest, violates the national treatment obligation in the TRIPS Agreement and the Paris Convention (1967).
>
> . . .
>
> . . . As the Panel rightly noted, in US – 1916 Act, we stated that a distinction should be made between legislation that mandates WTO-inconsistent behaviour, and legislation that gives rise to executive authority that can be exercised with discretion. We quoted with approval there the following statement of the panel in US – Tobacco:

... panels had consistently ruled that legislation which mandated
action inconsistent with the General Agreement could be challenged as such, whereas legislation which merely gave the discretion
to the executive authority of a contracting party to act inconsistently with the General Agreement could not be challenged as such;
only the actual application of such legislation inconsistent with the
General Agreement could be subject to challenge.

Thus, where discretionary authority is vested in the executive branch of
a WTO Member, it cannot be assumed that the WTO Member will fail
to implement its obligations under the WTO Agreement in good faith.
Relying on these rulings, and interpreting them correctly, the Panel concluded that it could not assume that OFAC would exercise its discretionary
executive authority inconsistently with the obligations of the United States
under the WTO Agreement. Here, too, we agree.

But here, the Panel stopped. We are of the view that, having reached the
conclusion it did with respect to the offsetting effect of OFAC practice,
the Panel should not have stopped but should have gone on and considered
the argument made by the European Communities about the "extra hurdle"
faced by non-United States successors-in-interest. For this reason, we do
so now.

. . .

The United States has not shown, as required under the national treatment obligation, that, in every individual case, the courts of the United
States would not validate the assertion of rights by a United States successor-
in-interest. Moreover, even if there is, as the United States argues, a
likelihood that United States courts would not enforce rights asserted by
a United States successor-in-interest, the fact remains, nevertheless, that
non-United States successors-in-interest are placed by the measure, on its
face, in an inherently less favourable situation than that faced by United
States successors-in-interest. And, even if we were to accept the United
States argument about the doctrine of non-recognition of foreign confiscation, presumably that doctrine would apply to those who are not nationals
of the United States as well as to those who are. Any application of this
doctrine would therefore not offset the discrimination in Section 211(a)(2),
because it would constitute yet another, separate obstacle faced by
nationals and non-nationals alike. Hence, it would not offset the effect of
Section 211(a)(2), which applies only to successors-in-interest who are not
United States nationals.

Accordingly, we conclude that Section 211(a)(2) imposes an additional
obstacle on successors-in-interest who are not nationals of the United
States that is not faced by United States successors-in-interest. And, therefore, we conclude that, by applying the "extra hurdle" imposed by

Section 211(a)(2) only to non-United States successors-in-interest, the
United States violates the national treatment obligation in Article 2(1) of
the Paris Convention (1967) and Article 3.1 of the TRIPS Agreement.

For this reason, we reverse the Panel's conclusion in paragraph 8.140 of
the Panel Report that "[b]ecause US nationals are unable to obtain licences
so as to become a successor-in-interest and OFAC has not granted any
such licence for such purpose . . . Section 211(a)(2) is not inconsistent with
Article 3.1 of the TRIPS Agreement and Article 2.1 of the TRIPS Agreement
in conjunction with Article 2(1) of the Paris Convention (1967)."

This is the latest pronouncement by the Appellate Body on the issue. The
cited passage is quite cryptic in the sense that it does not clarify under
what circumstances the burden of proof shifts to the defendant (in the
instant case, the US) to demonstrate that national treatment will be
observed in every transaction as the Appellate Body states.

The present case is a shift towards the "hard line" adopted by some
WTO adjudicating bodies whereby only legislation which always mandates
WTO-inconsistent behavior should be judged to be WTO-inconsistent:
in a nutshell, the Panel seems to suggest that it would have found violation
only in the case where the US legislation would explicitly preclude the US
competent authorities from acting upon prior unliquidated entries.

The distinction between mandatory/discretionary legislation is
judge-made law. The arguments advanced in its support are two-fold:
by sanctioning only mandatory legislation one avoids over-burdening
administratively the dispute settlement system of the WTO; on the
other hand, in presence of discretionary legislation which might or
might not eventually take the form of a WTO-inconsistent action,
one should not rush to the conclusion that an illegality will be committed anyway (some form of application of the *in dubio pro mitius*
maxim). Uncertainty, hence, is not punishable under this distinction.

This distinction implies that WTO Members can have the discretion to
behave in a WTO-inconsistent manner and will be punished only if they
do so. But retaining such discretion is at odds with the very idea of
entering into a contractual regime (with substantial in-built flexibilities)
where each participant promises the other WTO-consistent behavior at
all times for all issues covered by the WTO in accordance with the basic
pacta sunt servanda principle and Arts. 26 and 70 of the Vienna
Convention on the Law of Treaties. It should be pointed out that the
Section 301 case law cited above was a very honorable effort to bridge this
gap by requesting WTO Members to avoid, when appropriate, uncertainty as to their behavior.

3.2 Prospective against retrospective duty assessment mechanisms: does it really matter?

We have described above the two systems used by WTO investigating authorities for assessing dumping margins: the prospective and the retrospective system. Assume that an investigation occurs simultaneously in the US and the EC on allegedly dumped imports of maple leaf syrup (MLS) from Canada. Assume that both the US and the EC investigating authorities terminate their investigation on 1.1.2001 and find that Canadian MLS exporters have been dumping by 30% their exports of MLS to US and the EC. The US imposes the 30% rate provisionally and will recalculate the duty at the end of the year. They do so and on 31.12.2001 they find that Canadians continue to dump by 30% their exports of MLS to US. They hence release no funds to Canadian exporters and continue applying the 30% duty rate to all imports of MLS originating from Canada as from 1.1.2002. The EC applies as of 1.1.2001 the 30% duty rate in an uninterrupted manner to all imports of MLS originating in Canada.

Assume further that Canada introduces two complaints before the WTO and two WTO panels find that the duty should have been 15%. The panels consequently request that the US and EC bring their measures into compliance. Finally, assume that the panel is not appealed and that the reasonable period of time for both the EC and the US to bring their measures into compliance ends up on 31.12.2002.

The EC starts applying the 15% rate on all imports taking place as of 1.1.2003. In Canada's view, there is nothing wrong with such an implementation; in its view, the EC has faithfully implemented the panel's recommendations (and/or suggestions). The fact that the EC does not reimburse any duties for imports between 1.1.2001 and 1.1.2003 is not problematic in Canada's view.

The US does the same. It applies the 15% rate on all imports taking place as of 1.1.2003. Canada believes that the US has not implemented the panel's recommendations although the same transactions will be burdened by exactly the same dumping duty on the two sides of the Atlantic. The reason justifying Canada's nod to the EC implementation and Canada's nay to the US implementation is that the former applies the prospective whereas the latter the retrospective duty assessment scheme.

But should a domestic technique to assess duties matter? What matters is not how the US or the EC technically qualify the duties imposed. What matters should be which transactions should be burdened by which duty rate following a panel's finding that the duty had been mis-calculated in the original investigation.

It seems that Canada wants to avoid "rocking the boat" by entering into the sometimes contentious discussion of prospective vs. retroactive remedies in the WTO, but at the same time wants to benefit marginally (in the sense that it wishes to see, in case following a complaint to this effect a WTO panel finds that the US duty is excessive and requests the US to bring their measures into compliance, the WTO-consistent duty applied to all prior unliquidated entries: in case for example, a US 20% duty is in place for 3 years, and a WTO panel finds that the duty should be 10% instead, according to Canada's argument, the prior unliquidated entries, that is all imports taking place in the last of the three years, should benefit from the 10% duty) from retroactive remedies without naming them explicitly so.

It should be kept in mind that the WTO Antidumping Agreement does not impose *in this respect* a particular method to be used for calculating dumping margins (Art. 9.3 AD explicitly acknowledges the possibility of calculating final duties by having recourse to either the prospective or the retrospective system): Art. 2 AD requires from WTO Members to establish a dumping margin by observing its disciplines; and Art. 10 AD requires that in case provisional duties have been imposed and final duties are of a lesser value, then reimbursement should occur. The US system observes both these provisions.

For Canada to move and outlaw the US system, it would have to take the bold step and argue that in case a panel finds that duties should have been lower or never in place, such a recommendation (and/or suggestion) to revoke the order imposing duties should be understood as an obligation to implement retroactive remedies. In this case, the US would never be in a position to honor their WTO obligations, since the US Section 129 does not allow them to implement the WTO remedy in a retroactive manner as its unambiguous wording suggests. This is the step that Canada did not wish to take.

At the end of the day, however, irrespective of whether one qualifies a system as prospective or retroactive, the question is what is the time function of remedies? For a panel to accept Canada's argument, it would mean that the US is punished for committing crimes which would remain unpunished when committed by the EC or Canada or any WTO Member using the prospective system. Such an interpretation would run counter to the explicit acknowledgement in Art. 9.3 AD (indeed, the very provision the violation of which Canada asserted before the panel) that WTO Members can use either method when calculating dumping margins.

Canada was beating around the bush and the panel mimicked this dance. As we explain in what immediately follows, the panel, instead of trying to make some sense of Canada's (admittedly convoluted) arguments, beat around the bush itself, by establishing such a high burden of proof for the complainant that Canada would not be in a position to meet this burden. The panel thereby provided itself with the *deus ex machina* to avoid entering into a sensible understanding of Canada's claims.

3.3   Beating around the bush: the burden of proof ploy

The allocation of burden of proof is judge-made law: even in cases where one might intuitively presume that the burden of proof has been allocated in a particular way (like in the case of Art. 2.4 TBT), WTO adjudicating bodies have offered their own reading of the situation. GATT/WTO adjudicating bodies have more or less followed the maxims *actori incumbit probatio* (the party arguing something carries the burden of proof for its argument) and *jura novit curia* (the court of law is aware of the law applicable). From an economic perspective, it would seem that two considerations are of primordial interest when strategically allocating burden of proof:

(a) what is the objective of the adjudication?
(b) which party is best positioned to know a particular fact?

The response to (a) is quite straightforward: the WTO legal system does not know of *ex officio* complaints. Hence, its objective is not the discovery of the truth (however quixotic such a search might be). Its objective function is to accept or reject claims made by the participants. This is where (b) kicks in. However, since one cannot presume inconsistencies, the original burden of proof is always allocated to the complaining party. Burden of proof should be distinguished from *quantum of proof*: how much is needed to establish what is represented in legal terms as a *prima facie* case of violation is essentially a matter of appreciation by the adjudicating body (and a hardly quantifiable issue).

Let us entertain this discussion through two examples, keeping in mind that there is no dispute as to the mandatory nature of the legislation and as to the fact that Canada absolved its burden of proof in this respect. Under Scenario 1, Section 129 deals with all transactions but not with unliquidated entries, *and* there is another US domestic law provision which deals with such entries. Under Scenario 2, Section 129 deals with all transactions but not with unliquidated entries and there is no US domestic law provision dealing with such entries.[2] Presumably, the Panel's approach is that the burden of proof is the same in both scenarios.

Take Scenario 1: Canada shows what Section 129 does (as it did in the instant dispute), and we assume that the quantum of proof submitted by Canada by and large suffices for Canada to absolve its burden of proof. The burden of proof shifts to the US and all they have to do is show that there is another provision which does exactly what Canada requests (that is, that there is another US law dealing with prior unliquidated entries). The burden of proof shifts to the US since the US are in a better position to know their own legal regime. The downside to such allocation of the burden of proof is that it might incite too many legal challenges. It is to be rationally expected, however, that many cases will not go beyond the consultation stage (assuming that there is an obvious response to the claim, as it is in the present hypothesis).

Take now Scenario 2. Once again, assuming that Canada has shown that the legislation at hand is mandatory, if the burden of proof shifts to the US, Canada wins.

The Panel seems to suggest that for the US law at hand to be WTO-inconsistent it must not only state that it applies to post-USTR direction entries but further that it does not apply to prior unliquidated entries. The policy prescription which stems from this standard is that Canada could only complain about specific instances where prior unliquidated entries have been treated in a WTO-inconsistent manner and not about the legislation as such. But the Panel does not respond to a natural question emerging from this dispute: why would the US apply Section 129 to prior unliquidated entries when SAA, the natural legal context of Section 129 in the Panel's eyes, starts from the premise that all GATT recommendations are prospective? In this view bygones are bygones and there is nothing that one could do about them.

It seems that the Panel went out of its way to establish a very high evidentiary standard (the law must state that it applies to post-USTR direction entries *and* that it does not apply to prior unliquidated entries) in order to avoid discussing the issues before it. As discussed above, Canada's arguments before the Panel are not a monument of clarity and

---

[2] We assume for the study of both scenarios that Canada has proved that the legislation is mandatory.

if at all, the basis for Canada's complaint is much narrower (consistency of the retrospective duty assessment scheme) than the Panel's appreciation of it (retroactive remedies). Probably because the Panel failed to clarify what Canada was actually complaining about or probably because there is a fine line between Canada's arguments as presented before the Panel and the issue of retroactive remedies, the Panel decided to set such discussion aside by bringing forward an admittedly high evidentiary standard.

Of course Panels, by virtue of the maxim *non ultra petita*, cannot rule beyond what has been requested by the parties to the dispute. Since admittedly Canada did not explicitly request a ruling on the issue whether Section 129 does not allow reimbursement of retroactive duties, the Panel could not have addressed the issue in the first place. But Canada's arguments *could* be interpreted as going some way towards this direction:

(a) the retrospective duty assessment scheme practiced by the US concerns *final* and not *provisional* duties (this explains why Canada did not invoke Art. 10 AD for example);
(b) by arguing that Section 129 does not allow the US to apply the WTO-consistent regime to all imports during the last year, Canada is effectively arguing that all final duties applied on a provisional basis by the US should either be re-calculated and partially reimbursed (in a methodology case) or totally reimbursed (in a revocation case);
(c) true, Canada does not request full retroactive remedies. But Canada requests some form of retroactivity for duties perceived during the last year where imports were first burdened by a provisional and then by a definitive assessment.

Such an understanding of Canada's claims is not unthinkable in light of the arguments advanced by Canada. And it is precisely this understanding of Canada's claims that is thwarted once and for all by the panel's choice to impose such a high evidentiary standard for Canada so as to avoid entering into such a discussion.

3.4 The remedies issue

3.4.1 An unresolved issue in WTO law

The SAA starts with the premise that GATT panel recommendations apply only prospectively. As stated above, the Panel holds SAA to be the natural context (and hence relevant for the understanding and the interpretation) of Section 129.

The Panel does not take any formal position on this issue. In fact, the Panel, as we have highlighted in the previous sub-section, goes out of its way in this report to avoid taking any position. It is true that this endeavour of the Panel was to some extent driven by the claims put forward by Canada who did not ask squarely the question of whether this premise is WTO-consistent. A very reticent panel, like this one, found easy refuge behind the Canadian arguments of rather general nature and avoided the issue.

Since the issue was not formally discussed, we will refrain from addressing it in a comprehensive manner in this report. Suffice it to say, however, that

(a) the WTO primary law does not explicitly address the time-function of remedies;
(b) GATT/WTO practice evidences both cases of prospective and cases of retroactive remedies; and
(c) from a public international law perspective, it is far from clear that GATT recommendations are prospective, and there is some GATT/WTO panel-practice to the opposite (of the SAA) direction.[3]

In fact, some good economic arguments could be made in favour of introducing retroactive remedies into the WTO legal system. We turn to such arguments in what immediately follows.

3.4.2   Prospective remedies: enjoy the benefits of cheating without facing the costs of retaliation

In this sub-section, we first describe an economic framework within which the role of trade agreements may be understood. We then discuss remedies in the context of this framework.

We begin with a basic question: What is the purpose of a trade agreement? A satisfactory answer to this question must identify the reason that an appropriately designed trade agreement can offer governments greater political-economic welfare than they can achieve in the absence of a trade agreement (i.e., when trade policies are set unilaterally). In other words, we must identify an inefficiency (relative to governments' welfares) that arises when trade policies are set unilaterally and that is eliminated or reduced in an appropriately designed trade agreement.

---

[3] There are five reported cases in the GATT- and one in the WTO-era where panels recommended retroactive remedies. See Mavroidis (2001).

But what is this inefficiency? Consider a government that is evaluating whether to unilaterally impose an import tariff on some good. The government is aware that the tariff would create "winners" and "losers" in the domestic economy: the tariff would have the effect of raising the domestic price of the affected good, and so the domestic import-competing industry would be a winner while domestic consumers would be losers. Let's suppose that, after weighing the domestic political and economic consequences of the import tariff, the government decides to impose the tariff. Notice that the government's political-economic calcu-lation did not include the impact of the import tariff on the foreign export industry. If the import tariff lowers the profit enjoyed by foreign export-ers, then the foreign export industry – and thus the foreign government – is also a loser when the import tariff is imposed. When trade policies are set unilaterally, tariffs are thus inefficient and "too high," since each government does not internalize the cost of an increase in its own tariff on the welfare of the other government.[4]

From this perspective, it is now straightforward to see that an appro-priately designed trade agreement can eliminate or reduce this ineffi-ciency and raise the welfares of the participating governments beyond those which they would enjoy in the absence of an agreement. Reciprocity is a fundamental feature of such an agreement. A government is willing to make the concession of reducing its import tariff below its preferred unilateral level, provided that its trading partner does the same. In this general manner, a government's concern for its own export industry, in effect, motivates it to weigh in the impact of its import tariff on the foreign export industry.

This argument indicates that the trade-policy relationship between trading partners has a Prisoners' Dilemma structure. Governments could behave unilaterally and select high tariffs, but they would do better by agreeing to select lower tariffs. The enforcement of such an agreement is an important concern, however. This is because each government would gain from selecting a high tariff, if its trading partner's policy is held fixed. Thus, a trade agreement can be valuable as a means through which governments pursue their joint interests and negotiate lower tariffs; but the trade agreement must also include adequate enforcement provi-sions, as otherwise a government would be tempted to "cheat" and raise its tariff back toward the preferred unilateral level.

[4] For further analysis of this point, see Bagwell and Staiger (2002).

A trade agreement becomes enforceable through the possibility of retaliation. Naturally, a government will refrain from cheating with a tariff increase, if it anticipates that the short-run gain in welfare is small in comparison to the long-run welfare loss that occurs once its partner undertakes a retaliatory tariff increase. Like reciprocity, retaliation is thus also a fundamental feature in the design of a trade agreement.

With this framework at hand, we now return to the issue of remedies. Our point is most easily developed through an example. Let us suppose that the government of country A raises a tariff above its negotiated binding. As a result of this action, the government of country B complains that its negotiated benefits have been nullified or impaired. The government of country A disagrees, perhaps arguing that its tariff hike is justified as a safeguard. In any event, a panel is formed, the issue is debated, and ultimately the panel finds in favor of country B. The government of country A then files an appeal, and the case proceeds to the Appellate Body. Eventually, the Appellate Body upholds the panel's finding. At this point, the government of country A must withdraw the offending measure, offer acceptable compensation, or potentially face authorized retaliation by country B. Retaliation would take the form of a withdrawal of a concession by country B, and the magnitude of the corresponding tariff increase would be commensurate in prospective value to that of the tariff increase originally undertaken by country A.

This example points to the possibility that the government of country A may violate its binding, maintain the violation for some period of time (while panel and Appellate Body decisions are being reached), and then return its tariff to the bound level. As suggested by the economic framework sketched above, the government of country A may then enjoy the benefits of cheating without facing the costs of retaliation. Furthermore, even if the offending measure were not removed, the magnitude of the retaliatory response would be scaled relative to the prospective cost of this measure. In this case, too, the government of country A effectively enjoys the short-term benefits of cheating for free.

As this discussion suggests, a dispute settlement system that relies only on prospective remedies may have weak enforcement provisions and thus encourage violations. Such a system allows a government to contemplate a tariff increase without weighing in the full cost of the tariff increase on its trading partner. A better system would be attentive to the retroactive and prospective costs that are attributable to an offending measure. In the context of the example above, the government of country A would be less inclined to raise its tariff and claim a safeguard exemption, when its case is weak, if the remedy system included some penalty for retroactive costs as well. More generally, a remedy system in which the magnitude of any retaliatory response is scaled relative to the retroactive and prospective costs of the offending measure may enhance the enforcement of efficient trade policies.

4   Conclusions

In sum, this panel report suffers first and foremost from the lack of clarity of Canada's arguments. The WTO dispute settlement system is decentralized and panels cannot move and discuss claims not properly before them (Article 6.2 of the WTO Dispute Settlement Understanding, DSU). Hence, to the extent that Canada did not advance a claim, the Panel could not *ex officio* move ahead and discuss it.

This particular case, however, is a bit more complicated. Some of Canada's arguments could be interpreted as moving into the thorny issue of retroactive remedies. The Panel, probably in anticipation, established a high evidentiary standard which is hardly supported by any sort of reasonable allocation of the burden of proof grounds, and thus avoided entering into this discussion.

The fact that Canada did not appeal this report is probably an indicator of the value it attached to the issue.

References

Bagwell, Kyle and Robert W. Staiger. 2002. *The Economics of the World Trading System*, Cambridge, MA: The MIT Press.

Mavroidis, Petros C. 2000. Remedies In The WTO: Between A Rock And A Hard Place, 11 *European Journal of International Law*, 763–813.

3

United States – Tax treatment for "Foreign Sales Corporations" Recourse to Arbitration by the United States under Article 22.6 of the DSU and Article 4.11 of the SCM Agreement (WT/DS108/ARB) A Comment

BY

ROBERT HOWSE
(University of Michigan Law School)

AND

DAMIEN J. NEVEN
(Graduate Institute of International Studies, Geneva)

Some of the legal analysis in this study derives from joint work between Robert Howse and Susan Esserman on this ruling, "Trade disputes quire fairer arbitration," FT.com, Sep 12, 2002

1 Introduction

This chapter discusses the decision by the arbitrator on suspension of concessions ("retaliation") in the dispute between the US and the EU regarding the tax treatment of offshore corporate income under US legislation. By way of background, the first part of the chapter (section 2) describes the operation of the US scheme, including as revised after the first round of WTO rulings.

We observe that the arbitrators have adopted an unconventional approach with respect to the notion of countermeasures, which emphasizes the incentive to induce compliance while largely jettisoning proportionality between the countermeasure and the injury suffered by the wronged state as a meaningful normative constraint. Section 4 considers this approach from the perspective of established principles of international law and highlights a number of important shortcomings.

Section 5 takes this approach for granted and asks whether counter-measures could actually be relied upon in order to induce compliance. We conclude with respect to export subsidies, the incentives of complainants are such that under-enforcement can often be expected. The prospect of inducing compliance through countermeasures thus appears to be somewhat poor and at odds with established principles of international law.

2 Facts and procedure

This section first describes the operation of the US legislative scheme.

2.1 The original FSC scheme

A Foreign Sale Corporation (FSC) is a corporation established outside the United States or in some US possessions, which is involved in the sales of goods produced in the United States to foreign clients. These foreign sales corporations are typically subsidiaries of US companies and benefit from particular tax provisions under the US tax legislation. These provisions were established by the Deficit Reduction Act, adopted by Congress in 1984. In order to understand the tax benefit that flows from these provisions, some key features of the US tax system have to be described.

The US tax system is based on the residence principle, according to which the income of US residents is taxed in the US, whatever the geographical origin of the income. Hence, income generated outside the US is normally taxable in the US. Other countries apply the source principle, according to which income is taxed where it is generated. As a consequence, if income is generated in a country that applies the source principle but accrues to a beneficiary which is resident of a country applying the residence principle, income could be taxed twice. In order to avoid such double taxation, the US can either take into account the taxes paid in foreign countries by giving a tax credit[1] or can simply exempt the income earned in foreign countries.[2]

In the case of capital income, taxes are typically paid both on the profit of a corporation but also on the income of the shareholders of the

---

[1] This is referred to as the "capital export neutrality" principle – because capital is subject to the same tax, whether it is invested in the US or abroad.
[2] This is referred to as the "capital import neutrality" principle, because capital invested in a given country is subject to the same tax, whatever the location of its owner.

corporation when profits are distributed. Hence, the issue of double taxation arises both with respect to taxes of corporate profits (i.e. to what extent should the profit of a subsidiary or related company abroad be taxable in the US, where the parent is located) and taxes on shareholders' income (i.e. to what extent should the distribution of profits from a subsidiary or related company abroad to shareholders in the US be taxable).

Let us consider the first question, namely whether profits of a subsidiary or related company abroad should be taxable in the US. If those profits are taxed abroad and if the US adopts the approach of exempting foreign income, the definition of what can be considered as foreign income matters a great deal: under such system, US corporations will have an incentive to disguise income earned on domestic activities as foreign income (for instance, by shifting profits to foreign corporations), at least if the local tax on foreign income is very low. Hence, the US tax legislation stipulates a comprehensive set of rules to distinguish between income which is "effectively connected with a trade or business in the United States" and that which is not. Only income which is not connected with a trade or business in the United States can be exempted (will not be considered as part of the income of the US parent).

Turning to the taxes on shareholders, the US tax code stipulates that even if a foreign subsidiary or related company is not connected with a trade or business in the United States, dividends will be taxable in the US. There are also special provisions in the US tax code in order to avoid permanent deferrals of the taxes (that would arise if profits are accumulated abroad and never distributed). These provisions apply to companies that are controlled by a US parent and stipulate that US shareholders have to include their pro-rata share of profit of the foreign company in their own income. This provision effectively eliminates the opportunity of deferral for foreign companies that are controlled by shareholders resident in the US.

To sum up, the US tax legislation allows for the exemption of profits accruing to subsidiaries or related companies abroad from US corporate taxes as long as these companies are not connected with domestic activities but still impose taxes on dividends when these profits are repatriated. In addition, the payment of taxes on dividends cannot be deferred in the case of controlled companies.

The tax treatment of FSCs has four key features. First, a fraction of the income earned by an FSC is considered as "not effectively connected with a trade or business in the US" and is not subject to corporate taxes in the US. This fraction is at least 30% and is automatic.

Second, even though FSCs are typically controlled by US parents, the rule that US shareholders (the US parent) should include their prorata share of profit in their own income does not apply to FSCs. Hence, deferral of distributed profits can take place.

Third, dividends of the FSC will be taxed in the US as long as these dividends do not exceed the exempt income, i.e. the profit that is deemed not to be connected with a trade or business in the US. For instance, if that income accounts for 30% of the FSC's total profit, as much as 30% of the profit can be distributed to shareholders without taxes on dividends.

Fourth, the transfer prices between the FSC and its US parent are subject to special rules, which allow for more flexibility than would be allowed between domestic companies. These rules effectively enable the US parents to locate a particularly high share of profits with the FSC.

2.2   The WTO procedure

The original FSC scheme was found to be inconsistent with the Agreement on Subsidies and Countervailing Measures (SCM), both by the panel and the Appellate Body. The panel (upheld on this point by the AB), found that the FSC scheme constitutes a prohibited export subsidy under Art. 3 (1) a of the SCM agreement, essentially because in the absence of the FSC scheme, the US tax authorities would have obtained higher revenues (the tax exemptions under the FSC scheme result in the "foregoing of revenues") and because the financial benefit conferred by the FSC scheme was contingent upon export performance.

The DSB recommended that the US bring the disputed measures into conformity with the Agreement and in particular eliminate the export subsidy element that was found to exist in its taxation scheme.

The US passed a new law, the Extraterritorial Income Exclusion Act of 2000 (ETI Act). The United States and the EU disagreed as to whether this new legislation in fact eliminated the illegal export subsidy element that was impugned in the WTO proceedings.

The EU and the US had an understanding that (i) if the EU should decide to have recourse to Art. 21.5 (involving a compliance panel), it would also simultaneously request the imposition of countermeasures, using Art. 22.6, (ii) that the US would object to those measures, (iii) that the matter would be referred to arbitration and (iv) that the arbitration would be suspended until completion of a first round of 21.5 procedure (involving the adoption of a panel report and possibly an Appellate Body report). The parties thus committed to an arbitration procedure regarding countermeasures, but only following the 21.5 procedure.

In the 21.5 case, both the panel and the Appellate Body found that the ETI Act contained an export subsidy component and thus that the United States had failed to bring itself into compliance. The final step that remained was, then, a 22.6 arbitration on countermeasures, which is the subject of this chapter.

3 The ruling

We first describe the relevant legal provisions before turning to the concept of appropriate countermeasures developed by the arbitrators and evaluation of the countermeasures proposed by the EU.

3.1 Relevant provisions

The arbitration takes the view that the rules of the DSU with respect to the evaluation of the countermeasures apply to the SCM, except in the presence of specific rules (*lex specialis*).

In particular, Art. 22.7 of the DSU provides that

> The arbitrator acting pursuant to paragraph 6 shall not examine the nature of the concessions or other obligations to be suspended but shall determine whether the level of such suspension is equivalent to the level of nullification or impairment

Whereas, Article 4.11 of the SCM agreement provides that

> In the event a party to the dispute requests arbitration under paragraph 6 of Article 22 of the Dispute Settlement Understanding ("DSU"), the arbitrator shall determine whether the countermeasures are appropriate*
> (*original footnote n° 9. This expression is not meant to allow countermeasures that would be disproportionate in light of the fact that the subsidies dealt with under these provisions are prohibited).

The DSU provision thus focuses on the equivalence between the level of suspension and the level of nullification or impairment whereas the SCM focuses on whether countermeasures are appropriate. Much of the arbitrators' comments are concerned with the interpretation of this last provision, given that the parties proposed rather different interpretations.

The EU proposed countermeasures for about $4 billion, which corresponded to its own estimate of the amount of the subsidy granted by the

FSC legislation every year. The US considered that the trade impact on the Member country concerned was the relevant benchmark to determine whether the countermeasure was "appropriate". The US further considered that the value of the subsidy could be taken as a proxy for the trade impact and hence that the proportion of the subsidy which affects the EU would be appropriate (using the share of exports to the EU in total US exports as the relevant factor). The US also encouraged the arbitrators not to use more sophisticated estimates of the trade impact (beyond the value of the subsidy).

The EU argued that the SCM agreement stipulates a particular benchmark for what is appropriate which does not relate to the trade impact but rather emphasizes the incentive to comply. The EU further considered that the value of the subsidy is conservative in terms of this benchmark.

3.2   The concept of appropriate countermeasures

The arbitrators effectively adopted the approach advocated by the EU.

The arbitrators first note that countermeasures are meant (just as a matter of language) to neutralize a measure but that neutralization could be understood in terms of the measure itself or in terms of its effect.

The arbitrators then take the view that countermeasures in the context of Art. 4.10 cannot be confined to redressing or neutralizing effects only. The main argument in support of their approach relates to footnote 9 of the SCM agreement, which provides some guidance of how "appropriate" should be understood. They find support for their approach in the structure of the SCM agreement, which distinguishes between "prohibited" subsidies, and subsidies that are "actionable", i.e. that may be the subject of a complaint if it can be established that they cause certain kinds of trade effects, but otherwise do not attract state responsibility.

Let us consider some of these arguments in more detail. The main argument for not confining the evaluation of "appropriate" countermeasures to an effects test (of which a trade test is just one version) rests on the interpretation of footnote 9.

This footnote which indicates that "[appropriate] is not meant to allow countermeasures that are disproportionate in light of the fact that the subsidies dealt with under these provisions are prohibited", is a little convoluted. It reads as if it sets an upper bound on the countermeasures that can imposed (by not allowing them to be disproportionate). At the same time, it emphasizes the unlawful character of the measure at stake, which is an aggravating factor, and hence can be seen as warning against excessively low countermeasures or in other words as setting some lower bound on the countermeasures. The arbitrators effectively emphasize this second aspect. They observe that the measures at stake (export subsidies) are *per se* unlawful and hence that the imposition of such measures upsets the balance of rights and obligations under the WTO agreement, independently of their effects and in particular independently of the magnitude of their trade effects. According to the arbitrators "this emphasis on the unlawful character of the export subsidies invites . . . a consideration of the impact that this unlawful character may have in itself" (Para. 5.23). "It directs us to consider the appropriateness of countermeasures under Art. 4.10 from this perspective of countering a wrongful act and taking into account its essential nature as an upsetting of the rights and obligations as between Members. This, we conclude, is the manner in which we are directed to assess the matter. We are not, by comparison, actually directed to, e.g., consider demonstrated trade effects of the measure on the complaining Member."

Having established that appropriate countermeasures in the context of Art. 4.10 do not have to be restricted to an effects test, the arbitrators consider what alternative benchmark could be used. They find inspiration in the object and purpose of the SCM agreement in relation to Art. 4.10 and those of the DSB. They observe that in this context, the DSB can *only* recommend that the offending member withdraw its subsidy without delay, and hence that the countermeasures, which contribute to the objective of the DSB in the case of non compliance – should have the same objective. Hence, countermeasures should be considered as an incentive mechanism and whether they are "appropriate" should be assessed in terms of whether they induce compliance, i.e. contribute to the withdrawal of the subsidy.

The consequences of this determination should not be underestimated. It implies, in particular, that what matters in evaluating the appropriateness of countermeasures is not the effect on the importing country but rather the effect on the exporting country: indeed, the amount of countermeasure that will induce compliance should at least be equal to the benefit that the exporting country obtains from the export subsidy. Hence, it is perceived benefit to the exporting country that will provide an appropriate benchmark and not the cost incurred by the importing countries. That is also to say that the arbitrators have not only argued that the trade effects on importing countries cannot provide the only benchmark for evaluating countermeasures but also proposed that the effects on the exporting countries will provide a useful benchmark. This implication however seems to have been lost on the arbitrators (see below).

It is also worth noting that the concern about setting an upper bound on the amount of countermeasures in Art. 4.10 (such that measures should not be disproportionate) is of a second order if one takes the view that countermeasures should be used as an incentive mechanism. Indeed, only the lower bound will matter for the incentive mechanism: as long as the penalty is sufficient to induce compliance, the magnitude of the penalty will not matter – because it will not be applied (or it will be applied only during a transition period). Hence, the fact that the arbitrators emphasize the lower bound expressed in footnote 10, and tend to neglect the upper bound, is consistent with the incentive approach that they develop.

The approach which is developed by the arbitrators can also be characterized as one establishing a property rule rather than a liability rule. As emphasized by Schwartz and Sykes (2002), a property rule is a mechanism whereby a party needs to secure the permission of others before deviating from its obligations. By contrast, a liability rule is a mechanism whereby a party wishing to deviate from its obligations is only liable for the damages that the deviation causes. According to Schwartz and Sykes (2002), the main drawback of a liability rule is associated with the need to have a third party evaluate the damages. The property rule avoids this difficulty but may involve important transactions costs, associated with bargaining between the state wishing to deviate and its victims.

3.3   Assessment of the countermeasures proposed by the EU

In evaluating whether the amount of the export subsidy is an appropriate countermeasure, the arbitrators discuss whether it is in principle permissible, analyze the countermeasure in relation with the subsidy and discuss the extent to which the subsidy should be reduced by a factor that reflects the relative importance for the EU as an export market.

The arbitrators find that the proposed countermeasures are in principle permissible because "they are tailored to the initial wrongful act they are to counter" (Para. 6.11). The observation that countermeasures are "tailored" to the initial wrongful act arises, according to the arbitrators, from the fact that the amount of the subsidy "– the expense incurred – is the very essence of the wrongful act" (Para. 6.10).

Having established that a countermeasure which aims to "challenge the wrongful act in itself" (Para. 6.11) is in principle permissible, the arbitrators analyze the key elements of the wrongful act in order to check whether the proposed countermeasures are indeed "not disproportionate". In other words, the arbitrators attempt to derive some dimensions of the wrongful act along which proportionality can be assessed.

The arbitrators identify two dimensions, namely the financial contribution and the benefit to the recipients of the subsidy. With respect to the former, the arbitrators observe that the identity between the export subsidy and the countermeasure respects a form of proportionality (which goes beyond the superficial appeal that equal numbers may have). They note that the amount of the subsidy is the essential wrongful act of the US government. As the EU cannot "thwart these expenses at source," it proposes to suspend a "numerically equivalent obligation which it owes to the United States." According to the arbitrators, "it appears . . . that is a proper manner from which to judge the congruence of the counter-measure to the measure at issue, i.e. to view it under its legal category: on the one hand an expense to government of a certain value constituting an upsetting of the balance of rights and obligations; and therefore, on the other hand, a congruent duty imposed by a responding government as a mirror withdrawal of an obligation" (Para. 6.19).

With respect to the benefits accruing to recipients, the arbitrators note that the EU countermeasures could be viewed "as aiming to deprive US firms of an advantage that they would otherwise receive in relation to access to the EC market" (Para. 6.21). To the extent that the counter-measures impose a cost on US firms, they could be seen as annulling or "counteracting" the benefit that they receive through the export subsidy. The arbitrators note however that computing the amount of counter-measures that would annul the benefits is hardly feasible (especially at the firm level) but that a precise equivalence is not required given that the justification for the countermeasure is to counteract the "legal breach as a wrongful act" (Para. 6.22).

The arbitrators, observing that the EU has focused on the first dimension of the subsidy but that the US has not objected to that approach, conclude that the countermeasures proposed are not disproportionate to the initial wrongful act.

The approach followed by the arbitrators in evaluating the counter-measures is surprising, to the extent that it seems to depart from the principles established earlier. In particular, the arbitrators do not attempt to apply the principle that countermeasures are meant to act as an incentive mechanism to ensure compliance. They do not even refer to this principle any longer.

One would have expected that in line with the logic of an incentive mechanism, the arbitrators would have considered the penalty that is required in order to make it attractive for the US to withdraw the measure. The only oblique reference to the logic of incentive can be found in the discussion of benefits to US firms (Para. 6.21) – in which the arbitrators find that a cost imposed on US firms commensurate with the benefit that they receive from the export subsidy would be appropriate. Such a cost might presumably induce US firms to ask the US government to remove the subsidy – and hence induce compliance. However, the logic of the argument is not clearly spelled out.

As indicated above, the arbitrators also discuss whether the amount of the countermeasure – evaluated as the subsidy – should be reduced to reflect the relative importance of the EU as an export market. They consider that such an approach would be inconsistent with the nature of a *per se* obligation – which by definition is not a quantitative matter but one of principle.

The arbitrators recognize that this approach may be problematic if there were several WTO Members demanding countermeasures – but effectively escape the problem by suggesting that they do not have to consider a set of facts that is different from the facts that they are confronted with. They note at the same time that the EU is open to the possibility of sharing the "task" (sic) of applying countermeasures with other WTO Members affected by the subsidies.

4   Countermeasures, compliance, and proportionality

In this section, we first recall some principles of international law with respect to the definition of countermeasures. We subsequently consider the approach of the arbitrators in light of these principles.

4.1   Countermeasures in international law

It is a well-established principle of international law that countermeasures in response to an internationally wrongful act must be proportional to the injury suffered by the state taking the countermeasures. This is now reflected in Article 51 of the ILC Draft Articles on State Responsibility: "Countermeasures must be commensurate with the injury suffered, taking into account the gravity of the internationally wrongful act and the rights in question." While Article 49 of the ILC Articles states the purpose of countermeasures as inducing compliance of the violating state, the effect of Article 51 is to place an essential constraint on the quantity and nature of countermeasures, such that even if a higher amount of countermeasures might serve the goal of inducing compliance, counter-measures are limited to what is proportional to the injury suffered. As Crawford puts it: "Proportionality is, . . . , a limitation even on measures which may be justified under 49. *In every case* a countermeasure must be commensurate with the injury suffered, including the importance of the issue of principle involved, . . ." (Crawford (2002), p. 296; emphasis added). In Cannizaro's words, "the wording of Draft Article 51 clearly indicates that the ILC conceives proportionality as a factor mitigating the instrumental nature of countermeasures." (Cannizzaro (2001), p. 894).

Customary international law and general principles of international law govern the application and interpretation of WTO law, except where there is an explicit contracting out of such rules evidenced by a provision of the WTO treaties. (*Korea – Government Procurement*, Report of the Panel; see also *EC – Hormones*, Report of the Appellate Body, discussing the Precautionary Principle). Article 55 of the ILC Articles explicitly recognizes that the ILC Articles do not apply to the extent that state responsibility is governed by "special rules of international law."

As Crawford notes, "it will depend on the special rule to establish the extent to which the more general rules on State responsibility set out in the present articles are displaced by that rule." (Crawford (2002), p. 307).

There are a number of respects in which the WTO "special rules" on countermeasures obviously alter between the parties the law of counter-measures set out in the ILC Articles. First of all, breach of a primary obligation in a WTO treaty does not give rise to a right by the injured party to take countermeasures; instead, the matter must be taken to dispute settlement (DSU Article 23: *US – Section 301*, Report of the Panel). Then countermeasures are *only* available to the party or parties which have pursued dispute settlement proceedings, and *only* for the breach of the secondary obligation to *implement* a dispute settlement ruling that is binding on the parties. Such countermeasures must, further-more, be authorized by an arbitral panel, and must not exceed the nullification and impairment of benefits resulting from the failure to implement the ruling. Thus, countermeasures may not be backdated to the time of the breach of the primary obligation; the internationally wrongful act that these countermeasures respond to is the secondary obligation to implement a binding ruling of the DSB.

Countermeasures are available also for failure to implement a non-violation nullification and impairment ruling; this illustrates perhaps most dramatically of all the sense in which the internationally wrongful act at which countermeasures are aimed is failure to implement, because, of course, in non-violation nullification and impairment cases, by defini-tion, no violation of a primary obligation has been found.

The SCM Agreement contains an even more specialized set of rules on countermeasures that apply to cases of failure to implement rulings on prohibited subsidies under the SCM Agreement. Article 4.10 provides for the authorization of "appropriate" countermeasures, where the recom-mendation of the DSB is not followed within the time period specified by the panel. Footnote 10 to Article 4.10 states that the wording "appro-priate" is "not meant to allow countermeasures that are disproportionate in light of the fact that the subsidies dealt with under these provisions are prohibited."

In understanding this footnote, one must contrast the treatment of countermeasures with respect to prohibited subsidies under the SCM Agreement with that of another category of subsidies, labelled "action-able." The obligation of WTO Members in the case of "actionable" sub-sidies is one of result: in applying such subsidies, Members are required to avoid certain "adverse effects."[3] Where countermeasures are authorized for failure to comply with a ruling on actionable subsidies, these counter-measures must be "commensurate with the degree and nature of the adverse effects determined to exist, . . ." (Article 7.8).

Footnote 9 to Article 4.10 makes it clear that in applying the notion of proportionality in the case of prohibited subsidies commensurability of countermeasures need not be measured against the existence of the adverse effects that Members are obliged to avoid in respect of actionable, as opposed to prohibited, subsidies. Nothing in the language of Footnote 9, however, evinces a clear intent to do away, in the case of prohibited subsidies, with the principle stated in ILC Article 51 that countermeasures must be proportionate to the injury suffered. It is just that the drafters wanted to make it clear that in *applying* the principle of proportionality, the understanding of "injury" in the case of prohibited subsidies is not *limited* to the *kinds* of adverse effects that make actionable subsidies illegal. This makes sense when one considers that prohibited subsidies

---

[3] These adverse effects are defined in the following terms in Article 5 of the SCM Agreement as one or more of: "(a) injury to the domestic industry of another Member [footnote omitted]; (b) nullification or impairment of benefits accruing directly or indirectly to other Members under GATT 1994 in particular the benefits of concessions bound under Article II of GATT 1994 [footnote omitted]; (c) serious prejudice to the interests of another Member [footnote omitted]." The concept of "serious prejudice," defined in detail in SCM Article 6, ceased to apply after 1999, however, because of its provisional nature, as set out in SCM Article 31.

are export subsidies, whereas actionable subsidies are domestic subsidies; export subsidies may have adverse economic effects different and beyond those of domestic subsidies. In sum, "actionable" subsidies are *themselves* illegal and prohibited to the extent that they cause the adverse effects described in SCM Article 5; but because they are illegal *only to the extent that they cause those particular adverse effects*, an adjudicator must regard the adverse effects in question as an *upper limit* on countermeasures (SCM Article 7.8). Footnote 9 to Article 4.10 merely indicates that in the case of export subsidies, the proportionality of countermeasures must be assessed in light of the fact that these subsidies are "prohibited" per se, i.e. unlike "actionable" subsidies, prohibited *regardless* of whether *the kind* of adverse effects described in SCM Article 5 can be demonstrated by the complainant. But this hardly means that the injury to the defendant is *irrelevant* in assessing countermeasures in the case of "prohibited" subsidies; it is just that the adjudicator should not assume (as it is required to do in the case of actionable subsidies by SCM Article 7.8) that the injury is *limited* to the adverse effects described in Art. 5 in regard to "actionable" domestic subsidies.

4.2   The analysis of the panel

The arbitral panel in FSC misrepresented and misapplied this legal framework.

First of all, the panel took the reference to "prohibition" in Article 4.10, Footnote 9 not as a signal that the conception of economic injury for prohibited subsidies will be different from that for actionable subsidies, but rather as a basis for throwing out the window *any* effort to gauge the relationship of the subsidy to the injury suffered by the party requesting countermeasures.

The panel thus began its analysis of proportionality by reference to factors completely unrelated to the nature and extent of the injury suffered by the state requesting countermeasures. It noted that the US measure was "inherently destabilizing" or upsetting of the balance of legal rights and obligations. But defined in those abstract terms, so is any act in violation of a treaty norm; the whole basis of *pacta sunt servanda* is that violations of treaty norms undermine legal security, and the normative balance of rights and obligations. Such consequences therefore do not in themselves suggest a particular level of countermeasures, nor provide a basis for determining the gravity of a breach.

Thus, the panel was forced to make a leap of logic between the concept of security and stability of the balance of legal rights and obligations to the notion that this particular subsidy, being widely available, "creates systematic uncertainty and instability of expectations as to trading conditions" (para. 6.9). But there is nothing in the SCM Agreement that entitles a WTO Member to certainty and stability of trading conditions. Instead, it has again and again been emphasized in WTO jurisprudence that, as a general matter (and with the qualified exception of non-violation nullification and impairment complaints), WTO rules do not entitle Members to fixed expectations of trading conditions, but only to *legal* certainty; the expectation that Members will continue to act in compliance with the specific constraints placed on their conduct in the treaties. (See *US – Section 301*, Report of the Panel; *EC – LAN Equipment*, Report of the Appellate Body).

In considering the "gravity" of the breach the arbitral panel placed much weight on the fact that the export subsidies in question were "prohibited" per se under the SCM Agreement. But the categories of "prohibited" and "actionable" subsidies are merely terms of art in the SCM Agreement. The fact that the obligation with respect to the former category, export subsidies, is one of conduct whereas the obligation with respect to domestic subsidies is one of result (avoidance of certain adverse effects) does not in itself establish the special gravity of a violation of the SCM provisions on export subsidies. The panel here seems to be relying on a discredited notion in earlier versions of the draft ILC Articles that obligations of conduct are stricter than obligations of result; a view that, as Crawford explains, was explicitly rejected in the drafting of the final version of the Articles. (Crawford (2003), pp. 21–23; and see P.-M. Dupuy, "Reviewing the Difficulties of Codification: On Ago's Classification of Obligations of Means and Obligations of Result in Relation to State Responsibility").

The fact is that *both* prohibited and actionable subsidies attract state responsibility under the SCM Agreement.

In the case of actionable subsidies, there is a legal duty to "take appropriate steps to remove the adverse effects or . . . withdraw the subsidy" (7.8). As already noted, the failure to take such steps can result in countermeasures, which must be commensurate with "adverse effects" as defined in Articles 5 and 6 of the SCM Agreement. The *only* difference in the case of "prohibited" subsidies is that countermeasures are not limited by the concept of "adverse effects" in Articles 5 and 6. But it is a huge and unjustified leap to infer from this that "prohibited" subsidies are not subject to the general rules of international law on proportionality to the injury (admittedly a concept of injury that is not circumscribed by the *particular* meaning of "adverse effects" that is defined in the case of actionable subsidies in SCM 5 and 6).

It should be noted that most WTO obligations have been stated and interpreted as obligations of conduct or means, not result; and nevertheless, in respect of these hundreds or thousands of obligations of *conduct*, countermeasures are limited, under Article 22 of the DSU to measures of equivalent effect to the defendant Member's failure to implement. In sum, the general countermeasures regime of the WTO is inconsistent with the notion that the breach of an obligation of conduct has a special gravity to it, justifying countermeasures that may be in excess of the actual harm resulting from the failure to comply from a ruling.

This of course assumes that the panel was even correct in considering the gravity of the initial wrongful act, as opposed to the gravity of the failure to implement the panel ruling. Since under the WTO modification of the general international law of state responsibility and countermeasures, countermeasures are only available, as explained above, for the failure to comply with a *binding dispute settlement ruling*, it is arguable that the *relevant wrongful act*, the gravity of which must be considered, is this failure to comply, not the initial act of subsidization, though the two will have some relation, at least in certain cases.

Here it must be borne in mind that, as noted in the introductory section of this report, the United States attempted once to reform its FSC scheme to bring it into conformity with an initial Appellate Body ruling, but these changes were deemed inadequate by the 21.5 compliance panel, a finding upheld by the Appellate Body. When the revised scheme was found not to be adequate as an implementation measure, the United States engaged in serious negotiations with both domestic interests and the EC, to find a solution satisfactory to all parties. As far as the US behaviour goes after it was found not to be in compliance with its new scheme, there is nothing to suggest aggravation of the breach entailed in failing to implement. It should be noted that in any case the Appellate Body never characterized the US as acting in bad faith or pursuing an internationally wrongful purpose. Also, the FSC legislation is clearly a very complex piece of legislation that has economic implications that go beyond the context of trade, and relate to the entire corporate taxation approach of the US. This does not, of course, excuse the US for failing to implement the DSB ruling in a timely fashion; but it does suggest that there could be explanations for not doing so that do not suggest any particular element of "bad faith" or egregious violation in the US behaviour, as the panel sometimes suggests, for example, referring to the US as in "persistent violation" (paragraph 6.15).

Even if one sets aside these errors in applying the notion of gravity of breach, an analysis of the intrinsic gravity of the breaching act does not obviate the need to nevertheless consider, as well, the injury to the party requesting countermeasures. Thus, to revert to ILC Article 51, "Countermeasures must be commensurate with the injury suffered, taking into account the gravity of the internationally wrongful act and the rights in question (emphasis added)." This language cannot possibly justify the panel's conduct, which is to collapse the inquiry into injury, into an assessment of the gravity of the internationally wrongful act. If that were the intent, then Article 51 would refer only to commensurability with the internationally wrongful act; the reference to the injury suffered would be superfluous.

In any case, having ignored the basic notion of proportionality in international law, that of commensurability with the injury suffered, the panel invented its own conception of proportionality – how much it cost the *breaching* state to violate its international obligations! There is something odd in this reversal – the quantum of countermeasures being determined by the cost of the wrongful act to the perpetrator, not the cost to the victim. Of course, there is usually *some* relationship between the cost of a wrongful act to the perpetrator and the extent of harm to the victim state; the more that a state spends on chemical weapons, all things being equal, the greater the threat to other states. But the international law requirement of proportionality in countermeasures is not intended simply to establish some kind of arithmetic relationship – or ratio – between the wrongful act and the countermeasures, but rather to *limit* countermeasures so that they do not *exceed* the injury to the victim state.[4] The arbitral panel was required by international law to address itself to

---

[4] Countermeasures can almost always be expressed as some proportion or ratio: so for example, in a dispute over wrongful treatment of aliens, the home state could demand countermeasures of $1,000,000 for each alien improperly detained. There would be a "manifest relationship of proportionality" in the manner in which the panel understands proportionality, i.e. some kind of arithmetic ratio of countermeasures to the injury (the more aliens improperly treated the higher the quantum) but this would in no way answer the question of whether the countermeasures are disproportionate in the sense of excessive in relation to the injury taking into account the gravity of the breach, which is what is required by ILC Article 51.

whether, in using the amount of the entire subsidy it would be imposing an amount of countermeasures that *exceeded* the injury to the EC, properly understood. This the arbitral panel never did. By introducing other, mostly spurious or irrelevant meanings of proportionality, it simply avoided completely the question of the extent of injury to the state requesting countermeasures.

In turning to the costs of the subsidy as an appropriate benchmark for countermeasures, the arbitral panel sought to justify itself on the grounds that "financial contribution" was one of the elements of the internationally wrongful act in question, namely the continued provision of a prohibited export subsidy (para. 6.13). However, according to the SCM Agreement there is *no element of wrongfulness whatsoever* that attaches to the mere act of providing "financial contribution." *Only* where the financial contribution provides a "benefit" to a specific domestic firm or industry *can* any element of international wrongfulness attach to the act of subsidization. Thus no possibility of misfeasance arises by virtue of the "financial contribution" itself. The element of misfeasance is the conferral of a benefit on a domestic industry, through a subsidy contingent in law or in fact upon export performance. It is not as if some element or degree of wrongfulness arises from the "financial contribution" alone.

Thus, if the panel were to follow its own logic correctly it would relate the amount of countermeasures to the "benefit" – i.e. the competitive advantage over general market conditions conferred on domestic firms in consequence of the subsidy. Focusing on "benefit" would naturally lead to an analysis of the kind of economic harm to foreign firms competing with domestic US firms that was caused by the subsidy. And this in turn would have been much more consistent with, and indeed required, an inquiry into the nature and extent of the injury to the EC. At paragraph 6.21 of its ruling, the panel shows some dim awareness that "benefit" might be a more appropriate benchmark for assessing countermeasures than "financial contribution." The panel dismisses this concern by collapsing the notion of benefit into the notion of expense by the treasury, assuming benefit can be measured by the expended money that is granted to the firm. It is precisely such a move that was firmly rejected by the Appellate Body in *Canada – Aircraft*: "... we believe that Canada's argument that 'cost to government' is one way of conceiving of 'benefit' is at odds with the ordinary meaning of Article 1.1(b), which focuses on the *recipient* and not on the *government* providing the financial contribution." (para. 154; emphasis in original).

4.3 The prohibition of export subsidies as an "Erga Omnes" obligation

The failure of the panel to consider properly whether countermeasures in the total amount of the financial contribution would be disproportionate to the injury suffered by the EC is particularly egregious when one considers that the financial cost of the subsidy extended to all firms doing business everywhere in the world, not just the EC. In fact, the United States was prepared to go along with the use of an amount based upon financial cost of the subsidy, provided that amount was prorated to reflect the EC's total percentage of total trade with the US. In other words, the US was prepared to accept an amount of counter-measures that equalled the amount of subsidization that could reasonably have been expected to have an effect on the EC's markets.

At this point, the reasoning of the panel seems, at best, convoluted. To begin with, the panel stated that it viewed the prohibition on export subsidies as an *erga omnes* obligation to the entire community, of a kind such that the level of countermeasures should take into account the harm to the community, and not simply the injury to the state requesting the countermeasures.

A prohibition on export subsidies cannot plausibly be an *erga omnes* obligation. *Erga omnes* obligations are considered to be largely co-extensive with *ius cogens*, peremptory norms of international law such as the prohibitions on torture and genocide. (Pauwellyn (2002)).

What the panel had in mind was, more likely, the concept of an *erga omnes partes* obligation, i.e. an obligation owed not only to each Member of the WTO individually, but to the entire Membership as a collectivity. As Pauwellyn notes, according to the Commentary on the ILC Articles, "[the]. . . *principal* purpose [of *erga omnes partes* obligations] will be to foster a common interest, over and above any interests of the States concerned individually."(Commentary, pp. 320–321, para (7)). Obligations in human rights and environmental treaties have been considered *erga omnes partes*: these obligations embody some universal principle or seek some global public good.

While, according to Pauwellyn, there are some elements of collective interest in WTO obligations, in most cases their principal purpose is to serve and protect the interests of individual Member states. The Preamble to the WTO Agreement states some common purposes or interests such as "allowing for the optimal use of the world's resources in accordance with the objective of sustainable development, . . .", but makes it clear that the *way* in which the WTO contributes to such common interests is through *"reciprocal and mutually advantageous* arrangements directed to the substantial reduction of tariffs and other barriers to trade ..." (emphasis added). Thus, while they may *serve* some common interests and objectives, the *nature* of WTO obligations, generally speaking, is that they are "reciprocal and mutually advantageous."

Pauwellyn admits that there may be some obligations in the WTO Agreements (of an institutional framework nature) that could correctly be characterized as *erga omnes partes*; we do not necessarily agree with Pauwellyn's every characterization of a WTO obligation as bilateral. A full engagement with his position is beyond the scope of this Report. The panel, however, simply pulled out of a hat the notion that the prohibition on export subsidies is *erga omnes partes*. It failed to make any analysis whatever of the meaning of this concept (perhaps because it got the concept confused in the first place with *erga omnes*).

Is, then, the prohibition on export subsidies an *erga omnes partes*? Here, we return to the observation that export subsidization is only prohibited in the SCM agreement to the extent that it confers a "benefit"; in other words, such subsidization is only wrongful to the extent that it confers a competitive advantage beyond that which the entities in question would normally enjoy in the marketplace.

Why should conferring such a competitive advantage be internationally wrongful? This could only be so because of the effects on the economic interests of other states, i.e. the relative competitive positions of firms and industries in other WTO Member states. It is true that, in the case of export subsidies, unlike other subsidies, these effects are *assumed* once a benefit has been established, but such an assumption is reasonable where the subsidy is contingent on export. By knowing that a subsidy is a subsidy on exports, *and* that it confers a "benefit," i.e. a competitive advantage in respect of the exported products, we *know* that it is likely to affect competition in *foreign* markets.[5] It is for this reason that proof of adverse effects on other WTO Members is not required to establish a violation. Contrary to what the arbitral panel apparently thinks, it is not that export subsidies are somehow wrongful *regardless* of their effects on

---

[5] By contrast domestic subsidies may be aimed at capturing positive externalities (public goods) within the domestic market, e.g. R and D. They may be conferred on firms that do not trade internationally at all, or in areas of the economy where there is no significant import competition from other WTO Members. It is thus understandable that these domestic subsidies would only be wrongful, if *shown* to have the result of adverse affects on other WTO Members.

trade of individual WTO Members. It is that, taken together, the facts that exports are targeted and that a benefit (competitive advantage) is conferred lead to *Res Ipse Loquitur* with respect to adverse affects on other WTO Members.

The conclusion with respect to prohibition on export subsidies is that this WTO obligation is principally aimed at protecting the economic interests of individual WTO Members, by preventing a Member from providing its own exports with an artificial competitive advantage in the markets of other WTO Members or third countries where that Member's exports are competing with those of other WTO Members.

But, to return to an issue raised earlier in this Report, the panel merely assumes that the obligation for violation of which countermeasures can be authorized under WTO law is the primary obligation, i.e. prohibition of export subsidies and not the secondary obligation to implement an adopted panel and/or Appellate Body ruling that the primary obligation has been violated.

Is this secondary obligation *erga omnes partes*? There is a community interest in the rule of law that is served by implementation of adopted reports and disserved by non-implementation; this is reflected in DSU 21.1, which states "Prompt compliance with recommendations or rulings of the DSB is essential in order to ensure effective resolution of disputes to the benefit of *all* Members."(emphasis added). On the other hand, DSU describes dispute settlement as aiming at a "prompt settlement of situations in which a Member considers that any benefits accruing to *it* directly or indirectly . . . are being impaired by measures taken by another Member . . ." This language seems to make it clear that, while there is a community interest in compliance, the fundamental or primary interest at stake in dispute settlement is that of *individual* WTO Members in respect of measures taken by other Members. Thus, it is established in GATT/WTO practice that dispute settlement rulings are only legally binding between the parties, and not legally binding on the Membership as a whole, or the WTO as an organization (*Japan – Alcohol*).

Only a party to the initial proceedings may thus demand countermeasures; and this follows from the fact that the ruling that the defendant is failing to implement is binding on that Member only as a party to that proceeding, and not by virtue of being a Member of the WTO.

In sum, neither the primary nor the secondary obligation can reasonably be considered an obligation *erga omnes partes*.

In addition to the argument that the prohibition on export subsidies was an *erga omnes (partes)* obligation, the arbitral panel also justified its decision to not to adjust the total amount of countermeasures in light of the EC's percentage of global trade on the theory that the higher level of countermeasures would "have the practical effect of facilitating prompt compliance by the United States." However, as pointed out earlier in this analysis, proportionality as expressed in ILC Article 51 limits the level of countermeasures, even where a higher level might contribute to the legitimate objective of compliance.

Finally, disingenuously, the panel attacked the United States' argument that the amount of the countermeasures should be adjusted in light of the EC share of world trade on the grounds that this kind of method for calculating countermeasures would be "arbitrary." Why? "It simply presumes a one to one correspondence of dollar of subsidy to dollar of trade impact." (paragraph 6.9). But of course this is what the *panel itself* assumed in the first place in resorting to the *total* amount of the subsidy as the measure of injury (albeit to the entire Membership, on the *erga omnes partes* theory).

4.4   Alternative approaches to quantum

The Panel considered alternative approaches to calculating countermeasures, based on estimates of injury to the EC rather than the amount of subsidy; such approaches were in fact on the evidentiary record, presumably because the parties had some awareness that, in international law, proportionality cannot be evaluated without reference to injury to the victim state. The panel noted that at least on one approach to calculating the adverse effects on the EC, the amount could actually be higher than the total amount of the subsidy. It asserted that the United States had not been persuasive in showing that a better methodology would result in an amount of adverse effects on the EC below that of the total amount of the subsidy. Here the reasoning of the panel is as follows: the EC has proposed the entire amount of the financial contribution as the quantum of countermeasures; the United States has not proven that a clearly superior methodology for estimating the injury to the EC from the subsidy would result in a lesser amount; therefore, even if the amount of the subsidy is an arbitrary consideration in relation to injury, there is no compelling reason to reject the EC request. This seems to be an alternative basis for the panel's entire ruling, one that has nothing to do with the panel's earlier argument that the amount of the subsidy is directly related to the gravity of the breach and the injury, and that it is appropriate, because we are dealing with an *erga omnes partes* obligation, to base countermeasures on the injury to the entire WTO community.

While in fact this alternative theory of the ruling actually contradicts the prior analysis of the panel, it does at least have the advantage of being supported by precedent. In the *Brazil – Aircraft* case, the arbitral panel accepted the amount of the subsidy as the appropriate amount of countermeasures, observing that it was up to Brazil, the country challenging the amount of the countermeasures, to show that this amount was not "appropriate." The effect, according to the arbitral panel, was that in the case of the evidence being "in equipoise" Brazil would lose its claim of inappropriateness (Paras. 2.8–2.9).

Is this understanding of the burden of proof jurisprudentially sound? It is true that the effect of SCM 4.10–4.11 is that it will often be up to the state that is the target of countermeasures to challenge the quantum in arbitration; this is because 4.10 provides that the DSB shall directly authorize countermeasures, unless a Member seeks arbitration. Thus, where the DSB may be inclined to grant the countermeasures as requested by the Member that is victim of a breach, arbitration would only be likely to be invoked by the Member that is the target of the intended countermeasures to challenge the quantum. Thus, as a general matter it will be up to the party challenging the countermeasures to show that they are not "appropriate."

However, footnote 10 to 4.11 says that disproportionate countermeasures are not allowed; the arbitrator *must* not read the word "appropriate" in 4.11 to allow disproportionate countermeasures. This footnote, when considered in conjunction with the categorical requirement of proportionality in ILC Article 51, suggests that even if the party challenging the countermeasures has not as a general matter proven that they are inappropriate, the arbitrator must nevertheless insure that the countermeasures are not disproportionate. In other words, disproportionality is an exception to the general presumption that countermeasures proposed by the victim state are "appropriate" subject to the violator state showing otherwise. This would be consistent with the fact that, as Crawford puts it, "Article 51 establishes an *essential* limit on the taking of countermeasures"(p. 294). It is also consistent with the notion, suggested by Cannizzaro, that the principle of proportionality is aimed in some degree at curbing the traditional freedom of the victim state to assert countermeasures according to its own subjective standard (E. Cannizzaro (2002) p. 895).

5   Can countermeasures induce compliance?

As discussed above, the arbitrators suggested that countermeasures should be considered as part of a property rule, i.e. as an incentive mechanism, and imply in their ruling that considerations of proportionality between the countermeasures and the injury suffered are secondary and subordinate to the overall goal of achieving compliance. This section discusses how compliance could be induced by countermeasures, and in particular countermeasures that could be applied by several countries. Here we assume that proportionality does not constrain the capacity of a state to take all countermeasures that might contribute to the goal of compliance. We conclude that in many circumstances, the application of countermeasures will lead to insufficient compliance; that is, member countries will optimally select countermeasures which do not induce the removal of the unlawful export subsidy. Even if several members apply countermeasures simultaneously, under-enforcement will occur in equilibrium. The concern that countermeasures should be scaled by the importance of trade between the country imposing the countermeasures and the country granting unlawful subsidies in order to avoid excessive countermeasures thus appears to be unfounded. At the opposite, under-enforcement (lack of compliance) will occur even when several countries impose countermeasures simultaneously without upper bound on the amount of countermeasures that they impose. However, under-enforcement will also take place in circumstances where it is efficient (from a welfare perspective), i.e. when export subsidies increase welfare. Paradoxically, letting the "victims" of export subsidies choose countermeasures will lead to unlawful but efficient subsidies. That is also to say however that the implementation of a property rule would allow for efficient breach.

The intuition for this is straightforward: export subsidies often bring benefits to the country granting them which are in excess of the cost that they impose on importing countries.[6] To the extent that countermeasures take the form of export subsidies in another sector,[7] they will have the same property and hence bring benefits to the country imposing them that are larger than the cost that they impose on the offending

---

[6] We are not claiming that this property holds with respect to the export subsidies that the FSC scheme involves.

[7] Alternatively, countermeasures may take the form of import tariffs in the same sector (see below).

country.[8] In those circumstances, the country imposing countermeasures will find it optimal to set countermeasures at the highest possible level which does not induce compliance. When several countries are involved, there will be a continuum of Nash equilibria, where importing countries (acting as multiple principals towards a common agent[9]) jointly impose the highest level of countermeasures that does not induce compliance.

The argument is developed formally in box 1 but it can be illustrated with a numerical example. Assume that country C grants an export subsidy, which brings a net benefit (additional profits less the subsidy) of 100. This subsidy imposes a cost to countries A and B, equal to 40 for each country (hence, 80 overall, so that costs are 80% of the benefit). As long as the importing countries impose countermeasures which, collectively brings them a benefit which is less than 125 (i.e. 100/0.8), and hence impose a cost on country C which is less than 100 (assuming that costs are again 80% of the benefit), country C will not comply. If they achieve this they will obtain (collectively) a surplus of 45 (i.e. 125–80) and the country that has imposed an unlawful subsidy will have no surplus left. Can the importing countries achieve this outcome non-cooperatively? Yes, as long as each importing country imposes countermeasures which bring a positive net surplus, each country will prefer not to impose countermeasures which would trigger compliance (taking the countermeasure of the other countries as given). Hence, any pair of countermeasures which brings a positive net surplus to each country will constitute mutual best replies.

So far we have assumed that countermeasures take the form of export subsidies in another sector. Whether this form of countermeasure is allowed is however not clear. In principle, countermeasures can take the form of the suspension of tariff concessions or "other obligations". What "other obligations" may include has not been clearly delineated by the case law and may not exclude the obligation not to introduce export subsidies (so that retaliation could take the form of export subsidies). In any event, the argument presented above would seem to extend to the case of the suspension of tariff concessions. Indeed, the introduction of export subsidies will shift the industry equilibrium in a way which is favorable to the exporting country and damaging to importers. If importers are allowed to introduce import tariffs, they will always be in a position to implement the initial equilibrium (before the introduction of the export

---

[8] Here again, we are not claiming that the EU can implement countermeasures which have this property in the context of the case at hand.

[9] See Bernheim and Whinston (1986).

subsidies). This outcome will of course be preferable to them (they have the same consumer and producer surplus but gain some tariff revenues) so that they will fall short of inducing compliance.[10]

This reasoning has several implications. First, it suggests that complainants cannot be relied upon in order to induce compliance. When the incentive structure is such that the cost of an export subsidy is less than the benefit that it confers on the exporting countries, an arbitrator will have to grant countermeasures in excess of what the complainants seek in order to induce compliance. He will also face an issue of commitment as the complainants will have an incentive to implement a level of countermeasures short of what the arbitrators will decide. The arbitrators will have to monitor the imposition of countermeasures and compliance by the country imposing the unlawful export subsidy.

Second, the argument suggests that the implementation of a property rule does not necessarily imply large bargaining costs. The dispute settlement mechanism imposes a structure of move which yields an outcome in which the state wishing to deviate is left without surplus but in which breach takes place. Importantly, this outcome can take place even if the number of states that suffer from breach is large. These observations certainly suggest that the main drawback of a property rule, namely the importance of bargaining costs, may not be significant if bargaining is properly structured. By the same token, it suggests that a property rule may be superior to a liability rule.

Third, it appears that considering countermeasures in the context of a property rule would allow for efficient breach.

Finally, it appears that export subsidies and associated countermeasures can be used as a mechanism to induce multi-lateral export subsidies. Indeed, in the equilibrium that we describe, the country introducing the initial export subsidy is left without surplus while the complainants obtain (collectively and individually) a positive surplus. In equilibrium, all countries thus impose export subsidies. Consider now a repetition of "subsidy and countermeasure" stage game, where at each iteration one country imposes an export subsidy, which is subsequently subject to countermeasures falling short of inducing compliance. One expects to see the emergence of "collusive outcome" in such a repeated game where countries effectively introduce subsidies that yield no surplus in order to allow others to implement countermeasures which bring a positive surplus.

[10] We would like to thank Kyle Bagwell for pointing out this argument to us.

Box 1. A simple model of countermeasures

We first illustrate that export subsidies can bring benefits in excess of the cost that they impose. Consider for instance a Cournot duopoly with homogenous goods, such that firms sell only in the domestic economy. Let c_1 and c_2 be the marginal cost of respectively foreign and domestic firms and let s be the (unit) export subsidy granted to the foreign firm. Denote $\tilde{c}_1$ as the "effective" marginal cost of the foreign firm, i.e. its marginal cost less the unit subsidy. Welfare in the foreign country is given by profits less the subsidy and in the domestic economy it is given by the sum of the profit of the domestic firm and consumer surplus. Assume further that the marginal costs of the two firms are identical. Standard calculations confirm that in those circumstances, the fall in the domestic welfare following the imposition of a marginal subsidy (from zero) is less than the increase in foreign welfare. That is also to say that the export subsidy increases overall welfare. This arises because the export subsidy tends to correct the inefficiency associated with imperfect competition such that output is excessively low.

Consider now a game where at time t_1 country C can choose between a subsidy of zero and a subsidy of $\bar{s}$, which brings a net benefit $V(\bar{s})$. The cost incurred by two importing countries (A and B) are denoted respectively $c_A(\bar{s})$ and $c_B(\bar{s})$, with

$$c_A(\bar{s}) + c_B(\bar{s}) < V(\bar{s}) \qquad (1.1)$$

At time t_2, countries A and B can select countermeasures denoted s_A and s_B, which bring respective benefits of $V(s_A)$ and $V(s_B)$ and impose a cost on country C which is denoted $c(s_A)$ and $c(s_B)$, with $c(s_A) < V(s_A)$, $c(s_B) < V(s_B)$.

At time t_3, country C can decide to remove the subsidy. If subsidies are removed, all countries get a payoff equal to zero. If the subsidies are not removed, each country incurs the cost and obtains the benefit associated with prevailing subsidies and countermeasures.

The decision of country C at time t_3 is straightforward. It will remove the subsidy as long as

$$c(s_A) + c(s_B) > V(\bar{s}) \qquad (1.2)$$

We adopt the (technical) assumption that if the cost of countermeasure is equal to the benefit of the initial subsidy, country C will prefer not to comply. Consider now the decisions of countries A and B with respect to s_A and s_B at time t_2. We show that there is always an equilibrium $(\hat{s}_A, \hat{s}_B)$ such that neither A, nor B induce compliance, i.e. such that $c(\hat{s}_A) + c(\hat{s}_B) < V(\bar{s})$ and such that

$$V(\hat{s}_A) - c_A(\bar{s}) > 0, V(\hat{s}_B) - c_B(\bar{s}) > 0. \qquad (1.3)$$

Assume that country B imposes a countermeasure $\widehat{s}_B$ such that it prefers not to induce compliance, i.e. such that $V(\hat{s}_B) - c_B(\bar{s}) = 0$. We consider the best reply of country A, and show that it can obtain a positive payoff by not inducing compliance either. If it does not induce compliance, the best that country A can do is to choose a level of countermeasure such that (1.2) is met as a strict equality. Hence, using (1.1) and replacing $V(\bar{s})$ as an equality from (1.2), one obtains:

$$c_A(\bar{s}) + c_B(\bar{s}) < c(\widehat{s}_A) + c(\widehat{s}_B)$$

Using that $V(\hat{s}_B) = c_B(\bar{s})$, and, $c(\widehat{s}_A) < V(\widehat{s}_A)$ one obtains that:

$$c_A(\bar{s}) + V(\hat{s}_B) < V(\widehat{s}_A) + c(\widehat{s}_B)$$

And hence, given that $c(\widehat{s}_B) < ; V(\widehat{s}_B)$, we have that $c_A(\bar{s}) < V(\widehat{s}_A)$. Hence, country A will be better off not to induce compliance. Finally, note that if A does not induce compliance, it is indeed also a best reply for B not to induce compliance (i.e. to implement $\widehat{s}_B$). Hence, there is a Nash equilibrium in which neither A nor B induce compliance. One can also further describe the set of equilibrium countermeasures that do not induce compliance. Denote $\breve{s}_B$ as the optimal countermeasure imposed by B when country A imposes a countermeasure such that $V(\breve{s}_A) = c_A(\bar{s})$, i.e. such that it has no surplus. $(\breve{s}_A, \breve{s}_B)$ is also a Nash equilibrium. For any $s_A \in \left[\breve{s}_A, \widehat{s}_A\right]$, there will be some $s_B \in \left[\widehat{s}_B, \breve{s}_B\right]$, such that equilibrium conditions ((1.2) and (1.3)) hold. This follows simply by continuity of the equilibrium conditions. The shape of the frontier will be depend on the shape of $V(.)$ and $C(.)$.

Let us finally consider the decision of country C at time t_1. In equilibrium, it will obtain no surplus. We make the assumption that it prefers to introduce an export subsidy for instance because it obtains some transitory benefits in between t_1 and t_2.

6   Conclusion

Overall, this chapter has argued that a property rule approach to counter-measures does not sit comfortably with established principles of international law. The chapter has however also highlighted the attraction of such an approach, to the extent that it would allow for efficient breach even in the presence of a large number of parties.

The implementation of a property rule approach to countermeasures may still be difficult in practice. The distribution of rents between victims may for instance raise some difficult issues. As argued above, victims may be able to achieve an equilibrium where the countermeasures that they claim do not induce compliance. There are however many such equilibria which correspond to different distributions of countermeasures. This may very well lead to a race to the courthouse. To protect their interest in eventually being awarded countermeasures, WTO Members will want to sue now, lest some other Member get there first, and receive all the countermeasures.

References

Bernheim, D. and M. Whinston, (1986), Common Agency, *Econometrica*, 54 (4), 923–942.

Bond, E., (1996), Competition Policy in Customs Unions: a Natural Experiment using State Level Antitrust Enforcement, mimeo, Pen State.

Cannizzaro, E., (2001), The Role of Proportionality in the Law of International Countermeasures, *European Journal of International Law*, 12.

Crawford, J., (2002), *The International Law Commission's Articles on State Responsibility: Introduction, Text, and Commentaries*, Cambridge: Cambridge University Press.

Mavroidis, P., (2000), Remedies in the WTO Legal System: between a Rock and a Hard Place, *European Journal of International Law*, 11 (4), 763–813.

Pauwellyn, J., (2002), "The Nature of WTO Obligations", Jean Monnet Working Paper, at www.jeanmonnetprogram.org, p. 8.

Schwartz, W. and A. Sykes, (2002), The Economic Structure of Renegotiation and Dispute Resolution in the World Trade Organisation, *The Journal of Legal Studies*, 31 J.

4

United States – Countervailing Duties on Certain Corrosion-Resistant Carbon Steel Flat Products from Germany (WTO Doc. WT/DS213/AB/R): The Sounds of Silence*

BY

GENE M. GROSSMAN
Princeton University

AND

PETROS C. MAVROIDIS
University of Neuchâtel and Columbia University

1 Facts of the Case

On August 17, 1993, the United States Department of Commerce (USDOC) imposed definitive countervailing duties (CVDs) on carbon steel originating in Germany. The imposition of these duties was based on an investigation by USDOC in which it was determined that certain German producers had benefited from five countervailable subsidy programs at a total *ad valorem* rate of 0.60 percent.

On September 1, 1999, the USDOC gave notice of the automatic initiation of a sunset review of these duties, in accordance with Article 21.3 of the *Agreement on Subsidies and Countervailing Measures* (the *SCM Agreement*).[1] The United States found, in the course of its review, that

* We are grateful to the ALI reporters and especially to Richard Baldwin, Bill Ethier, Bernard Hoekman and Jasper-Martijn Wauters for useful comments on previous drafts. Remaining errors are our own.
[1] Article 21.3 of the *SCM Agreement* reads, in relevant part: "...any definitive countervailing duty shall be terminated on a date not later than five years from its imposition (or from the date of its most recent review under paragraph 2 if that review

withdrawal of CVDs would have led to a recurrence of subsidization and injury. The USDOC calculated the amount of countervailable subsidy to be 0.54% *ad valorem*, inasmuch as two of the original five subsidy programs had been terminated between the time of the original investigation and that of the administrative review.

2 Issues raised before the Panel

The European Communities complained that the US review was inconsistent with US obligations under the *SCM Agreement*. In the view of the European Communities, the United States should have withdrawn the CVDs when they found that the amount of countervailable subsidy to be 0.54% *ad valorem*. The European Communities argued that Article 11.9 of the *SCM Agreement* provided support for its argument in this respect; Article 11.9 obliges WTO Members to terminate original subsidy investigations when the amount of subsidy is calculated to fall below a *de minimis* standard of 1% *ad valorem*. According to the European Communities, the same standard ought to apply to subsequent sunset reviews as well. Not only was US practice in violation of the *SCM Agreement*, argued the European Communities, but the US law, which prescribes a *de minimis* standard of 0.5% *ad valorem* for sunset reviews, was illegal as well. Thus, the European Communities claimed that the United States had violated both Article 21.3 and Article 32.5 of the *SCM Agreement*, the latter requiring that each Member take measures to ensure the conformity of its laws and procedures with the terms of the Agreement.

The European Communities further complained about the evidentiary standard set out in US law and applied in its sunset reviews. In its opinion, the standard used by the United States for automatic self-initiation of sunset reviews falls short of the requirements of Articles 21.3 and 10 of the *SCM Agreement*.

Finally, the European Communities complained that the United States had violated its obligations under Articles 21.4 and 12 of the *SCM Agreement* when it considered the likelihood of continuation or

has covered both subsidization and injury, or under this paragraph), unless the authorities determine, in a review initiated before that date on their own initiative or upon a duly substantiated request made by or on behalf of the domestic industry within a reasonable period of time prior to that date, that the expiry of the duty would be likely to lead to continuation or recurrence of subsidization and injury. The duty may remain in force pending the outcome of such a review."

recurrence of subsidization in the event of removal of countervailing duties by not allowing ample opportunity for interested parties to present their views in the context of the sunset review.

3   The Panel Decision

The WTO Panel rejected the EC arguments that US evidentiary standards were inconsistent with Article 21.3 of the *SCM Agreement*, that US law concerning the obligation to determine the likelihood of continuation of recurrence of subsidization in sunset review is inconsistent with Article 21.3 of the *SCM Agreement*, and that the United States had violated its obligation under the *SCM Agreement* by failing to provide interested parties with an opportunity to present their views. Regarding the last of these findings, the Panel noted that the European Communities had not included the issue among its list of complaints when requesting the establishment of a panel, and thus the issue did not fall within its terms of reference per Article 6.2 of the *Dispute Settlement Understanding*.

On the other hand, the Panel found that the United States had violated its obligations under the *SCM* Agreement by not adhering to a *de minimis* standard of 1.0% in its sunset review. The Panel ruled that the United States had violated both Article 21.3 of the *SCM Agreement* in the specific instance under review, and also had violated Article 32.5 by failing to bring its laws into conformity with the terms of the Agreement.

Finally, the Panel found that the United States had failed to determine properly the likelihood of continuation or recurrence of subsidization in its sunset review and thus had acted in a manner inconsistent with Article 21.3. It should be emphasized that the Panel's finding in this respect concerns US practice and not the US law as such, which the Panel found to be consistent with the US obligations under the *SCM Agreement*.

4   The Appeal and the Appellate Body Decision

Both sides appealed aspects of the Panel decision, although the United States did not contest the Panel ruling that it had failed to determine properly the likelihood of continuation or recurrence of subsidization *in this particular case*. The United States appealed the Panel findings that a 1.0% *de minimis* standard applies to *ad valorem* subsidy rates in a sunset review. The European Communities contested the Panel finding that the evidentiary standards used by the United States in its sunset review are not inconsistent with its WTO obligations, and that the US laws concerning the procedures to be used in determining likelihood of continuation of recurrence of subsidization in sunset review are not inconsistent with the *SCM*.

In *United States – Countervailing Duties on Certain Corrosion-Resistant Carbon Steel Flat Products from Germany* (WTO Doc. WT/DS213/AB/R, henceforth *Carbon Steel*), the Appellate Body upheld all but one of the Panel's findings; it reversed only the finding that the United States had acted in a manner inconsistent with its obligations by failing to apply a *de minimis* standard 1% *ad valorem* in its sunset review of the case under dispute. According to the AB, the *SCM Agreement* imposes no restriction on the size of a subsidy that can be subject to continued countervailing measures, provided the subsidies continue to cause or threaten to cause injury in the importing country.

Since the Panel had ruled that the United States had failed to determine properly the likelihood of continuation or recurrence of subsidization in the particular sunset review at issue in this case, and since this finding generated no appeal from the United States, the AB requested that the United States bring its measures in *Carbon Steel* into conformity with its WTO obligations.

5 Discussion of the AB Decision

5.1 The function of sunset reviews

In a report last year [see Grossman and Mavroidis (2003)], we discussed the role of countervailing duties in the global trading system. We concluded that

> ... the effect of a subsidy on aggregate welfare in another Member country is *a priori* ambiguous. Therefore, if the Members had intended the *SCM Agreement* to discourage actions that would inflict welfare losses on others, they would have directed the "test" for actionable subsidies toward identifying conditions where aggregate loss is most likely to occur. For example, an external welfare loss is more likely to occur when a government subsidizes firms that sell in an imperfectly competitive market. So the test for an actionable subsidy might have made reference to the competitive conditions of the subsidized industry. Similarly, a welfare loss is more likely when wages are sticky in the importing country than when they are flexible; so the Agreement might have made reference to the labor-market conditions there. The Agreement might also have allowed for countervailing measures in Member countries that export goods in competition with the

subsidized good, inasmuch as these countries are quite likely to suffer welfare losses as a result of a foreign subsidy.

In fact, the *SCM Agreement* does not confine the use of CVDs to situations in which an importing country has established the presumption of a welfare loss. The Agreement makes no reference to labor-market conditions, to market structure, or even to consumer welfare. And the Agreement makes no allowance for countervailing measures in countries that export the subsidized good, where the presumption of welfare losses surely exists.[2] Rather, countervailing measures are permitted only when there has been (or threatens to be) injury to a domestic industry in an importing country.

The observation that injury to import-competing interests provides the sole basis for countervailing action points to a different interpretation of the objective of the *SCM Agreement*. Evidently, the signatories meant to discourage certain policy actions that would harm competing *producer* interests in the importing country. This objective is understandable in the light of recent literature on the political economy of trade policy, which has emphasized that governments often set their trade policies with objectives other than the maximization of aggregate economic welfare in mind. The policies that are chosen typically reflect a compromise among competing constituent interests. Moreover, some interests – especially those that are relatively concentrated – receive more weight in the political process than others. Less concentrated groups are not so successful in the political arena, in part because they have difficulty in overcoming the free-rider problems that plague collective political action (Olson, 1965). Thus, governments often are induced by political pressures to give more weight to producer interests than to consumer welfare when making their decisions about trade policy.

(emphasis in the original)

The *SCM Agreement* provides for two means of terminating a countervailing duty (CVD). First, the imposition of a CVD might end following a self-initiated or requested administrative review, as provided for in Article 21.2.

---

[2] Although the Agreement recognizes the possibility of serious prejudice to the interests of another Member that may arise due to the displacement of exports of a like product to the market of the subsidizing Member or to a third-country market, it does not allow serious prejudice to exporting interests to be a basis for countervailing action. Rather, in such cases, the Agreement calls for consultations between the Member that is granting or maintaining a subsidy and the Complaining Member, followed by a panel review in the event that consultations do not result in a mutually agreed solution. Only after a report by a panel or Appellate Body has been adopted in which it is determined that a subsidy has resulted in adverse effects to the interests of another Member, and the subsidizing Member has failed to take appropriate steps to remove the adverse effects of the subsidy may the complaining Member take such countermeasures as have been authorized by the Dispute Settlement Body (see Articles 7.8 and 7.9 of the *SCM Agreement*).

Second, a CVD might be allowed to lapse after five years or be terminated following a sunset review conducted at that time. Article 21.3 stipulates that

> any definitive countervailing duty shall be terminated on a date not later than five years from its imposition... *unless* the authorities determine... that the expiry of the duty would be likely to lead to continuation or recurrence of subsidization and injury
>
> (emphasis added)

Thus, the Agreement incorporates a rebuttable presumption that protection will no longer be needed after a period of five years. In order to continue a CVD beyond that time, the competent authorities must conduct a review in which they find that continued application of the duty is necessary to prevent a recurrence of the injurious effects of the subsidy.

Our analysis of the role of CVDs applies to sunset reviews just as it does to the initial investigation inasmuch as the injury standard is the same in both cases. We find support for this claim, for example, in footnote 45 of the *SCM Agreement,* which reads:

> Under this Agreement the term 'injury' shall, *unless otherwise specified,* be taken to mean material injury to domestic industry, threat of material injury to a domestic industry or material retardation of the establishment of such an industry and shall be interpreted in accordance with the provisions of this Article
>
> (emphasis added)

Since Article 21.3 of the *SCM Agreement* concerning sunset reviews does not specify otherwise, we must conclude that the Members intended the same standards to apply in such reviews.

5.2   De minimis *standards in sunset reviews*

5.2.1   The Panel's reasoning

Whereas the SCM *Agreement* provides for a *de minimis* threshold of 1% *ad valorem* in all original investigations of countervailable subsidies,[3] it makes no explicit reference to any such standard in the body of Article 21, which provides for the sunset reviews. The US trade law respects the

---

[3] Article 11.9 states that "...There shall be immediate termination [of an initial investigation] in cases where the amount of a subsidy is *de minimis,* or where the volume of subsidized imports, actual or potential, is negligible. For the purpose of this paragraph, the amount of the subsidy shall be considered to be *de minimis* if the subsidy is less than 1 per cent *ad valorem.*"

stipulated 1% threshold for original subsidy investigations, but provides for a lower 0.5% threshold for all subsequent reviews.

The Panel nonetheless found that the United States had acted in a manner inconsistent with its obligations under the *SCM Agreement* by employing a *de minimis* threshold of 0.5% *ad valorem* in its sunset review of a CVD on certain corrosion-resistant carbon steel products from Germany. The Panel ruled that the WTO Members intended the 1% threshold to apply not only in original investigations, but also in all subsequent reviews. According to the Panel, the Members could not have meant for there to be two different standards at the different points in time. Rather, the Panel interpreted the silence in Article 21.3 of the *SCM Agreement* as tacit acceptance of the standard laid out in the earlier Article 11.9.

The Panel supported its interpretation by asserting that the *SCM Agreement* aims, *inter alia*, to counteract injurious subsidies.[4] Since the Members had decided to set a *de minimis* standard of 1.0% *ad valorem* for the original investigation, they must have believed that subsidies at less than this rate could not cause injury sufficient to warrant countervailing measures. Arguably, a subsidy at less than 1% *ad valorem* also could not cause such injury at a later stage.[5] The Panel concluded that, since only subsidies that are causing injury can be subject to CVDs, *de minimis* subsidies that cannot cause sufficient injury (as defined in Article 11.9) cannot be deemed countervailable.

5.2.2   The AB reversal: silence must mean something

The AB rejected the Panel's reasoning on the issue of *de minimis* thresholds in sunset reviews. The AB advanced several arguments to support its position.

First, the AB argued that the Agreement's silence in Article 21 on the issue of *de minimis* thresholds for sunset reviews must have meaning. In

---

[4] In support of this point, the Panel pointed to a negotiating document prepared by the WTO Secretariat during the Uruguay Round multilateral trade negotiations. This document offered two rationales for the introduction of *de minimis* standards, one of which was to ensure that CVDs would counteract only injurious subsidies; see para. 77 of *Carbon Steel.*

[5] The preparatory work for the *SCM Agreement* suggests that the *de minimis* standard was incorporated into the agreement to preclude the use of its provisions as a form of harassment. The signatories felt that Members should not be allowed to proceed with an investigation in situations where, arguably, the injurious effects of a subsidy could not have been great in view of the low rate of subsidization. It is impossible to discern from the preparatory work, however, the basis for setting the threshold at 1% rather than at some other level.

particular, the AB notes that cross-referencing would have been an option, and indeed has been used quite frequently in the *SCM Agreement*. The AB interprets the absence of such cross-referencing to mean that the Members did not intend the threshold requirements incorporated into Article 11.9 to apply also to the reviews discussed in Article 21.

Second, the AB dismissed the relevance of the negotiating document cited by the Panel inasmuch as the documents list the counteracting of injurious subsidies as only one of two rationales for the introduction of *de minimis* thresholds in the original investigation. The AB notes in para. 78 of its report on *Carbon Steel* that there is no reason for the interpreter of Article 21 to rely on this particular rationale for *de minimis* thresholds while dismissing the other. The AB further argues (in paras. 79–81) that, as a matter of general matter, subsidy and injury are two distinct concepts in the *SCM Agreement* and the latter is not defined with reference to any minimum *ad valorem* subsidy rate. The Agreement also distinguishes the original investigation and subsequent reviews as two distinct processes with their own rules and procedures. The AB sees no *a priori* reason why the requirements for invoking countervailing duties should be the same in the two processes.

The AB concludes that the US law, which provides for a *de minimis* threshold of 0.5% *ad valorem* for a subsidy to be countervailable following a sunset review, is not inconsistent with US obligations under Article 21.3 of the *SCM Agreement*.

5.2.3   In support of the AB ruling

There are additional arguments that support the AB ruling on the use of *de minimis* thresholds in sunset reviews. First, the maxim of *in dubio pro mitius* favors the Appellate Body's interpretation of the *SCM Agreement*. According to this maxim of public international law, the international judge, because of his/her function (as an agent, not a principal) cannot presume a transfer of sovereignty when none is present. The interpreter, when in doubt (*in dubio*), must interpret an international agreement narrowly; that is, assuming that sovereignty remains with the states rather than assuming that it has been transferred to the international regime (*pro mitius*). Legislative silence presents at least genuine doubt as to whether sovereignty has been transferred. The maxim of *in dubio pro mitius* reflects an intellectually coherent proposition in the light of the frequent challenges of the purview of the international regime that are brought before international courts. And whereas an ill-advised judgment by a domestic court in a national context can readily be overturned via subsequent legislative action, a poor decision by an adjudicating body of the WTO will require, before it can be corrected, a consensus among 146 Member countries. Since agency costs associated with poor judicial decisions are especially high in an international context, it behooves an international court to let sovereignty remain with the Member countries whenever a legitimate doubt exists.

Second, the interpretation favored by the AB may well be consistent with the overall objectives of the *SCM Agreement* as applied to the issue of *de minimis* thresholds. As we explained in Grossman and Mavroidis (2003) and rehearsed in Section 5.1 above, CVDs play an important role in the international trading system not only to offset injury, but also to discourage countries from implementing subsidies that might cause harm to a domestic industry in an importing country in the first place. Subsidies are not per se illegal in the international trading regime. Rather, countervailing duties are permitted to ensure that governments have adequate incentive to consider the externalities that their national policies impose on their trading partners. The longer lasting the CVDs, the greater the disincentive to a government to implement subsidies that do harm to their trade partners. It is at least plausible that the WTO Members intended to allow countervailing measures against small subsidies as a way to discourage governments from keeping subsidies in place longer than is necessary. Since the Agreement is silent on the issue of whether *de minimis* thresholds ought to apply in sunset reviews, it is enough that a plausible case can be made that no such thresholds were intended to justify the overturning of the Panel's ruling by the AB.

Finally, the wording of footnote 52 (to Article 21.3 of the *SCM Agreement*) seems to lend support to the Appellate Body's approach. It provides that

> [w]hen the amount of the countervailing duty is assessed on a retrospective basis, a finding in the most recent assessment proceeding that no duty is to be levied shall not by itself require the authorities to terminate the definitive duty.

If a finding that no duty should be levied does not in and of itself require that the authorities terminate the duties imposed, then by inference a finding of *de minimis* subsidization should lead to the same result.[6]

---

[6] This point was made to us orally by Jasper-Martijn Wauters. We should probably note that our comments here assume the legal text as a constraint on the Appellate Body's decision. In fact, we can see some good arguments in favor of the Panel's position (that was overturned by the AB) that a subsidy scheme, when below a *de minimis* level defined in the *SCM Agreement*, should be regarded as non-injurious during both the original investigation and subsequent reviews. However, the language of Article 21.3 of the *SCM Agreement* does not lend sufficient support to these arguments.

5.3 Evidentiary standards in self-initiated sunset reviews

The US law provides for *automatic* self-initiation of sunset reviews 30 days before the fifth anniversary of the original imposition of a CVD, regardless of whether the USDOC is in possession of any relevant evidence or not. The European Communities disputed the consistency of the US legislation with the terms of the *SCM Agreement*. According to the European Communities, the evidentiary standards stipulated in Article 11.6 of the *SCM Agreement* as requirements before an investigatory authority can itself initiate an original investigation of a foreign subsidy ought to apply as well to the self-initiation by such authorities of a sunset review. Specifically, the European Communities claimed that the United States, if it wishes to self-initiate a sunset review, should possess the same level of information as would be required in a "duly substantiated request" for a review by the domestic industry. The Panel rejected the EC claims, ruling that Article 21.3 of the *SCM Agreement* dictates no specific evidentiary standards for the self-initiation of sunset reviews.

The AB upheld the Panel's ruling on appeal. It pointed to the wording of Article 21.3, which mandates the elimination of CVDs after five years "unless the authorities determine, in a review initiated before that date on their own initiative or upon a duly substantiated request made by or on behalf of the domestic industry." The AB argued that the adjective "duly substantiated" modifies only the "request made by or on behalf of the domestic industry" and not the alternative method described for initiating a sunset review, namely self-initiation by the investigating authorities. Again, the AB interpreted silence to mean that the provision places no limitation on the manner in which the Member country may take the indicated action.

In our view, the most persuasive argument in support of the Panel's decision was not mentioned in the report on *Carbon Steel*. When it comes to the original investigation, Articles 11.2 and 11.6 of the *SCM Agreement* establish a balance between investigations initiated following a request by the domestic industry and self-initiated investigations. Whereas an industry petition can generate a subsidy investigation whenever certain substantive requirements are satisfied, government-initiated investigations are reserved for exceptional cases. On this point, Article 11.6 of the *SCM Agreement* states that

> If, in special circumstances, the authorities concerned decide to initiate an investigation without having received a written application by or on behalf

of a domestic industry for the initiation of such investigation, they shall
proceed only if they have sufficient evidence of the existence of a subsidy,
injury and causal link, as described in paragraph 2, to justify the initiation
of an investigation

Article 21.3 of the *SCM Agreement* does not, however, treat self-initiated
sunset reviews as exceptional procedures. A coherent argument could be
advanced in favor of a parallelism between the two provisions: absent an
abiding interest by the domestic industry (the entity which has the
incentive to request protection) an investigating authority should neither
initiate an investigation nor review duties to evaluate whether they are still
needed, except in unusual circumstances. In other words, if the domestic
industry fails to take the initiative to request the application of a CVD or
its continuation, the competent authorities should take this as a signal
that trade protection would not be especially beneficial to the industry. In
such circumstances, no CVD should be applied or continued, considering
that such protection confers negative externalities on a Member's trading
partners.

But whereas Article 11.6 of the *SCM Agreement* treats the initiation
of an investigation by the government authorities as an exceptional
event, Article 21.3 of the *SCM Agreement* does not do so. This discrepancy provides a rationale for a looser evidentiary standard during the
review stage. The degree of leniency that should be allowed relative to
the requirements of Article 11.2 of the *SCM Agreement* is a matter
that must be addressed on a case-by-case basis. The AB chose to interpret silence literally as an absence of any requirement whatsoever, so
that competent authorities may choose to conduct sunset reviews
even when they are in possession of no evidence to suggest that the
CVD is still needed. Their interpretation certainly cannot be rejected
based on a contextual reading of the text of Article 21.3 of the *SCM
Agreement*.

5.4   The likelihood of continuation or recurrence of subsidization

The European Communities further argued that US law and practice
essentially prohibit the USDOC from examining changes to the subsidy
programs that may occur subsequent to an initial investigation. Several of
the EC claims were rejected by the Panel and the AB, because they were
not properly raised during the dispute process. The AB also rejected the
appeal by the European Communities that faulted the Panel for failing to
condemn a "consistent practice" on the part of the United States as

regards changes to subsidy programs. The AB noted that, in making this assertion, the European Communities had relied primarily on the US conduct in the case under review. Such US actions, whatever they may have been, could not amount to a "consistent practice."

The European Communities had argued that US trade law [Section 752(b)(1) of the US Tariff Act] does not allow the USDOC to consider changes in subsidy programs when determining the likelihood of continuation or recurrence of subsidization. The Panel relied on the language of the law to conclude that it did not, in fact, mandate behavior inconsistent with Article 21.3 of the *SCM Agreement*. The AB upheld this ruling, and we concur.

5.5   The opportunity to present evidence in sunset reviews

The European Communities complained that, during the Panel proceedings, the United States had violated its obligations under Article 12 of the *SCM Agreement* by not providing interested parties with ample opportunity to present their views. The United States objected to this claim, arguing that it fell outside the Panel's terms of the reference inasmuch as the issue had not been raised at the time that the European Communities invoked the dispute resolution process. The United States referred to Article 6.2 of the *Dispute Settlement Understanding* (DSU) for support on this issue.

In reviewing the EC request for the establishment of a panel, the Panel found only a reference to an objection to "certain aspects of the review procedure." The Panel did not find this reference to be sufficiently specific to identify the issue at hand. In the case law on the issue of the Panel's terms of reference, the WTO adjudicating bodies have consistently interpreted Article 6.2 of the DSU as requiring complainants to identify the factual situation about which they complain and the legal provision that allegedly has been violated in the document submitted to request a panel. Accordingly, the Panel ruled in favor of the United States on this issue.

On appeal, the AB upheld the Panel ruling, on the grounds that the EC request for establishment of a panel had failed to identify Article 12 of the *SCM Agreement* as the basis for its contention that its rights had been violated. We agree with the Panel and the AB on this finding, noting that were Article 6.2 of the DSU to be interpreted otherwise, complainants would be able to surprise defendants with new allegations at all the stages of the dispute settlement proceedings.

6 Conclusions

We concur with the AB findings about the non-applicability of *de minimis* thresholds in sunset review and have developed some additional arguments to support its ruling. We also concur with the AB findings on evidentiary standards during reviews. Both of our conclusions are predicated on our understanding of the function of (or, the objectives pursued by) the *SCM Agreement* as currently drafted.

This does not mean, however, that we agree with the current drafting of the *SCM Agreement* on the issues under review. In fact, we see good arguments in favor of a re-drafting of Article 21.3 of the *SCM Agreement* in two respects.

(a) The Agreement should make clear that, the absence of *de minimis* standards notwithstanding, if the level of subsidization is found to have fallen over time, then the size of the CVD should shrink as well after the sunset review (since the purpose of a CVD is to offset the "distortion" caused by the subsidy and not to (over-)compensate the affected domestic industry). As Article 21.3 of the *SCM Agreement* now stands, it is unclear whether, in case the level of subsidization changes over time, the size of the countervailing duty must change as well.

(b) The evidentiary standards during the sunset review stage should be changed to restore parallelism with the standards used during original investigations initiated by industry petition and those initiated by the investigating authority. A lack of interest by the domestic industry in continuing a CVD action should be used as a signal that no further protection is warranted. As the text now stands, it is difficult to advance a convincing legal argument in favor of such parallelism.

7 Post Scriptum

We note that, in a subsequent dispute concerning a review of antidumping duties, the AB reached a conclusion that might be regarded as being at odds with the decision discussed here. Like the *SCM* Agreement, the *AD Agreement* incorporates a *de minimis* threshold for the dumping margin at the investigatory stage leading to the original imposition of duties, but contains no explicit reference to any *de minimis* standards that must be applied during a sunset review. In its report on *United States – Sunset*

Review Of Anti-dumping Duties On Corrosion-resistant Carbon Steel Flat Products From Japan (WTO Doc. WT/DS244/AB/R of 15 December 2003) the AB reaffirmed in §§ 124–127 its view that a competent authority is not obliged by the agreement to calculate precise dumping margins during a review of antidumping duties. It went on, however, to specify that in case a WTO Member does choose to calculate margins in such a review, it must do so in accordance with the procedures stipulated in Article 2 of the AD. Article 2 regulates the procedures for calculating the dumping margin during an original investigation and constitutes one of the three prerequisites for the lawful imposition of antidumping duties under Article 1 of the AD. But Article 1 further stipulates that Article 5 must govern the conduct of an investigation, and Article 5.8 contains the *de minimis* rule that obliges WTO Members to discontinue any investigation if they find the dumping margin to be below 2%. Consequently, any definition of the dumping margin that accords with Article 2 of the AD must obey the *de minimis* threshold reflected in Article 5.8. In short, it is possible to interpret the AB ruling in the AD case as requiring the *de minimis* standard for an initial investigation also to be observed in any sunset review that involves the calculation of dumping margins.

References

Grossman, Gene M. and Petros C. Mavroidis. 2003. Here Today, Gone Tomorrow? Privatization and the Injury Caused by Non-Recurring Subsidies. A Discussion of the Appellate Body Report on *United States – Imposition of Countervailing Duties on Certain Hot-Rolled Lead and Bismuth Carbon Steel Products Originating in the United Kingdom* in H. Horn and P. C. Mavroidis, eds., *The WTO Case Law of 2001*. Cambridge: Cambridge University Press.

5

United States – Countervailing Measures Concerning Certain Products from the European Communities (WTO Doc. WT/DS212/AB/R): Recurring Misunderstanding of Non-Recurring Subsidies*

BY

GENE M. GROSSMAN
Princeton University

AND

PETROS C. MAVROIDIS
University of Neuchâtel and Columbia University

1   Facts of the Case

In *United States – Countervailing Measures Concerning Certain Products from the European Communities* (WTO Doc. WT/DS212/QB/R, henceforth *Certain Products*), the Appellate Body (AB) of the World Trade Organization was called upon to revisit the issue of whether the United States can legally impose countervailing duties following the privatization of state-owned enterprises that had received non-recurring subsidies. In twelve cases, the United States Department of Commerce (USDOC) had applied either the "*gamma* method" or the "same-person method" in assessing the impact of a change of ownership on the continued existence of a benefit from a countervailable subsidy. The European Communities challenged the legality of these methods.

Under the *gamma* method, the USDOC applied an "irrebuttable presumption" that the benefits from a non-recurring subsidy remain in existence for the entire useful life of the assets purchased with benefit of

* We are grateful to Henrik Horn, Doug Irwin, Arun Venkataraman and Jasper-Martijn Wauters for helpful discussions on the issue treated in this report.

a subsidy. The USDOC did not undertake any inquiry into whether and to what extent a non-recurring subsidy continued to benefit the producers during the useful life of the assets. Rather, when confronted with a change of ownership, the USDOC simply allocated the subsidy benefit between seller and purchaser to match the fraction of the assets that had been transferred.

Following the AB ruling in *United States – Imposition of Countervailing Duties on Certain Hot-Rolled Lead and Bismuth Carbon Steel Products Originating in the United Kingdom*, (WTO Doc. WT/DS138/AB/R, henceforth *Lead and Bismuth*) that the *gamma* method is inconsistent with US obligations under the Agreement on Subsidies and Countervailing Measures (the *SCM Agreement*), the United States introduced the new, same-person method. Under this method, the USDOC conducts a two-step test to assess the continued existence of a benefit from prior subsidization. First, the agency decides whether the post-privatization entity is the "same legal person" as that which received the subsidy prior to privatization. To render this assessment, the USDOC considers whether there has been a continuity of general business operations, a continuity of production facilities, a continuity of assets and liabilities, and a retention of personnel. If, based on these criteria, the USDOC concludes that the privatization created no new legal person, it automatically concludes that the benefit from the subsidy still exists irrespective of the price paid by the new private owners for the assets of the state-owned enterprise. If the privatization has created a new legal person, then the benefits of the original subsidy are considered to have been extinguished.

The USDOC applied the *gamma* method in 11 of the 12 cases at issue in *Certain Products*. Of these, six were original investigations, one was an administrative review, and four were sunset reviews. The USDOC applied the same-person method in one case, which was an administrative review.

2   Panel Ruling

The European Communities argued before the WTO Panel that both the *gamma* method and the same-person method violate US commitments under the *SCM Agreement* to apply countervailing measures only when the removal of such measures would likely lead to continuation or recurrence of subsidization that causes or threatens to cause injury to domestic interests. Under Article 1.1 of the *SCM Agreement*, a subsidy can be deemed to exist only if a financial contribution by a government confers a "benefit" on the recipient. The European Communities argued, as it had done previously, that a firm cannot benefit when it purchases assets at arm's length and for fair-market value. Thus, according to the European Communities, a privatization of state-owned assets and for fair-market value creates an irrebuttable presumption that a subsidy no longer exists and so renders any countervailing measure imposed by another Member country illegal.

The United States conceded in the case before the Panel that it had acted in a manner inconsistent with its WTO obligations in seven of the twelve determinations; namely, those that involved application of the *gamma* method in original investigations or administrative review. In these cases, the United States acknowledged, the USDOC should have examined the continued existence of a benefit from the non-recurring subsidy. The United States denied having taken any actions inconsistent with its commitments in the four cases that involved sunset reviews, claiming that where no administrative review has taken place, its investigatory authority is under no obligation to consider any evidence when deciding whether the expiry of a countervailing duty would likely lead to a continuation or recurrence of subsidization causing injury. Finally, the United States argued that the same-person method addresses the objections raised by the AB in its rulings on the *gamma* method. Using the same-person method, the United States argued, the USDOC had considered whether a benefit from a subsidy continued to exist, as required by Article 21 of the *SCM Agreement*.

The Panel ruled in favor of the European Communities on both accounts. Concerning the four sunset reviews in which the USDOC had applied the *gamma* method, the Panel ruled that the United States was indeed obliged in such cases to examine the continued existence of a benefit. Without doing so, the USDOC could not have properly considered whether there would likely be continuing or recurring subsidization that would cause or threaten to cause injury absent the countervailing duty.

The Panel further judged the same-person method to be inconsistent with the *SCM Agreement*. The Panel in fact concluded that privatization at arm's length and for fair-market value will always necessarily extinguish the remaining portion of any benefit from a prior non-recurring subsidy paid to a previously existing state-owned enterprise. The Panel's central finding is put quite clearly in para. 8.1d of its report, which states in part:

> [o]nce an importing member has determined that a privatization has taken place at arm's-length and for fair market value, it must reach the conclusion

that no benefit resulting from the prior financial contribution (or subsidization) continues to accrue to the privatized producer.

3   US Appeal and AB Ruling

The United States argued on appeal that the Panel had erred by failing to distinguish between a firm and its shareholders. According to the United States, a benefit received by a legal person cannot be redeemed by its shareholders. Thus, if a state-owned enterprise (a legal person) benefits from a financial contribution and if that same legal person continues to exist following privatization, then the benefit also continues to exist until it has been fully amortized or repaid. Privatization at whatever price – even if at arm's length and for fair-market value – cannot eliminate the benefit of a prior contribution as long as the same legal person continues to exist. By this argument, the fact that private owners pay a fair-market price indicates only that these individuals have not received a windfall gain, but not that the legal person producing the subject merchandise is not still benefiting from the original subsidy.

The United States also appealed the Panel finding that its investigating authority is obliged to consider whether there is continuing benefit from a financial contribution whenever it conducts a sunset review, but it failed to advance supporting arguments on this point.

On the critical issue of whether a privatization at fair-market value might or must extinguish the benefit from a non-recurring subsidy, the AB accepted neither the claims advanced by the United States of the total irrelevance of the price at which assets are transferred, nor the ruling by the Panel that a sale at a fair-market price creates an irrebuttable presumption that the subsidy has been eliminated. In so doing, the AB reversed the position it had taken in *Lead and Bismuth* that privatization at fair-market prices inevitably extinguishes the benefit from a prior government contribution.

In its report, the AB drew upon its interpretation of the word "benefit" in *Canada – Measures Affecting the Export of Civilian Aircraft* (WTO Doc. WT/DS70/AB/R). There it had ruled that the word implies some kind of comparison, and that "the marketplace provides an appropriate basis for comparison . . . because the trade-distorting potential of a 'financial contribution' can be identified by determining whether the recipient has received a 'financial contribution' on terms more favorable than those available to the recipient on the market" (*Certain Products*, para. 157).

Whereas the United States had argued that the *utility value* of the assets acquired with the benefit of the government's financial contribution had not been eliminated as a result of the transfer of these assets to new private owners, the AB saw the utility value as irrelevant for the legal purpose of assessing the continued existence of a "benefit". Rather, the AB insisted that the marketplace should be used as the starting point for any such assessment.

The AB rejected entirely the United States' argument to the effect that the price at which assets are acquired is irrelevant to a firm's use of these assets, and the other decisions it makes subsequent to that acquisition in regard to the prices and quantities of its production. On this point, the AB wrote in *Certain Products,* para. 103, that

> [w]e fail to see the basis for the assumption by the United States that, regardless of the sale price of the firm, its costs and volume of production will remain the same, since these costs include, as a necessary component, the cost of capital. Indeed, the Panel noted that private investors are "profit-maximizers", who will seek to "recoup[] through the privatized company . . . a market return on the full amount of their investment." For example, if a government makes a "financial contribution" that "benefit[s]" a state-owned enterprise, and then sells that enterprise for *less* than its fair market price, would this not normally result in a "better off" return for the private capital newly invested in that enterprise? Would that not suggest, as a consequence, that the under-priced enterprise may then attract more investment than it would have attracted otherwise, if the government had sold it for fair market price? Why would this government-induced add-itional investment not then reduce the enterprise's cost of raising capital (either by borrowing it from the bank or from, say, shareholders) and, ultimately, reduce the firm's overall costs of production?

However, the AB disagreed with the Panel's judgment that a benefit from a prior financial contribution to a state-owned enterprise can never continue to exist following the privatization of the enterprise's assets at arm's length and for fair-market value. To reach this conclusion, the AB drew a distinction between the *exchange value* of goods and services and their *scarcity value*. It noted that, "[u]nder certain conditions (e.g., unfettered interplay of supply and demand, broad-based access to information on equal terms, decentralization of economic power, an effective legal system guaranteeing the existence terms of private property and the enforcement of contracts), prices will reflect the relative scarcity of goods and services in the market" (*Certain Products,* para. 122). Under these conditions, the AB opined, the "actual exchange value of

the continuing benefit of past non-recurring financial contributions
bestowed on the state-owned enterprise will be fairly reflected in the
market price."

But the AB noted that it could imagine circumstances in which the
market price of the assets would not reflect "the exchange value of
the continuing benefit." Such circumstances might arise, for example,
if the government were intervening in the market to induce certain outcomes that it deemed socially or politically desirable. Then, in the view of
the AB, the value of the assets might be altered by the government policies
or by the conditions in which the private owners would subsequently be
allowed to make use of the assets. When the fair-market value diverges
from the "actual exchange value of the continuing benefit," an investigatory authority could legitimately find that a benefit of past non-recurring
financial contributions to a state-owned enterprise continues to exist
beyond the time of an arm's-length privatization. The AB gave no con-
crete example of the sort of situation it had in mind.

In sum, the AB affirmed the Panel's ruling that the United States had
acted inconsistently with its obligations under the *SCM Agreement* in the
twelve specific determinations at issue in *Certain Products*. In so doing,
it ruled that the same standards ought to apply for showing continuing
existence of benefits from financial contributions in sunset reviews as
in original investigations or administrative reviews. However, the AB
overturned the Panel's finding that privatization at arm's length and for
fair-market value presumptively extinguishes any benefit from a non-
recurring financial contribution bestowed upon a state-owned enterprise.
Rather, it ruled that whereas such a privatization creates a rebuttable
presumption that a benefit ceases to exist, there may be circumstances in
which an investigatory authority can find otherwise.

4 Discussion of the AB Ruling

In our report last year on *Lead and Bismuth*, we concluded in relevant part
that[1]

> The AB ruled incorrectly that a change in ownership of assets at fair market
> value provides per se evidence of an absence of subsidy, because it precludes
> 'benefit' to the acquiring firm. A consistent interpretation of the *SCM*

[1] See Gene M. Grossman and Petros C. Mavroidis, "Here Today, Gone Tomorrow? Privatization
and the Injury Caused by Non-Recurring Subsidies," in Grossman and Mavroidis (2003).

Agreement calls for a 'but for' test for continuing injury from a non-recurring subsidy. The authorities in the importing country should periodically
review whether its domestic producers of like products are suffering harm
relative to what would be their economic condition but for the prior non-
recurring subsidy. To effect this test, the authorities must ask whether or
not the subsidized investments have become infra-marginal in the light of
subsequent events in the industry

(p. 34).

In *Certain Products*, the AB has reversed its position that a change in
ownership at fair-market prices provides per se evidence of the absence of
subsidy. We concur on this issue. However, we find fault with the reasoning used by the AB in reaching this conclusion. And we disagree with its
finding that a change in ownership at fair-market prices provides a
rebuttable presumption that a subsidy no longer exists.

By insisting that the sales price at which a privatization takes place is
relevant to the determination of the continued existence of benefit from a
subsidy, the AB has failed to understand the economic concept of a sunk
cost. The United States is correct when it argues that the price at which a
profit-maximizing enterprise acquires an asset will not affect its subsequent production and pricing decisions. The fact that such an enterprise
will wish to "recoup a market return on its investment" is simply irrelevant to its subsequent business decisions. Consider, for example, an art
dealer who misjudges the public appeal of a painting and pays €1000 for
an acquisition. Such a dealer may well *wish* to recoup a market return on
his investment, but if the amount collectors are willing to pay for the
painting is only €500, the dealer would be well advised to sell at that price.
Now compare this dealer to another who has been lucky enough to
acquire a similar painting for €100. If this second dealer is a profit
maximizer, he will not sell the painting for €120 and be satisfied with a
fair-market return on his investment. Instead, he will hold out for the full
€500 that collectors are willing to pay. In short, the dealer who acquires
an asset for €1000 and another who acquires one for €100 – if they are
both profit maximizers – will indeed follow similar pricing strategies.
Once the dealers have purchased the paintings, the amounts they
paid become *sunk costs*; they have no bearing on subsequent, profit-
maximizing behavior.

Similarly, a firm that acquires assets in a privatization of a state-owned
enterprise will maximize profits by producing up to the point where the
marginal revenue from the last unit of output is just equal to the marginal
cost. Inasmuch as the marginal cost of production is not affected by the

price paid for machinery and equipment, the profit-maximizing behavior will not be affected by such bygone considerations.

The logical difficulties that stem from the AB interpretation of the word "benefit" in Art. 1.1 of the *SCM Agreement* in terms of the market value of the privatized assets can be seen in a comparison of two hypothetical occurrences. Imagine a machine that can be used to create €50,000 in present discounted profits. A private, profit-maximizing firm would be willing to pay up to €50,000 to acquire such a machine. Let the production cost of the machine be €100,000. Then no firm will be willing to buy the machine absent any government inducement. Now consider Event 1, in which the government offers a subsidy of €50,000 to any firm willing to buy and install the machine. Such a subsidy is sufficient to induce one or more private firms to make the purchase. In the event, and if the machine is used in a way that causes injury to firms in importing countries, surely the *SCM Agreement* would recognize the existence of a subsidy and permit a countervailing duty.

But now consider Event 2, in which the government buys the machine itself in the name of a state-owned enterprise. On the next day, it offers to privatize the enterprise by selling the firm's assets to the highest bidder. The privatization – which occurs at arm's length – will take place at a fair-market price of €50,000. But, in this case, the AB would deny the existence of a subsidy, and deny Member countries the right to countervail. In both Events, the private firm that eventually makes use of the machine pays €50,000 for the acquisition. In both cases, the firm uses the machine to produce profits of €50,000 and, in the process, inflicts injury on firms in importing countries. In both cases, the government's net financial contribution is €50,000. Yet the AB construes a benefit from a financial contribution in one situation but not the other. It seems unlikely that this was the intention of those who drafted the *SCM Agreement*.[2]

The AB interpretation of "benefit" also creates logical difficulties for the treatment of non-recurring subsidies paid directly to private enterprises.[3] The ownership shares of such enterprises turn over regularly in

---

[2] Of course, we cannot be sure that those who drafted the agreement did not intend to draw a distinction between these economically equivalent events. To assess their intentions, we must analyze the apparent objectives of the agreement in the light of its various provisions. We have conducted just such an analysis in Grossman and Mavroidis (2003), where we concluded that the only interpretation of the text that accords with the apparent objectives of the agreement is one that associates "benefit" with a gain in competitive advantage.

[3] We are grateful to David Palmeter for this observation.

transactions on private equity markets. Such sales take place at arm's length and for fair-market value. And those who purchase the shares subsequent to the payment of the subsidy do not personally benefit from the original subsidy. Does the AB consider a part of the "benefit" to be extinguished with each such private equity sale?

As we argued in Grossman and Mavroidis (2003), the only interpretation of the term "benefit" in Article 1.1 of the *SCM Agreement* that is consistent with the aims and objectives of those who drafted the Agreement is one that attributes benefit whenever a firm's competitive position is advantaged relative to what it would have been *but for* the government's financial contribution. We view the main objective of the *SCM Agreement* as being to discourage subsidies that threaten harm to competing producers in importing countries. To achieve this objective, it makes no sense to interpret "benefit" in terms of the financial wealth of the owners of a firm. Rather, the potentially adverse effects of a subsidy on producers in an importing country can be avoided only if a subsidy is deemed to exist whenever a government's financial contribution impacts the competitive situation in an industry. And, as we have argued, the price at which a change in ownership takes place has no bearing on the subsequent competitive conditions.

In Grossman and Mavroidis (2003), we also found fault with the procedures used by the United States for assessing whether the removal of a countervailing measure would likely lead to a continuation or recurrence of subsidization causing injury. Our arguments there – which related to use of the *gamma* method – apply with equal force to the same person method that was subsequently developed by the USDOC. The US methods presume that the benefits from a non-recurring subsidy necessarily survive for the full average useful life of the assets, provided that the legal person that purchased the assets with benefit of the subsidy continues to exist. We do not agree. Events that occur subsequent to the payment of a subsidy may render inframarginal an investment that was formerly unprofitable. If an investment becomes inframarginal, it is impossible to argue that the subsidy is the cause of ongoing injury. In such circumstances, the injury would be present even if the subsidy had never been paid. We therefore conclude that the same person method does not fulfill the United States' obligation under Article 21.1 of the *SCM Agreement* to ensure that

> a countervailing duty shall remain in force only as long as and to the extent necessary to counteract subsidization which is causing injury.

To fulfill this obligation, the USDOC should conduct a review that addresses the hypothetical question of what industry conditions would have been but for the payment of the non-recurring subsidy. We do concur with the AB ruling that the obligations imposed on an investigatory authority by the *SCM Agreement* apply with equal force to the reviews mandated by Article 21 of the Agreement. The Agreement defines a countervailable subsidy in terms of the cost to the government, the benefit to a recipient, and specificity to an enterprise or industry. Since the existence of a benefit forms part of the definition of a subsidy, and countervailing duties can be continued only if there is a subsidy that *is causing* injury (emphasis added), the obligation to identify a beneficiary applies not only to the original investigation, but also to subsequent review proceedings.

5 Conclusions

We believe that privatization at arm's length and for fair-market value does not presumptively extinguish the benefits from a non-recurring subsidy to a state-owned enterprise. Rather, an investigatory authority should periodically review whether the prior subsidy continues to affect competitive conditions in such a way as would cause or threaten injury to a domestic industry in an importing country in the absence of a counter-vailing duty. The investigatory authority should compare conditions in the industry to those that would have prevailed but for the subsidy payments.

As we noted in last year's report, there is no need to amend the *SCM Agreement* in order that it might be applied in an economically-friendly manner.

References

Grossman, Gene M. and Petros C. Mavroidis. 2003. Here Today, Gone Tomorrow? Privatization and the Injury Caused by Non-Recurring Subsidies. A Discussion of the Appellate Body Report on *United States – Imposition of Countervailing Duties on Certain Hot-Rolled Lead and Bismuth Carbon Steel Products Originating in the United Kingdom* in H. Horn and P. C. Mavroidis, eds., *The WTO Case Law of 2001.* Cambridge: Cambridge University Press.

6

Canada – Export Credits and Loan Guarantees for
Regional Aircraft (WT/DS222/R)
A Comment

BY

ROBERT HOWSE
(*University of Michigan Law School*)

AND

DAMIEN J. NEVEN
(*Graduate Institute of International Studies, Geneva and CEPR*)

1 Introduction

This panel report represents another installment in the long-standing
litigation between Canada and Brazil over subsidization of sales of commuter jets by both countries. The report addresses a set of claims by Brazil
closely related to prior claims concerning the practices of the Export
Development Corporation as well as industrial policy entities in the
Canadian province of Quebec. Brazil specifically challenged certain recent
transactions where these federal and provincial entities provided certain
kinds of financing assistance in connection with the sale of Bombardier
aircraft (namely to Air Wisconsin, Atlantic Coast Airlines, Comair,
Kendell, and Air Nostrum). For the most part the panel applied existing
jurisprudence on export subsidies to the factual record. In particular, the
panel applied a "private investor principle", verifying in all instances
whether the conditions that were granted by the export development
and industrial policy agencies were more favorable than the conditions
that were available from alternative private sources. However, it is

extremely difficult to provide an adequate commentary on the panel's comparison between the conditions available in the market and those granted by the agencies because vital factual information concerning the transactions in question has been removed from the panel report for reasons of commercial confidentiality.

Thus, in our Report, we focus on several specific areas, largely of a procedural and preliminary nature, where the panel made apparently novel findings of law that have some systemic or general significance for WTO jurisprudence and practice.

Some preliminary comments on the general approach of the panel may however be in order. It is striking that the panel paid a lot of attention to the distinction between programs that leave some discretion to the authorities granting subsidies which may be unlawful and programs which instruct the authorities to do so. According to the panel, only programs which instruct the authorities to grant unlawful export subsidies are as such unlawful, despite the fact that the declared objective of these programs is to grant export subsidies (which are likely to be unlawful). Hence, everything appears as if the programs are not unlawful because one can exclude that they may not pursue the objective that has been assigned to them.

The apparent contradiction between the objectives assigned to the agencies and the behavior that they are meant to pursue in order to comply with the WTO framework is reinforced by the application of the private investor principle. According to this benchmark, particular loans and guarantees are lawful if they could have been obtained from private investors. Here again, the behavior of the agency is lawful where it mimics the behavior of private sources of funds − which suggests that they should not have been public agencies in the first place or at the very least that their public status (and the particular objectives that they are supposed to pursue in light of this status) should be seen as irrelevant.

Overall, one can thus wonder about the effectiveness of a legal framework that imposes behavioral norms on an institution that are in contradiction with its "raison d'être".

This raises the broader question of whether the constraints imposed by the SCM agreement are reasonable. A discussion of this issue goes much beyond the scope of this chapter. It is worth mentioning however that subsidies can sometimes be highly desirable (see Besley and Seabright, 2000, for a discussion) and that the blanket prohibition on export subsidies contained in the SCM agreement may not be warranted.

2   Jurisdiction of 21.5 Panels in Relation to Panels Seized of a New Matter

In its Request for a Panel Brazil included claims related to the alleged non-compliance of Canada with previous panel rulings. This was particularly evident with Claim 3, which alleged: "Canada, in defiance of the rulings and recommendations of the Dispute Settlement Body, continues to grant or offers to grant export credits to the regional aircraft industry . . ."

Article 21.5 of the DSU provides: "Where there is disagreement as to the existence or consistency with a covered agreement of measures taken to comply with the recommendations and rulings such dispute shall be decided through recourse to these dispute settlement procedures, including wherever possible resort to the original panel." Canada argued that, to the extent that Brazil was making a claim concerning "existence or consistency" of measures taken to implement a pre-existing DSB ruling, it was required to make that claim under 21.5, and thus that the present panel did not have jurisdiction to adjudicate.

The panel responded in several different ways to this argument of Canada. First of all, the panel observed that Brazil was not, strictly speaking, asking it to examine the measures in question to determine their consistency with a prior ruling of the DSB, but rather to determine their consistency with provisions of the WTO SCM Agreement. In other words, even though Brazil was asserting the inconsistency of Canada's measures with earlier rulings, it was asking the panel for de novo review of those measures, not findings concerning their consistency with the earlier rulings.

The problem with the distinction the panel draws here, upon Brazil's suggestion, is that, according the Appellate Body, it is *precisely* the role of a 21.5 panel to examine, in respect of measures that were the subject of previous panel rulings, whether the subsequent conduct of the defendant relating to those measures is consistent with the provisions of covered Agreements (*Shrimp/Turtle 21.5*, para. 85, *Brazil – Aircraft 21.5*, para. 35.).

The logic of the panel here would seem to have the following result: where a previous panel found a measure inconsistent with certain provisions of the covered Agreements, and the defendant changed the measure such that it now fell afoul of different provisions, not dealt with in the original panel report, this would not be a matter for a 21.5 panel, but an entirely new panel, based on new terms of reference.

If this were so, then a defendant could avoid the expedited procedures under 21.5 simply by redesigning its measure so as to make it inconsistent with different provisions of the covered Agreements than those dealt with in the original panel proceeding. It may be in part for this reason that, repeatedly, the Appellate Body has made it clear that the 21.5 panel can and must consider the consistency of any new or modified measure with the covered Agreements, not just with the previous rulings and recommendations of the panel.

Secondly, the panel noted that Brazil said it was simply seeking a factual finding that since the adoption of the prior 21.5 report Canada had not made any changes in one of the measures in question, the so-called Canada Account. The panel relied on Article 11 of the DSU to simply refuse to consider this question of fact on the grounds that it would not assist in the panel's determination of Brazil's claims of violation of the SCM agreement in the present proceeding.

This reasoning of the panel is rather hard to follow. Given that the 21.5 panel had found the Canada Account in violation of the prohibition of export subsidies in the SCM agreement, a factual finding that the measure was unchanged since that previous ruling would seem to have cardinal importance for resolving Brazil's *new* claim of violation in respect of the same measure. It would mean that *res judicata* would arguably apply, since the new claim of violation concerns a measure found, as a matter of fact, to be identical to one previously ruled in violation.[1]

Where a measure is identical to one that has already been adjudicated and is the subject of an adopted DSB ruling, it does not seem appropriate for a later panel to assess *de novo* whether that measure is consistent with the very same provisions that were the subject of the previous

---

[1] See the *India – Autos* panel, where the first step in the analysis in determining whether there could be *res judicata* was to consider whether certain legal claims *and* measures already adjudicated were *identical* to those now before the panel. (paras. 7.83–7.103). The *India – Autos* panel never reached the issue of whether *res judicata* actually applies in WTO proceedings but began with investigating whether, *assuming res judicata* did apply, the criteria of identity of claims and measures could be met in this particular case. Having determined that they could not, the panel considered it unnecessary to provide a definitive answer to the question of whether *res judicata* is available in WTO law. In the *Argentina – Poultry* case the panel rejected an argument that *res judicata* applied with respect to previous proceedings in a *non*-WTO forum, MERCOSUR, but it also seemed to question whether *res judicata* could exist even as between an earlier and later WTO proceeding. In *Argentina – Poultry*, the panel seemed to confuse the issue of whether the *res judicata* could apply in later proceedings between the same parties on the same matter, with the question of whether panel rulings have binding precedential authority, i.e. are *stare decisis* in different matters between different parties (which of course they are not).

adopted ruling. This would be inconsistent surely with the principle of finality of adopted DSB rulings, as between the parties. Thus, it was arguably important, assuming that it was correctly seized at all with the issue, for the panel to determine whether the Canada Fund was unchanged, in order to be able to decide whether the matter was indeed *res judicata.*

Thirdly, the panel, in attempting to distinguish the kind of claim Brazil was making from a 21.5 claim, noted that "Brazil's claims in this proceeding do not concern the specific financing transactions "at issue" in the [earlier] *Canada – Aircraft* case. Rather, different transactions are at issue. Moreover, the legal framework under which the Canada Account is operated has changed, as noted below" (Paragraph 7.18).

But the Appellate Body has made it clear that it is precisely the mandate of a *21.5* panel to consider the measure as modified and applied *subsequent* to the original panel ruling (*Shrimp/Turtle 21.5*). This will normally and naturally involve new transactions, to the extent that the application of the measure is at issue. So why the existence of different transactions or changes in legal framework would take the claims of Brazil out of the jurisdiction of a 21.5 panel or make it appropriate for a new panel instead to seize itself of the matter is entirely obscure.

One could regard the panel's findings on the issue of the relationship of its jurisdiction to that of a 21.5 panel in two different ways. The panel might have been saying that there is some overlap between 21.5 jurisdiction and the jurisdiction of an entirely new panel in cases where the new complaint concerns both measures that were already adjudicated by a prior panel and some measures that have not been the subject of the prior adjudication. Or alternatively it could be taken as saying that certain defined features of Brazil's claim in this case would make 21.5 jurisdiction inapplicable (new transactions, changes in legal framework). If it is the latter, the panel's ruling seems clearly inconsistent with the view of the AB on the appropriate scope of a 21.5 panel's inquiry.

On the former interpretation, the main systemic issue that arises is one of forum shopping. This is especially so given the apparent avoidance of the panel of *res judicata*, with the implication that it can review *de novo* on-going conduct that was the subject, in part, of a previous panel ruling. If a complainant did not find the ruling of a panel sufficiently favorable, including a 21.5 panel, it could start a new proceeding and have a different panel examine the same on-going conduct. While the new panel could presumably only address those aspects of the on-going violation that are subsequent to the first panel's ruling, nevertheless the complainant might now achieve legal and factual rulings that lead to a recommendation that the on-going measure be removed, thus achieving a prospective remedy, which is really the only kind (generally speaking) the WTO dispute settlement system can offer. Such forum shopping seems at odds with a number of principles stated in the DSU, including the notion of prompt settlement (3.3). One curb on such forum shopping may arise from the ruling of the AB in *Shrimp/Turtle 21.5* that where an adopted Appellate Body report has found a measure or an aspect of a measure to be **not** in violation, it is appropriate for the 21.5 panel not to re-examine the issue, but to rely on the earlier finding of non-violation. Thus, in the *Shrimp/ Turtle 21.5* appeal, Malaysia sought to re-open the issue of whether the United States measure, as opposed to its application, violated provisions of the covered agreements.

The AB had previously found that the measure itself was consistent with the GATT obligations of the United States and it noted in the 21.5 appeal:

> As we see it, then, the Panel properly examined Section 609 as part of its examination of the totality of the new measure, correctly found that Section 609 had not been changed since the original proceedings, and rightly concluded that our ruling in *United States – Shrimp* with respect to the consistency of Section 609, therefore, still stands. We wish to recall that panel proceedings under Article 21.5 of the DSU are, as the title of Article 21 states, part of the process of the *"Surveillance of Implementation of Recommendations and Rulings"* of the DSB. This includes Appellate Body Reports. To be sure, the right of WTO Members to have recourse to the DSU, including under Article 21.5, must be respected. Even so, it must also be kept in mind that Article 17.14 of the DSU provides not only that Reports of the Appellate Body "shall be" adopted by the DSB, by consensus, but also that such Reports "shall be . . . unconditionally accepted by the parties to the dispute. . . ." Thus, Appellate Body Reports that are adopted by the DSB are, as Article 17.14 provides, ". . . unconditionally accepted by the parties to the dispute", and, therefore, must be treated by the parties to a particular dispute as a final resolution to that dispute. In this regard, we recall, too, that Article 3.3 of the DSU states that the "prompt settlement" of disputes is essential to the effective functioning of the WTO.
>
> (paragraphs 97–98)

Assuming this reasoning were also to apply to adopted panel reports, a complaining Member would effectively be prevented from going to a new panel in order to seek a ruling of violation that it was not able to get from an earlier panel or AB decision, at least in respect of the same on-going measure.

3   The Mandatory/Discretionary Distinction and Brazil's Claims

Brazil argued that the Canadian legal framework for export financing itself violated the prohibition on export subsidies in the SCM Agreement, inasmuch as that framework at least implicitly contained a *mandate* to responsible officials to engage in export subsidization. In addition, Brazil argued that the way the framework was applied was itself a violation of the SCM Agreement. Finally, Brazil challenged the practices and policies adopted with respect to a set of specific transactions.

The panel took a very formalistic view of whether the Canadian legal framework mandated export subsidization, looking only at the face of the Canadian law, which, not surprisingly, did not contain any explicit instruction to officials that they must provide export subsidies of a kind prohibited by the SCM Agreement. The panel choose to ignore, or consider irrelevant to the issue of mandatory legislation, the various arguments of Brazil that the legal framework had to be read in light of the policy context, and the inherent nature of the activities that the export financing entities were funded to engage in. In effect, Brazil was saying that when one examined the overall nature of the Canadian government's commitment to export promotion, the mandate of for example the EDC went along with very serious "cues" that it would be expected to confer a non-market competitive advantage on Canadian exports.

Whether or not Brazil could make that case persuasively, the panel's exclusive emphasis on the form or face of the legal framework in assessing whether it mandated a violation of the SCM Agreement is not consistent with the more contextual approach of panels in other situations where they have looked at whether there was a mandatory or regulative government action in a particular situation, for example the *Semi-Conductor* and *Kodak-Fuji* cases. A legislative framework may mandate a WTO violation, we would argue, even if none is required by its facial provisions, if the legislative framework creates strong disincentives or incentives on officials or other actors to engage in behavior violating WTO rules. At one level, the panel may be right that Brazil on the facts did not bear the burden of proof in showing this to be the case. But at numerous points in its ruling, the panel appears to be going further, suggesting that the case must be made exclusively on the basis of the formal juridical character of the Canadian law.

This may have been an instance where Brazil would have been better off not admitting as apparently it did that the distinction between mandatory and discretionary legislation should be dispositive of its claim against the

Canadian legal framework "as such". That is, Brazil might well have argued that the appropriate approach to state responsibility in a case like this, which relates to intense competition in a single product market, would be to employ the kind of test utilized by the panel in the S. 301 case, namely whether the kind of legal insecurity with respect to WTO rights created by the legislation is such as to give rise, in the context, to state responsibility based on the legal framework alone. Certainly, Brazil would have had a plausible case that the signals sent by the kind of programs established by Canada as such were sufficiently strong as to induce in Canada's Brazilian competitor a strong sense that it could not rely simply on market competitiveness to survive in the marketplace, due to the likely intervention of Canadian authorities to provide financing that would make the competing Canadian product more attractive to buyers, all other things being equal. This sense of insecurity would induce Embraer itself to invest resources in obtaining assistance from its own government, especially given that Embraer could not know exactly what Canada might, or might not, be offering to a given purchaser. In other words, the legal insecurity created by Canada's programs as such (and reinforced by Brazil's experience with their application to *past* trans-actions) would undermine one of the basic purposes of the SCM Agreement and binding dispute settlement in subsidies cases – to provide a viable response to a party concerned about the export subsidy practices of another party, which avoids the concerned party protecting the inter-ests of its producers by resorting to competitive subsidization or attempted "matching".

Brazil may have had a good argument that when one looked to the Canadian legal framework, especially "as applied", one could dis-cern patterned, norm-based conduct that attracts state responsibility, even apart from individual discrete discretionary decisions on particular transactions.

Because Brazil did not make this argument through the conceptual optic in the *301* case, it was largely lost on the panel, especially what it would mean to find a violation in the legal *scheme* "as applied" as opposed to or distinct from violations arising from individual acts of discretion in respect of particular transactions.

To recall *301*, there the panel found that, although the scheme on its face gave rise to legal insecurity of a kind such as, in the circumstances, to attract state responsibility, the broader legal context was such as to remove this insecurity, i.e. to give sufficient confidence that the scheme would not be interpreted and applied as if it mandated a violation of WTO rules. Here, Brazil was making an argument that was sort of a mirror image of that analysis – even if the formal elements of the Canadian legal framework did not, on their own, create the kind of legal insecurity that implicates state responsibility, when one considered the *pattern* of application or interpretation of the export financing entities' mandates, these schemes themselves did function such as to create the relevant level of legal insecurity, thus justifying a finding of violation, independent of the discretionary decisions of officials on particular transactions.

4 The Relationship of the SCM Agreement to the OECD Arrangement

The Panel revisited this issue, which has been addressed in earlier panel reports and Appellate Body rulings in the *Canada – Brazil* aircraft dispute.

Canada argued that its subsidies fell within the "safe harbor" of Annex I paragraph (k) in the SCM Agreement, which provides that export credit practices "in conformity with" the interest rate provisions "an international undertaking on official export credits to which at least twelve original Members of this Agreement are parties as of 1 January 1979", i.e. the *OECD Arrangement* by any other name. According to Canada the *OECD Arrangement* permitted matching of concessional interest rates, either those offered by a competing country on the basis of provisions of the *OECD Arrangement*, or as was relevant here, in derogation from the *Arrangement*.

While not definitively concluding that the *OECD Arrangement*, taken on its own, prohibits "matching" of derogations, the panel concluded that it would be inappropriate to incorporate into WTO law such an expansive understanding of the *OECD Arrangement*.

The panel suggested that the matching of a derogation would itself be a derogation and therefore not "in conformity with" the *OECD Arrangement*, unless it were understood as a permitted form of self-help. While the notion of self-help might be consistent with the nature of the OECD Arrangement as a "gentleman's agreement", it was not consistent with the WTO system, which prohibits self-help (7.170).

This is clearly erroneous. If the WTO system prohibited self-help, then it would prohibit countervailing duty actions against prohibited subsidies.

The panel also suggested that if the *OECD Arrangement* were incorporated into the SCM Agreement such as to permit matching of derogations of participants, non-participants in the OECD Arrangement would be at a disadvantage, as they would lack knowledge of such derogations, and thereby the opportunity for matching them. On the other hand, where what was being matched was an interest rate permitted under an explicit exception in the *OECD Arrangement*, the non-participants would be able to know what they needed to match, since the explicit exceptions are in a public document, the *Arrangement* itself. As Canada attempted to explain to the panel, this distinction is largely false, because the public document contains only notice of the theoretical possibility of concessional financing being offered on the basis of the exceptions in question, but does not provide information about what might actually be offered in any given transaction, i.e. the information needed for effective "matching".

In addition, the panel expressed the concern (7.177) that if "matching" of derogations were permitted, and a derogation were taken by a non-WTO Member, the benchmark for whether a export subsidy was permitted or not under the WTO rules would be the conduct of that non-Member. The panel found it unacceptable that the limits of WTO rights could be determined by non-Members. Nevertheless, the latest version of the *OECD Arrangement* does not list any non-WTO Members as participants, so this concern appears to be entirely hypothetical (in theory, non-WTO Members could be invited to join the arrangement, however unlikely this is in the current situation). Moreover, where an export subsidy is "matching" the subsidy of a non-WTO Member, it is difficult to see an issue arising under the SCM Agreement in the first place, since the non-WTO Member would not have any standing to challenge the "matching" subsidy. Assume for the sake of argument that Brazil is not a Member of the WTO – Canada matches Brazil's alleged derogation from the *OECD Arrangement*, but since Brazil has no rights under the SCM Agreement, nor Canada any obligations towards Brazil, it is not really the case that the limits of WTO rights and obligations are being determined by the conduct of a non-Member.

Of course, Brazil and Canada could be competing hypothetically with a third country, a WTO Member (let's say South Africa) for commuter jet sales. Canada legally matches Brazil's derogation, and so arguably this limits in effect its obligation to South Africa under the SCM Agreement. But doesn't the same problem arise with respect to matching of an interest rate explicitly permitted under an exception in the *OECD Arrangement*, namely, the conduct of a non-WTO Member, Brazil, triggers a legal right to match, which limits the rights of South Africa, a WTO Member, under the SCM Agreement?

Now it is true that because the exception is explicitly detailed and circumscribed in the OECD Arrangement, there is a fixed outward limit, as it were, on how much South Africa's rights could ultimately be limited by Brazil's conduct, which doesn't so obviously exist in the case where it is derogations that are matched. This fixed outward limit is itself however determined in a body participation in which does not have WTO Membership as a prerequisite.

7

United States – Definitive Safeguard Measures on Imports of Circular Welded Carbon Quality Line Pipe From Korea Not for Attribution*

BY

GENE M. GROSSMAN
Princeton University

AND

PETROS C. MAVROIDIS
University of Neuchâtel and Columbia University

1   Facts of the Case

This dispute concerns the imposition of a definitive safeguard measure by the United States on imports of circular welded carbon quality line pipe ("line pipe") from Korea (WTO DOC. WTO/DS 202/AB/R). The measure was imposed following an investigation conducted by the US International Trade Commission (USITC). The USITC determined in a safeguard investigation initiated on 29 July 1999 that "circular welded carbon quality line pipe . . . is being imported into the United States in such increased quantities as to be a substantial cause of serious injury or the threat of serious injury."[1] In its investigation, the USITC identified a

---

* This study reviews the WTO Appellate Body report *United States – Definitive Safeguard Measures on Imports of Circular Welded Carbon Quality Line Pipe From Korea* (WT/DS202/AB/R 15 February 2002). We are grateful to Henrik Horn and Jasper-Martijn Wauters for helpful discussions and to Alan Sykes, whose paper (Sykes, 2003) profoundly influenced our thinking about these issues.

[1] The Appellate Body report on *United States – Definitive Safeguard Measures on Imports of Circular Welded Carbon Quality Line Pipe From Korea* (WT/DS202/AB/R 15 February 2002; henceforth, *Line Pipe*) that we discuss in this paper notes (p. 1) that three Commissioners made a finding of serious injury, two Commissioners made a finding of threat of serious injury and that the affirmative vote of these five Commissioners

number of factors apart from increased imports that might have caused serious injury or threat of serious injury to the domestic line pipe industry. The Commission concluded that increased imports were "a cause which is important and not less than any other cause" and that, therefore, the statutory requirement of "substantial cause" had been met.[2]

By Proclamation of the President of the United States dated 11 February 2000, the United States imposed a definitive safeguard measure on imports of line pipe in the form of a duty increase for three years applicable to imports above 9,000 short tons from each source country, effective 1 March 2000.[3] The applicable duty was increased by 19 percent *ad valorem* in the first year, 15 percent in the second year, and 11 percent in the third year. The measure was applied to imports from all countries, including Members of the World Trade Organization (WTO), but excluding imports from Canada and Mexico, the NAFTA partners of the United States.

Korea requested consultations with the United States pursuant to Article 4 of the *Understanding on Rules and Procedures Governing the Settlement of Disputes* (DSU), Article XXII:1 of the *General Agreement on Tariffs and Trade 1994* (GATT) and Article 14 of the *Agreement on Safeguards* (SGA), with regard to the safeguard measures on line pipe.[4] When the two sides failed to resolve a number of disputed issues, Korea requested that a WTO panel be established to examine US actions in this case. The Panel concluded that the US safeguard measure for line pipe was inconsistent with certain of the provisions of the GATT and the SGA.[5] The Panel found, *inter alia*, that the United States had acted inconsistently with Article 4.2(b) of the SGA by failing to establish a causal link between the increased imports and serious injury to a domestic industry, or threat thereof. The Panel however rejected an argument by Korea that the United States had acted inconsistently with its obligations under Art. 5.1 of the SGA by imposing a safeguard measure intended to

---

constituted the majority in support of the "affirmative determination" of the USITC. A single Commissioner made a negative determination that there was neither serious injury nor threat of serious injury. The views of that Commissioner are not part of the USITC determination.

[2] See *Line Pipe* at p. 2.

[3] "Proclamation 7274 of 18 February 2000 – To Facilitate Positive Adjustment to Competition From Imports of Certain Circular Welded Carbon Quality Line Pipe," *United States Federal Register*, 23 February 2000 (Volume 65, Number 36), pp. 9193–9196; Panel Report, para. 7.176, also reflected on p. 3 of the AB report on *Line Pipe*.

[4] WTO Doc. WT/DS202/1, G/L/388, G/SG/D10/1, 15 June 2000.

[5] WTO Doc. WT/DS202/5, 22 January 2001.

counteract the whole of the injury suffered by the import-competing industry rather than only the part that could be attributed to increased imports.

Both the United States and Korea appealed aspects of the Panel's ruling. The United States claimed *inter alia* that the Panel was wrong in its ruling about causality, because the USITC had explicitly addressed that issue and had found that imports were a substantial cause of serious injury, meaning a "cause that is important and no less so than any other cause." Korea argued *inter alia* that the Panel had erred in sanctioning a safeguard measure meant to offset the entire injury to the industry and not just the part due to increased imports. In this chapter, we will focus on just these two issues and not on a number of relatively less important questions that were also in dispute.

The remainder of the chapter is organized as follows. In Section 2, we describe the relevant legal provisions in the GATT and the SGA and the prior WTO jurisprudence that bears on this case. In Section 3, we discuss the possible objectives of the escape clause in the GATT and the SGA. Ideally, we would hope to use the objectives of the agreement to inform our interpretation of the treaty text. However, we will argue that the parties' intentions in these agreements are by no means clear. Section 4 outlines in greater detail the issues concerning attribution of injury and the extent of safeguard measures that are at issue in this case. Here, we also recount the Panel and AB rulings. Section 5 contains our critique of the AB ruling. We argue that a redrafting of the relevant provisions of the GATT and the SGA is badly needed. We summarize and conclude in Section 6.

2   Relevant Legal Provisions and Prior Jurisprudence

2.1   *The relevant provisions of GATT and SGA*

The WTO treaty allows a signatory to abrogate its obligations to other Members for a proscribed period of time under certain conditions. The conditions describe changes in the health of a domestic industry that competes directly with imports (i.e., that produces a "like product") and the causes of those changes. In particular, Article XIX.1a of the GATT states that

> If, as a result of unforeseen developments and of the effect of the obligations incurred by a Member under this Agreement, including tariff concessions, any product is being imported into the territory of that Member in such

increased quantities and under such conditions as to cause or threaten serious injury to domestic producers in that territory of like or directly competitive products, the Member shall be free, in respect of such product, and to the extent and for such time as may be necessary to prevent or remedy such injury, to suspend the obligation in whole or in part or to withdraw or modify the concession.

The SGA provides further detail on the nature of the investigation that must be used to determine injury, the nature of the required link between imports and injury, and on many procedural matters.[6] Among the provisions that are germane to this case is Article 2.1 of the SGA, which stipulates that

> A Member may apply a safeguard measure to a product only if that Member has determined, pursuant to the provisions set out below, that such product is being imported into its territory in such increased quantities, absolute or relative to domestic production, and under such conditions as to cause or threaten to cause serious injury to the domestic industry that produces like or directly competitive products.

Article 4.2a of the SGA adds that

> In the investigation to determine whether increased imports have caused or are threatening to cause serious injury to a domestic industry under the terms of this Agreement, the competent authorities shall evaluate all relevant factors of an objective and quantifiable nature having a bearing on the situation of that industry, in particular, the rate and amount of the increase in imports of the product concerned in absolute and relative terms, the share of the domestic market taken by increased imports, changes in the level of sales, production, productivity, capacity utilization, profits and losses, and employment.

Finally, Article 4.2b requires that

> The determination referred to in [Article 4.2a] shall not be made unless this investigation demonstrates, on the basis of objective evidence, the *existence of the causal link between increased imports of the product concerned and serious injury or threat thereof. When factors other than increased imports are causing injury to the domestic industry at the same time, such injury shall not be attributed to increased imports.*
>
> (emphasis added)

---

[6] In *Argentina – Safeguard Measures On Imports Of Footwear* (WTO Doc. WT/DS121/AB/R of 14 December 1999) and elsewhere the AB has ruled that safeguard measures must be consistent with *both* Article 19 of GATT and the SGA; see paras. 83, 84, 93 and 94.

Concerning the dispute over the nature and extent of the US safeguard measure, the relevant text is contained in the first sentence of Article 5.1 of the SGA. This sentence reads that

> A Member shall apply safeguard measures only to the extent necessary to prevent or remedy serious injury and to facilitate adjustment.

2.2   Prior WTO case law

The AB has not as yet attempted to define what the treaty requires as a standard for "serious injury," nor has it delineated the factors that should be considered as possible contributors to that injury. Concerning Article 4.2 of the SGA, where it states that "the competent authorities shall evaluate all relevant factors of an objective and quantifiable nature having a bearing on the situation of that industry, in particular, the rate and amount of the increase in imports of the product concerned in absolute and relative terms, the share of the domestic market taken by increased imports, changes in the level of sales, production, productivity, capacity utilization, profits and losses, and employment," the AB has ruled in *Argentina – Safeguard Measures on Imports of Footwear* (WT/DS121/AB/ R 14 December 1999; henceforth *Footwear*) that the text requires that the entire list of factors must be "evaluated" in every case. Also, in *United States – Definitive Safeguard Measures on Imports of Wheat Gluten From the European Communities* (WT/DS166/AB/R 22 December 2000; henceforth *Wheat Gluten*), the AB has ruled that an investigating authority faced with multiple potential causes of injury must, in accordance with Article 4.2a of the SGA, examine every factor known to it and not only those raised by the interested parties.[7]

---

[7] Para. 55 of *Wheat Gluten* states, in part, that:

> "... in our view, that does *not* mean that the competent authorities may limit their evaluation of 'all relevant factors', under Article 4.2(a) of the *Agreement on Safeguards*, to the factors which the interested parties have raised as relevant. The competent authorities must, in every case, carry out a full investigation to enable them to conduct a proper evaluation of all of the relevant factors expressly mentioned in Article 4.2(a) of the *Agreement on Safeguards*. Moreover, Article 4.2(a) requires the competent authorities – and *not the interested parties* – to evaluate fully the relevance, if any, of 'other factors'.

Much of the argumentation in disputes concerning the use of safeguard measures has centered on the meaning of the words "cause" and "causal" in Article XIX.1 of the GATT and Articles 2.1 and 4.2 of the SGA, and on the meaning of the requirement in Article 4.2b of the SGA that, in situations where it is deemed that factors other than increased imports have contributed to an industry's ill health, "such injury shall not be attributed to increased imports." The AB has indicated in *United States – Safeguard Measures On Imports Of Fresh, Chilled Or Frozen Lamb Meat From New Zealand And Australia* (WTO Doc. WT/DS177 and 178/AB/R of 1 May 2001; henceforth *Frozen Lamb*) that it considers a two-step analysis to be appropriate: first, the competent authority must ensure that injury due to other factors is not attributed to imports and then it must find evidence of a causal link between increased imports, and injury. The AB wrote in para.180 of *Frozen Lamb*:

> . . . the 'causal link' between increased imports and serious injury can only be made *after* the effects of increased imports have been properly assessed, and this assessment, in turn, follows the separation of the effects caused by all the different causal factors.
>
> (emphasis in the original)

The AB has not been at all clear about what a competent authority must do to comply with the requirement that injury due to "other factors" should not be attributed to increased imports. For example, in *Wheat Gluten* (para. 70) the AB ruled that

> The need to ensure a proper attribution of injury under Article 5.2(b) indicates that competent authorities must take account, in their determination, of the effects of increased imports *as distinguished from* the effects of other factors.
>
> (emphasis in the original)

while in *Frozen Lamb* (para. 181) the AB wrote:

> We emphasize that the method and approach WTO Members choose to carry out in the process of separating the effects of the other causal factors is not specified by the *Agreement on Safeguards*. What the Agreement requires is simply that the obligation in Article 4.2 must be respected when a safeguard measure is applied.

Nonetheless, the AB has repeatedly found fault with investigations carried out by the competent authorities, especially the USITC, ruling on several occasions that they have failed to comply with the requirement for non-attribution. In *Wheat Gluten* (para. 19), the AB concluded that the USITC had not "adequately evaluated the complexities" and had not "ensured that injury attributable to other factors is not attributed to imports." In *Frozen Lamb*, the AB wrote (para. 185) that

> ...we see nothing in the USITC Report to indicate how the USITC complied with the obligation found in the second sentence of Article 4.2(b) and, therefore, we see no basis for either the Panel or us to assess the adequacy of the USITC process with respect to the "non-attribution" requirement of Article 4.2(b) of the *Agreement on Safeguards*. The USITC Report, on its face, does not explain the process by which the USITC separated the injurious effects of the different causal factors, nor does the USITC Report explain how the USITC ensured that the injurious effects of the other causal factors were not included in the assessment of the injury ascribed to increased imports.

and (para. 186)

> In the absence of any meaningful explanation of the nature and extent of the injurious effects of these six 'other' factors, it is impossible to determine whether the USITC properly separated the injurious effects of these other factors from the injurious effects of the increased imports. It is, therefore, also impossible to determine whether injury caused by these other factors has been attributed to increased imports.

If an investigating authority somehow could convince the AB that it had met the requirements for non-attribution, it seems it could rather more easily meet the standards for establishing causality. In principle, the AB recognizes the distinction between correlation and causation; for example, in *Footwear* (para. 144) it concurred with the Panel that "coincidence by itself cannot prove causation." But, in practice, the AB has not grappled much with the difficulty of demonstrating causal relationships between economic events. Rather, it has been content to accept co-temporal movements (i.e., correlation) as evidence of causality in most situations. In *Footwear*, the AB noted in para. 141 that "if causation is present, an increase in imports normally should coincide with a decline in the relevant injury factors" and in para. 144 it concurred with the Panel that

> ...in an analysis of causation, 'it is the relationship between the movements in imports (volume and market share) and the movements in injury factors that must be *central* to a causation analysis and determination.' (emphasis added) Furthermore, with respect to a '*coincidence*' between an increase in imports and a decline in the relevant injury factors, we note that the Panel simply said that this should 'normally' occur if causation is present.

Although the AB has been adamant about the need for an investigating authority to separate the injury caused by increased imports from those caused by other factors, it has ruled that the SGA does not require that the authority show that increased imports alone would have been sufficient to cause serious injury. To the contrary, the AB stressed in *Frozen Lamb* (para. 70) that

> ... the *Agreement on Safeguards* does not require that increased imports be 'sufficient' to cause, or threaten to cause, serious injury. Nor does the Agreement require the increased imports 'alone' be capable of causing, or threatening to cause, serious injury.

To summarize, the AB has noted the distinction between causation and correlation, but has not provided guidance on how the two should be distinguished in practice. The AB has insisted that the Members ensure that injury caused by other factors not be attributed to increased imports, but has not suggested an acceptable method for ensuring non-attribution. And the AB has indicated that an import surge normally should be contemporaneous with injury to the domestic industry, but has ruled that the surge need not be sufficient to have caused serious injury without other, contributing factors.

2.3   Discussion of previous jurisprudence

The AB rulings prior to *Line Pipe* create a number of difficult problems for this and subsequent interpretation of the Safeguards Agreement. The difficulties have been rehearsed at length by Horn and Mavroidis (2003), Sykes (2003), Irwin (2003), and others, so the discussion here can be reasonably brief.

First, the AB has failed in all of its rulings to confront the meaning of the words "cause" and "causal" as they apply in the context of safeguard proceedings. This is very problematic, because the text makes clear the need to establish that increased quantities of imports have been a cause of serious injury to the domestic industry and yet, as Grossman (1986), Kelly (1988), Rousslang (1988), Horn and Mavroidis (2003), Sykes (2003), Irwin (2003), and others have argued, the volume of imports of a particular product into a particular country is an endogenous outcome that cannot logically be considered to be the cause of other economic outcomes. That is, a number of supply and demand factors combine to determine equilibrium outcomes in an industry. Among these are the factor and input prices faced by national and foreign producers, the technologies available for producing the good at home and abroad, consumers' tastes for the goods produced by the industry, the prices of goods produced by competing industries, the overall levels of demand in the national and international economies, etc. These factors jointly determine the location of the supply and demand curves for the product of the import-competing industry and the supply and demand curves for imports. The supplies and demands in turn determine the sales of the national industry, the prices of national and imported products, and (importantly!) the volume of imports. Thus, a change in the underlying conditions of supply or demand will affect not only the health of the domestic industry (sales, employment, profits, rates of return on capital, etc.) but also the quantity of imports. So, it is simply impossible to ascribe a causal relationship between an increased quantity of imports and injury to a domestic industry when the two outcome variables are determined simultaneously by the same set of fundamental variables. Yet, this is exactly what Article XIX of the GATT and Article 4.1 of the SGA requires the competent authority in a safeguard investigation to do.

Sykes (2003) has argued that the historical context of the GATT gives some hints as to what the negotiating parties might have meant by their wording of the text. At the time that they wrote that "If, as a result of unforeseen developments *and* of the effect of the obligations incurred by a contracting party under this agreement, including tariff concessions, any product is being imported into the territory of that contracting party in such increased quantities and under such conditions as to cause or threaten serious injury . . ." the multilateral tariff reductions that were being considered by the parties were unprecedented and so their likely consequences were unknown. It makes sense in this context that the negotiating parties might have intended to draw a link between the "effects of the obligations incurred by a contracting party under this agreement" and the "increased quantities" of imports that might "cause or threaten serious injury." In other words, it is possible to interpret the sentence as meaning that the investigating authorities should look not for a causal relationship between increased imports per se and the conditions of the domestic industry (which would be impossible), but rather between the increased imports that resulted from the obligations incurred in the 1947 GATT Agreement and the injury that might result soon thereafter as a direct consequence thereof.

However, the wording has remained unchanged for fifty-six years and it is no longer sensible to look for injury caused by obligations incurred in 1947. Moreover, the AB has ruled explicitly that the requirement that injury be a result of "the obligations incurred by a contracting party under this agreement, including tariff concessions" means only that the importing party must have taken on some obligations as a result of its participation in the trade treaties.[8] As Sykes (2003) concludes, and we agree, the passage of time and the AB interpretation of the first clause of Article XIX of the GATT combine to eliminate the possibility of an economically coherent interpretation of the entire sentence. If it is not increased imports resulting from some specific exogenous event that is considered to be a possible cause of injury, but rather increased imports as a whole, then it is logically impossible to perform the separation of causes stipulated by the non-attribution provisions of the SGA.

It is not surprising, then, that the AB has failed to provide any clear guidance about what sort of analysis would qualify to meet its requirements for non-attribution. While the AB insists that the investigating authorities must provide a "reasoned and adequate explanation" (*Frozen Lamb* at para. 103) for their conclusion that injury due to other factors has not been attributed to an increase in imports, no such explanation is possible in the absence of a coherent interpretation of what it means for imports to cause injury.

2.4   The legal context for Line Pipe: summary

The discussion of causality and non-attribution in the *Line Pipe* dispute takes place in the context of a deeply flawed legal environment. Concerning the text of the pertinent agreements, Sykes (2003, p. 21) summarizes well:

> ... it is important to focus on the fundamental problem: neither Article XIX nor the Safeguards Agreement offer a coherent foundation for safeguard measures. The Appellate Body has consistently emphasized fidelity to text in its decisions, but that approach simply cannot work when the text is so fundamentally deficient.

Moreover, the prior case law has done little to resolve the questions raised by the text and much to add uncertainty about what an investigating

[8] Another interpretation with some intellectual appeal would be to read Article XIX of the GATT as providing an instrument to compensate losses that might result from the most recent round of trade liberalization. Such an interpretation suffers, however, from at least two important shortcomings: first, the language to support this interpretation is absent from the text of the SGA and Article XIX of the GATT; second, such an interpretation would deprive Members of the right to introduce safeguards when imports surge in sectors in which tariffs were not reduced in the most recent trade round.

authority must do to fulfill its obligations to its WTO partners in safe-guard proceedings. Evidently, such an authority must (i) examine all relevant factors that may have affected conditions in an industry, including those not raised by the interested parties themselves, (ii) establish the existence of serious injury by examining (at least) all of the industry factors mentioned in Article 4.2a of the SGA, (iii) provide an explicit, reasoned and adequate explanation for how it has distinguished the injury caused by increased imports from the injury caused by other factors, and (iv) determine that increased imports bear a causal relationship to deteriorating industry conditions at least by showing co-movement of these variables. How it can do so in a world where imports and industry conditions are simultaneously determined by other exogenous factors remains unclear.

3   Possible Objectives of the Safeguards Agreement

Before we proceed to our discussion of the issues concerning causality and non-attribution that arise in *Line Pipe*, we pause to consider the objectives of the Safeguards Agreement. As we argued in Grossman and Mavroidis (2003), it is important to understand the objectives of an agreement and what behaviors it is meant to discourage or tolerate in order to interpret the meaning of the text and discern how it ought to be applied in circumstances that are not explicitly discussed. Unfortunately, we will find in this case that the objectives of the agreement are no more clear than is the text or the prior case law. Although there are several possible economic rationales for including an escape clause in a multilateral trade agreement, the Safeguards Agreement is not structured in a way that indicates any particular one of them as the intended or proper purpose. Accordingly, economic theory provides relatively little guidance as to how the Agreement ought to be interpreted when adjudicating disputes.

3.1   Safeguards as compensation for losers

The opening of trade via multilateral negotiations will generate aggregate efficiency gains in many situations, but there are bound to be individuals and groups that are harmed. The inclusion of safeguard measures in a trade agreement might be rationalized as a means to compensate the losers from trade liberalization (see Deardorff, 1987). A safeguard measure can be used to restore relative prices to what they would have been but for the trade liberalization and thereby preserve jobs and incomes for workers in the import-competing industry. To the extent that the protection is temporary, the compensation will only be partial. But the burdens imposed on displaced workers might be mitigated if these workers have a longer period to retrain and seek new employment.

However, as Burtless et al. (1998), Sykes (2003), and many others have argued, trade protection is a clumsy tool for effecting redistribution. Empirical studies have found repeatedly that import-restraining policies impose very high costs on the importing country per job saved or per dollar transferred due to the productive inefficiencies that result from such measures and the great burdens they impose on consumers (see, for example, Feenstra (1992)). The total cost of these measures is even larger when the interests of the exporting country are taken into account, as they presumably will be in any negotiated agreement. Protectionist responses are poorly targeted policies for the purposes of effecting redistribution to disadvantaged groups inasmuch as they boost incomes not only of displaced workers and others with specific human capital, but also of well-diversified (and often quite wealthy) shareholders who own the firms and capital in the import-competing industry. Also, it is hard to see why a society would find it desirable to compensate the losses from unexpected import surges, but not those resulting from other economic events that affect the fortunes of individuals working in or invested in a particular industry.

There is nothing explicit in the way that the text of GATT Article XIX or the SGA is written to suggest that the intended purpose of the safeguard provisions is to compensate the losers from trade liberalization. First, the preferred interpretation of Article XIX of the GATT that has been offered by the AB does not limit the use of safeguards measures to situations in which losses are attributable to trade liberalization per se, but rather to import surges that occur for any reason. Second, Article XXVIII of the GATT, which provides for renegotiation of concessions, would seem a preferable tool for protecting the interests of those that are harmed by trade protection, inasmuch as such renegotiation allows for a more permanent restoration of competitive conditions to what they were before the tariff concessions or other effects of an agreement. Third, as Sykes has argued, the text of Article XIX of the GATT limits application of safeguards to injury that results from "unforeseen developments"; if redistribution were the rationale for these provisions, it is difficult to see why the Members would not have wished also to compensate losers also for the anticipated consequences of their trade concessions.

3.2   Safeguards to promote restructuring or facilitate adjustment

3.2.1   Promoting investments to restore competitiveness

Industry representatives often seek to justify their pleas for escape clause protection on the grounds that such measures will provide the wherewithal for reinvestment and restructuring to restore competitiveness. Temporary protection can increase profitability so that firms have more funds available to invest in retooling, while the respite from foreign competition can give them time for their new investments to come on line. In this way, proponents argue, viable firms can be saved when otherwise they might be driven from the market by cheap imports.

Although this argument may resonate with some politicians and lay persons, it makes little economic sense. Firms that are viable in the long run should be able to finance their investments in restructuring by borrowing funds or raising equity in the capital markets. For an investment to be socially warranted, it must yield expected discounted profits (or other social benefits) at free-market prices that equal or exceed the cost of the project plus any risk premium. Firms with potential projects that meet this criterion should be able to borrow at prevailing interest rates, unless there are imperfections in the capital market. Those that do not meet the criterion and that become profitable only with the help of elevated prices during a period of import protection should be rejected as economically inefficient. And capital markets, at least in the developed countries, are widely thought to be reasonably efficient, at least in most cases. Even if they are not, a targeted program that would provide subsidized capital or loan guarantees to firms and industries that are unable to obtain financing at socially appropriate rates would be a far superior policy to one of protection, which affects the allocation of all resources and not just capital, and which imposes avoidable burdens on domestic consumers.

If Article XIX of the GATT and the Safeguards Agreement were intended to promote investments in restructuring, one would expect to find certain provisions in them that are missing. Investments in restructuring ought to be limited to cases in which the domestic industry is viable in the long run, and in which the private capital markets would charge an unjustifiable premium to firms attempting to raise external funding. Thus, a test for the applicability of safeguards would begin with an examination of whether the conditions in the domestic industry have changed temporarily or permanently, and whether new investments reasonably could be expected to restore profitability. It would also include an investigation to establish the existence of capital market imperfections that prevent the domestic industry from financing profitable investments by borrowing or issuing new shares. It might reasonably include a requirement that trade policies be used only when less trade distorting measures (such as credit subsidies or loan guarantees) are unavailable. Finally, it might include provisions to ensure that the excess profits generated from the temporary protection are in fact invested in restructuring and not used to generate windfall gains to shareholders and bondholders. Article XIX of the GATT and the SGA contain none of these features.

3.2.2   Promoting efficient adjustment

Safeguard measures might also be rationalized as a means to promote efficient and orderly reallocation of resources (especially labor) in situations in which adjustment is costly. As Mussa (1982, 1984) has shown, the mere fact that resource movements are costly provides no presumption that a free-market adjustment process will be inefficient. If workers have rational expectations about the future of their industry and have access to capital markets to finance temporary income shortfalls at interest rates close to the social discount rate, and if real wages are reasonably flexible and an individual's job search creates no externalities for others, then workers will move from a declining industry to another (and bear the associated costs of search and re-training) at the rate that is socially warranted. Of course, labor markets may be distorted due to the existence of short-run wage rigidities or congestion in the search process. Then, as Lapan (1976), Neary (1982), Cassing and Ochs (1978) and Davidson and Matusz (2001) have shown, the free-market rate of adjustment can easily be too rapid, with excessive unemployment or sub-optimal matching of workers to jobs.

Horn and Mavroidis (2003) have built a case for including safeguard provisions in trade agreements around the presence of distortions in the labor market.[9] They describe a situation in which an unanticipated, permanent shift in the foreign supply curve of imports indicates a decline in the efficient, long-run employment level in a domestic industry. Following such a shock, a temporary safeguard measure could be expected to raise social welfare if the size of total adjustment costs depends positively on the speed of adjustment, and if there is a gap between the private and social

[9] See also Sykes (1991) and, for a more formal treatment, Davidson and Matusz (2002).

costs of adjustment. The positive link between the speed of adjustment and the size of adjustment costs would arise, for example, if wages are inflexible, so that a fall in labor demand results in displacements rather than wage cuts, and if the number of workers that can be absorbed by new employers rises gradually over time. In such circumstances, with unemployment caused by wage rigidities rather than optimal search for new employment, the private and social costs of unemployment are bound to diverge.

Horn and Mavroidis (2003) note some potential pitfalls in the use of safeguard measures to promote more efficient adjustment, which might account for *some* of the features of Article XIX of the GATT and the SGA. First, governments might be tempted to invoke safeguard protection any time they feel political pressure from special interests in an industry, and not just in response to shocks that necessitate fine-tuning of the adjustment process. A test for serious injury might be incorporated into the safeguard provisions as a means to discourage such opportunistic behavior. Also, if safeguard measures could be invoked to cushion any negative shocks, firms in the domestic industry might face insufficient incentives to exercise due diligence in avoiding unnecessary job displacements. To eliminate this moral hazard for the domestic industry, the escape clause provisions could require a causal link between external events and injury to the industry, and preclude the use of safeguard measures when the need for adjustment is entirely due to the poor performance of domestic firms.

While the adjustment-cost rationale for safeguard provisions is consistent with certain features of the WTO Safeguards Agreement, it is hard to interpret the Agreement as a whole as being a response to this particular economic problem. First, as Horn and Mavroidis (2003) themselves point out, a protectionist measure is hardly a first-best response to the labor market imperfection that they (and others) have identified. It would be far more efficient to treat adjustment problems with a program of "adjustment assistance" that would provide income insurance for displaced workers plus worker training and perhaps some wage subsidies. In fact, empirical studies by Hufbauer and Elliot (1994), Sazanami et al. (1995), Messerlin (2001), among many others, suggest that, in practice, the costs of trade protection in a variety of countries far outweigh the possible efficiency gains attainable from slowing the rate of worker relocation. Second, as Sykes (2003) points out, a safeguard provision intended to promote more efficient adjustment would include an investigation of industry conditions to determine whether they suggest that it would be beneficial to stretch out the adjustment process. At the least, a high rate of industry unemployment might seem a sensible pre-requisite for safeguard measures intended to slow the departure of workers from an industry. But the SGA explicitly requires that competent authorities examine a variety of indicators of industry health and not just unemployment. Third, the SGA has no provisions to ensure that adjustment actually takes place during the period of temporary protection. Indeed, many industries have used safeguard protection as a way to avoid contraction, and many have returned for second and third doses of "temporary" relief after having failed to adjust.

3.3   Safeguards as political safety valves

A third possible objective of the safeguard provision in trade agreements is to serve as a political safety valve. If a Member knows that it can "escape" from its commitments in the face of intense political pressures, it may be willing to make greater concessions in its multilateral negotiations than would be the case if its liberalization was irreversible. Moreover, if an agreement gives a Member the option to roll back prior concessions in times of political need, this may dissuade the Member from resorting to extra-legal measures or from scrapping the agreement altogether. This rationale for safeguard provisions has been developed most fully by Sykes (1991, 2003), who goes on to argue that "serious injury" might be a proxy for intense political pressure in the importing country, while increased quantities of imports suggest that the foreign industry is not suffering similarly. Sykes suggests that when an import surge coincides with serious injury to an industry in an importing country, safeguard measures might be used to create surplus for the two governments, inasmuch as the government in the importing country could gain more political support from a market-closing measure than the other would lose.

To some extent, it is tautological to argue that safeguard provisions have been included in trade agreements to provide a political safety valve. The provisions would not be part of the agreement had the negotiators not perceived that allowing them to be invoked in certain circumstances would create political surplus for the Member governments. The issue of concern is whether taking this perspective provides guidance on how the treaty text ought to be interpreted. Surely, Members cannot be allowed to escape from the agreement any time they claim a political benefit from doing so, for this would invite opportunistic behavior and would in no way ensure that the provisions are invoked only when the political gains to the government of the importing country exceed the losses to those of the exporting country. And whereas Sykes (2003) argues that "serious injury" and correlation of injury with increased imports suffices to identify the relevant circumstances, we question whether this is so. Grossman and Helpman (1994) show, for example, that access to a foreign market may be especially valuable to special interests in an exporting industry when those firms are highly productive and enjoy low costs. In such circumstances, a safeguard measure might impose greater political costs on the government of the exporting country than it provides benefits to that of the importing country.[10]

In short, it is not enough to recognize that the safeguard provisions are intended as a political safety valve to be invoked whenever the continued application of bound tariffs would cause more political harm to the government of the importing country than would their temporary suspension cause to the government of the exporting country, for this would amount to a legal test with little if any normative guidance, and hence would be unsuitable in the context of international adjudication. We, as interpreters of the agreement, still need to know how the negotiating parties meant to identify such circumstances and what limitations they intended to impose on the importing country to protect the political interests of the government of the exporting country. In reviewing this and other potential objectives of the safeguard provisions, we find little to guide us in interpreting the language of the text or in adjudicating disputes such as *Line Pipe*. The SGA is silent about what the Members intended to achieve by their incorporation of safeguard provisions in the trade treaty.

We are thus faced with a situation in which an agreement that is opaque about its intended objectives contains an incoherent conditions test. Under the circumstances, it is almost impossible for us to render a cogent interpretation of the text that could be used to determine when safeguard measures are permissible and when they are not. But this question is the essence of the *Line Pipe* dispute, to which we now turn.

---

[10] Sykes argues that when exporters are especially profitable, the special interests in the exporting industry will not value market access highly, because any potential rents will be dissipated by entry; see also Baldwin and Robert-Nicoud (2001). But this argument rests on the assumption that there are no quasi-fixed factors of production in the industry that might limit entry and thereby create rents for those who have entered first.

4   Issues and Rulings in *Line Pipe*

4.1   *USITC investigation and findings*

The safeguard provisions in US trade law are contained in Sections 201 to 204 of the Trade Act of 1974. These Sections allow interested parties in an import-competing industry to petition the USITC requesting an investigation as to whether a product is being imported into the United States in such increased quantities as to be a substantial cause of serious injury, or threat thereof, to the domestic industry producing an article that is like or directly competitive with the imported article. The statute defines a "substantial cause" to be a "cause which is important and not less than any other cause." It defines "serious injury" as a "significant overall impairment in the position of a domestic industry." Sections 201 to 204 do not require that injury be linked to any trade liberalization or concessions made by the United States in an international agreement, nor do they stipulate any explicit effort on the part of the USITC to ensure that injury caused by other factors is not attributed to increased imports.

The USITC instituted a Section 201 investigation of line pipe on 30 June 1999 following receipt of a petition from seven domestic producers and the United Steelworkers of America. As required by US law, the Commissioners considered whether the domestic industry producing line pipe had suffered serious injury or threat thereof, and if so, whether increased imports were a substantial cause of that injury. In their report of December 1999, the Commission reported its findings that there were increased quantities of imports during the five years preceding the investigation, that the domestic industry had suffered serious injury, and that imports were a substantial cause of that injury.[11] In making its determination of serious injury, the Commission considered a variety of indicators of industry conditions, including all of those listed in Article 4.2a of the SGA. As possible causes of injury, the Commission considered the role of increased imports, of decline in the demand for line pipe due to reduced oil and natural gas drilling, of competition among domestic producers, of changes in the market for oil country tubular goods (also produced by domestic producers of line pipe) that may have caused domestic line pipe producers to switch production out of these goods,

---

[11] Three commissioners found that the industry had suffered serious injury, two found that the industry was threatened by serious injury, and one found that there had been no injury. According to USITC rules, this constitutes a finding in favor of serious injury.

of contraction in US producers' export markets, of increase in per-unit overhead resulting from shrinking production, and of declines in raw material costs. The Commission ruled that the decline in demand for line pipe resulting from reduced oil and natural gas drilling and production activities indeed had contributed to the industry's poor performance, but that the effects of increased imports on the domestic industry were as great or greater. It also ruled that the other factors either had no adverse effect on the industry, or had an effect that was very much smaller than that of imports. Finally, concerning the attribution of injury to its various causes, the Commissioners wrote:[12]

> Respondents also argued that we may not attribute injury caused by [the other] factors to the imports. We have not done so. As required by the statute, after evaluating all possible causes of injury, we have determined that the imports are an important cause of serious injury and are not less important than any other cause.

In the light of its positive finding that increased imports were a substantial cause of serious injury to the domestic line pipe industry, the USITC recommended various remedies to the President of the United States. The President introduced a safeguard measure by proclamation, without providing an explicit justification for the extent of the measure or any evidence that the measure was limited to that which was necessary to address the injury that could be attributed to increased imports.

4.2   The Panel ruling

A WTO Panel was established on 23 October 2000 to consider complaints by Korea regarding the line pipe measure. Korea argued before the Panel *inter alia* that the USITC had violated its obligations under Article 4.2b of the SGA by failing to demonstrate properly that injury caused by other factors had not been attributed to increased imports. In particular, Korea asserted that the USITC had not properly distinguished the injurious effects caused by other factors from those caused by imports and thus it could not assure the non-attribution required by Article 4.2b of the SGA. Korea also claimed that the United States had violated its obligations contained in Article 5.1 of the SGA to ensure that its safeguard measure was applied "only to the extent necessary to prevent or remedy serious

---

[12] See the USITC investigation of *Circular Welded Carbon Quality Line Pipe* (USITC Investigation No. TA-201-70, Publication 3261, December 1999) at p. I–30.

injury and to facilitate adjustment." Korea contended that a safeguard measure must be limited in size to at most what would counteract the injurious effects of the increased imports. According to Korea, because the USITC had not ensured that injury caused by other factors was not attributed to increased imports, it could also not ensure that the safeguard measures introduced subsequently were applied only to the extent necessary to offset the injury attributable to imports.

The Panel ruled in favor of Korea on the first point, rejecting in the process the US argument that the USITC had properly distinguished the effects of other factors from the effects of increased imports by examining six factors other than increased imports as possible causes of serious injury and determining that none was a more important cause of injury. The Panel concluded on this point that the USITC "did not adequately explain how it ensured that injury caused to the domestic industry by factors other than increased imports was not attributed to increased imports."[13]

The Panel rejected Korea's claims about the permissible extent of the safeguard measure, ruling that it had failed to make a *prima facie* case showing that the United States had violated Article 5.1 of the SGA. The Panel noted (para. 7.11) that "Korea has failed to identify any aspect of the line pipe measure which would suggest that it was intended to address the injurious effects of the decline in the oil and gas industry" and added that even had the remedy recommended by the USITC been intended to do so, this did not mean that the line pipe measure that was eventually applied by the United States was illegal, because the latter differed substantially from the remedy recommended by the Commission. The panel concluded that "[s]ince Korea has failed to establish any factual basis for its argument, it is not necessary for us to consider the substantive issue of whether or not safeguard measures should be confined to addressing the injurious effects of imports." Evidently, the Panel did not find merit in Korea's claim that the failure by the USITC to distinguish the injury due to other factors from that due to increased imports implies, as a matter of logic, that the United States could not have succeeded in limiting the extent of the safeguard measure so as to counteract only the injurious effects of the increased imports.

---

[13] See *United States – Definitive Safeguard Measures on Imports of Circular Welded Carbon Quality Line Pipe From Korea* (WT/DS202/R 29 October 2001) at para. 7.290.

4.3 Appellant arguments and the AB ruling

The United States appealed the Panel's ruling on non-attribution, arguing that the Panel had simply presumed without any factual analysis that the USITC had not complied with Article 4.2b of the SGA in this case. This presumption, the United States claimed, was based on a misinterpretation by the Panel of the AB rulings in *Frozen Lamb* and *Wheat Gluten*. The United States contended that the USITC had in fact identified and distinguished the effects of other factors and did not attribute injury caused by those factors to imports, but that the Panel failed to acknowledge or review those findings and analysis. In the view of the United States, the Panel had simply assumed that the USITC's relative injury causation analysis could not possibly have entailed separation and assessment of the injurious effects of factors other than imports, because the methods used in the case were similar to those found faulty in previous cases.

Korea appealed the Panel's ruling on the proportionality of the line pipe measure on the basis that the Panel had failed to recognize a link in the SGA between the causation analysis that a competent authority must perform in order to justify the use of a safeguard measure and the permissible extent of that measure. According to Korea, the SGA limits the extent of a safeguard measure to that which would offset the serious injury attributable to increased imports. If the USITC had failed to ensure that injury due to other factors was not attributed to increased imports, it must have also failed to ensure that the safeguard measure was applied only to the extent of the injury that could be attributed to the increased imports.

The AB upheld the ruling of the Panel on the issue of non-attribution. Essentially, the AB found that the US analysis of causation did not provide a reasoned and adequate explanation of how it had ensured that injury caused by other factors had not been attributed to increased imports. First, the AB reiterated its understanding of the requirements imposed by Article 4.2b of the SGA:

> We have previously ruled, and we reaffirm now, that, to fulfill this require-
> ment, competent authorities must separate and distinguish the injurious
> effect of the increased imports form the injurious effects of the other factors.
> As we ruled in *US – Hot-Rolled Steel* with respect to the similar requirement
> in Article 3.5 of the *Anti-Dumping Agreement*, so, too, we are of the view that,
> with respect to Article 4.2(b), last sentence, competent authorities are
> required to identify the nature and extent of the injurious effects of the
> known factors other than increased imports, as well as explain satisfactorily

the nature and extent of the injurious effects of those other factors as distinguished from the injurious effects of the increased imports.

(para. 215)

Accordingly, the AB noted,

> ... competent authorities must establish explicitly, through a reasoned and adequate explanation, that injury caused by factors other than increased imports is not attributed to increased imports. This explanation must be clear and unambiguous. It must not merely imply or suggest an explanation. It must be a straightforward explanation in express terms.
>
> (para. 217)

The AB accepted Korea's argument that, although the USITC had recognized that a decline in oil and gas drilling and production had caused injury to the domestic line pipe industry, it had not explicitly identified the nature and extent of the injury attributable to this cause and so it could not have properly separated and distinguished these effects from the effects of increased imports. The AB concluded that

> Our examination [of the US appellant's submissions and of the cited parts of the USITC report] leads us to conclude that those cited parts of the USITC report do not *establish explicitly*, with a *reasoned and adequate explanation*, that injury caused by factors other than the increased imports was not attributed to increased imports. The passage on page I–30 of the USITC report highlighted by the United States is but a mere assertion that injury caused by other factors is not attributed to increased imports. A mere assertion such as this does not *establish explicitly*, with a *reasoned and adequate explanation*, that injury caused by factors other than the increased imports was not attributed to increased imports. This brief assertion in the USITC Report offers no reasoning and no explanation at all, and therefore falls short of what we have earlier described as a reasoned and adequate explanation.
>
> (para. 220, emphasis in the original)

Apparently, the AB ruling compels the competent authorities to provide a full accounting of the causes of all injury suffered by an industry to establish explicitly that the injury attributed to imports does not include parts due to other causes.

The AB also ruled in favor of Korea on the issue it raised concerning the permissible extent of the safeguard measure. The AB first emphasized that the treaty allows only limited safeguard measures, namely those that are "necessary to prevent or remedy serious injury and facilitate adjustment."

Since the measures are limited to what is necessary to achieve a certain objective, it becomes imperative to identify the objective. The answer clearly is to offset serious injury, but which serious injury? The AB answers its own question, when it opines that

> [i]n our view, the 'serious injury' to which Article 5.1, first sentence, refers is, in any particular case, necessarily the same 'serious injury' that has been determined to exist by competent authorities of a WTO member pursuant to Article 4.2. We think it reasonable to assume that, as the Agreement provides only one definition of 'serious injury', and as the Agreement does not distinguish the 'serious injury' to which Article 5.1 refers from the 'serious injury' to which Article 4.2 refers, the 'serious injury' in Article 5.1 and the 'serious injury' in Article 4.2 must be considered as one and the same. On this, we agree with the United States. But, contrary to what the United States argues, the fact that these two provisions refer to the same 'serious injury' does not necessarily lead to the conclusion that a safeguard measure may address the 'entirety' of the 'serious injury,' including the part of the 'serious injury' that is attributable to factors other than increased imports.
>
> (para. 249)

Next, the AB notes that the meaning of "serious injury" here must be understood in the context of the agreement. The AB sees the non-attribution language in Article 4.2b of the SGA as a central part of the architecture of the SGA and thus as providing the appropriate context for interpreting Article 5.1 of the SGA. The AB argues that

> ... the non-attribution language of the second sentence of Article 4.2b has two objectives. First, it seeks, in situations where several factors cause injury at the same time, to prevent investigating authorities from inferring the required 'causal link' between imports and serious injury or threat thereof on the basis of the injurious effects caused by factors other than increased imports. Second, it is a benchmark for ensuring that only an appropriate share of the overall injury is attributed to increased imports. As we read the Agreement, this latter objective, in turn, informs the permissible extent to which the safeguard measure may be applied pursuant to Article 5.1, first sentence. Indeed, as we see it, this is the only possible interpretation of the obligation set out in Article 4.2b, last sentence, that ensures its consistency with Article 5.1, first sentence. ...
>
> (para. 252)

From this, the AB concluded that "... the phrase 'only to the extent necessary to prevent or remedy serious injury and to facilitate adjustment' in Article 5.1 of the SGA, first sentence, must be read as requiring that safeguard measures may be applied only to the extent that they address serious injury attributed to increased imports" (see para. 261 on p. 83).

5   Critique of the AB Rulings

5.1   Attributing the causes of injury

The GATT and the SGA – especially when taken in combination with the prior rulings on escape clause cases by the WTO Appellate Body – do not provide a coherent framework for determining the legality of a safeguard measure. The text requires that the competent authorities find imports to be a cause of serious injury to a domestic industry and that, in so doing, they do not attribute to imports the ill effects of other factors that may be contributing to the industry's poor health. Yet simple economic reasoning reveals that an increased quantity of imports cannot *per se* be a "cause" of injury, inasmuch as the quantity of imports is determined as an equilibrium outcome along with the various indicators of industry health. For an economic variable to be the "cause" of some effect, it must be possible for that variable to move exogenously and independently of other possible causes. But imports are endogenous, responding as they do to conditions of supply and demand in the domestic and foreign markets.[14]

In principle, it might be possible to ascertain the Members' intended meaning in Article XIX.1 of the GATT and Article 4 of the SGA by considering their objectives in structuring these agreements. But, as we have argued in Section 3 above, the objectives themselves are not clear. The intended role of the safeguard provisions might be to ensure compensation of losers from trade liberalization, to promote efficient readjustment in the face of industry shocks, or to provide a "safety valve" to relieve political pressures. One can readily construct an economic rationale for safeguard provisions that would serve any one of these objectives, but a sensible treaty aiming to achieve each such objective would have to include additional features that are absent from the SGA. Moreover, one would not structure an agreement aimed largely at compensation, for example, in the same way as one intended to promote efficient adjustment. Thus, without knowledge of the primary purpose and intended function of the agreement, one cannot be sure how to structure an

---

[14] For an elementary exposition of this point, see Kelly (1988) or Horn and Mavroidis (2003).

appropriate causality test (if, in fact, the inclusion of such a test is indicated at all).

Let us return to the case at hand. In the absence of a clear text and in the light of the jurisprudential history that has involved repeated findings of illegality, it would have behooved the AB to provide guidance about what sort of investigation would satisfy the requirements of the SGA as currently written. Admittedly, such guidance would only serve as a palliative until the text of the agreement can be improved; but without it, the competent authorities are faced with a text apparently demanding an attribution exercise that cannot meaningfully be performed.

One possible way to lend coherence to Article XIX.1 of GATT and Article 4.1 of the SGA is suggested in a paper by Grossman (1986). In that paper, Grossman confronted the question of how one should interpret the requirement in Section 201 of the US Trade Act of 1974 that safeguard measures be reserved for situations in which increased imports are shown to be a substantial cause of injury to the domestic industry. Since the quantity of imports *per se* cannot meaningfully be considered to be an exogenous event, Grossman proposed that the USITC seek to identify an event that is "trade-related" and truly exogenous with respect to the health of the domestic industry. A change in trade policy (e.g., a tariff concession) might constitute such an event, but such an interpretation of injury caused by imports would be too narrow in the context of US trade law, because Section 201 makes no reference whatsoever to trade policy when describing the circumstances that would justify a safeguard measure. As an alternative, Grossman noted that a shift in the supply curve of imports is exogenous to the health of the domestic industry and that such a shift could legitimately be considered as a potential cause of injury.[15] The import supply curve shifts whenever the United States lowers a trade barrier, but also when foreign producers acquire a new technology, become more efficient, experience a fall in factor prices, or install new capacity. Thus, a shift in the import supply curve is distinguished from an increase in the quantity of imports inasmuch as the former reflects events that occur *outside* the US industry and thus is independent of the "other factors" that impinge upon the industry's health, whereas the latter is the result of events that occur *inside* the industry as well as those that take place abroad.[16]

---

[15] See also Kelly (1988), who adopts a similar approach.

[16] Put differently, it is possible to separate the effects of a shift in the import supply curve from the effects of other factors that impact the health of an import-competing industry,

The "import supply curve" approach lends economic coherence to Section 201 by asking whether changing conditions of import supply, rather than increased quantities of imports, have been a substantial cause of injury to the US industry.[17] Since a "substantial cause" in the US trade is defined to be a cause that is "important and not less so than any other cause," Grossman proceeds in his paper to enumerate a list of potential exogenous variables that might have caused injury to the US steel industry during the period that he considered, and develops a methodology to compare the amount of injury attributable to each one.

Article XIX.1 of the GATT does not require the competent authorities to show that increased imports have been a substantial cause of injury to a domestic industry. Rather, it requires the authorities to assess whether "...as a result of unforeseen developments and of the effect of the obligations incurred by a Member under this Agreement, including tariff concessions, any product is being imported into the territory of that Member in such increased quantities and under such conditions as to cause or threaten serious injury to domestic producers." It is possible to interpret the exogenous event here as being "the obligations incurred by a Member under this Agreement, including tariff concessions." Indeed, Sykes (2003) suggests that this may have been the meaning intended by the negotiators of the original agreement, wherein "the obligations

---

as is required to ensure non-attribution. But it is not possible to separate the effects of an increase in the quantity of imports from the effects of these other factors, because the other factors will alter the quantity of imports even as they cause injury to the domestic industry.

[17] Sykes (2003) recognizes this virtue of the import supply curve approach, but criticizes it for "effectively rewriting the statute" without providing a legal theory to support its interpretation of the text. We would respond that the incoherence of the text makes some rewriting by the interpreter unavoidable. Absent some imaginative interpretation, the WTO judge would, in the face of the incoherence of the causality-requirement as currently reflected in the SGA, effectively have to deprive WTO Members of the possibility to use safeguards until a new re-negotiated SGA is put in place of the existing text. This would be the case if the WTO judge were to conclude, having exhausted the interpretative elements of Articles 31 and 32 of the Vienna Convention on the Law of Treaties, that the current test is unreasonable or absurd. The other possibility would be for the judge to pick one of the three possible rationales for a safeguards clause that we have advanced *supra* and define the permissible extent of safeguards by using such a benchmark. Our preferred interpretation can be defended over such an approach with reference to the moral hazard that would exist if domestic factors were to play a role in determining the legitimacy of safeguards. For more on this point, see Horn and Mavroidis (2003). Eventually of course, a clear rewriting of the SGA in this respect has the advantage of providing upfront clarity as to what was actually intended by the Member countries.

incurred" referred to the entirety of the commitments made under the new treaty. Since the treaty remains in force fifty-six years later, it is no longer possible to associate the "obligations incurred" with the original concessions made in 1947. But the "obligations incurred" might now be read to mean any (or perhaps the most recent) concessions made by a Member of the WTO as a part of the multilateral negotiating process. These policy changes are exogenous events as far as the industry is concerned, and they might give rise to unforeseen developments, including an increase in imports that causes injury.

It would also be possible to take a broader view, such as the one proscribed by the AB. The AB prefers to read the second part of the first sentence of Article XIX.1 of the GATT (i.e., "the obligations incurred by a Member under this Agreement, including tariff concessions") as providing only the context in which the injury takes place. With this reading, it is not possible to use a change in trade policy as the exogenous event that might precipitate injury. But then the import supply curve approach could be used to provide a coherent interpretation of the remainder of the sentence. In other words, the statute might be read to require an assessment of whether unforeseen shifts of the import supply curve that have induced growth in the volume of imports, were also responsible for having serious injury or threat thereof to a domestic industry. The US statute and Article 4.2 of the SGA can then be seen as mandating a "but for" analysis by the competent authorities, who would need to compare the actual health of the domestic industry with that which would have prevailed *but for* the change in the conditions of import supply (with all else the same). A safeguard measure would be permitted if and only if the difference between the actual and hypothetical state of the industry was found to be sufficiently great to meet the standard for "serious injury" or threat thereof.

Note that the approach of considering shifts in the import supply curve as the exogenous events that might precipitate injury is distinct from the methods that might be used to carry out the but-for analysis indicated by such an approach. Grossman (1986) has illustrated one possible approach to the counterfactual analysis. He posits a model of the US steel industry in which indicators of industry health are determined by demand trends in the US demand for steel, the aggregate level of industrial production, the world price of iron ore, the world price of energy, and the world price of imported steel. The last of these variables is taken to reflect the location of the import supply curve under the assumption that the United States consumes a relatively small share of the world output of steel. Grossman establishes econometrically a statistical relationship between the indicators of industry conditions and current and lagged values of the exogenous variables. He then performs counterfactual simulations to assess how changes in each exogenous variable had contributed to deteriorating conditions in the industry, given the time paths of the others. Grossman was able to evaluate the claim that increased imports of steel (due to changes in import supply conditions) were a substantial cause of injury to the US steel industry by comparing the magnitude of the injury attributable to each factor. Although not conceived for this purpose, his results could also be used to evaluate claims that increased imports resulting from exogenous changes in import supply had caused serious injury to the US industry. Note that the econometric methodology ensures that injury due to other factors besides imports is not attributed to imports; it does so by examining the partial effect of one independent variable on the dependent variable while holding constant the effect of all others.

The econometric methodology proposed by Grossman (1986) is not the only one that might be used to implement the import supply curve approach. Kelly (1988) proposes an alternative method based on the empirical calibration of a simple model of supply and demand for imports and imperfectly-substitutable domestic products. The important point is that the competent authorities should adopt *some* method that yields a "reasoned and adequate explanation" of the partial effect of changed conditions of import supply on industry health, holding constant the values of other exogenous variables that might also have affected conditions in the domestic industry.

We return now to *Line Pipe*. Clearly, the AB did not provide the sort of guidance and interpretation of the statutes that we feel would have been appropriate. Did they also err in finding that the United States had acted inconsistently with its obligation under Article 4.2b of the SGA by failing to ensure that injury caused to the domestic industry by factors other than increased imports was not attributed to increased imports? We think not. We have offered two possible interpretations of Article XIX.1 of the GATT, one that treats the exogenous event that might cause injury to a domestic industry as a change in trade policy resulting from obligations incurred under a multilateral agreement and another that treats the exogenous event as a shift in the import supply curve that occurs for any reason. Under either interpretation, Article 4.2b of the SGA still demands objective evidence of a causal relationship that does not attribute to increased imports any injury that may have been caused by other factors. Our reading of the USITC report has been hindered by the censoring done to preserve confidentiality. Still, we find no evidence that the USITC carried out the sort of but-for analysis that we would deem necessary for the purpose. For example, nowhere in the document do we find an estimate of the injury caused by any exogenous event related to trade, holding constant the paths of other variables such as the level of oil and gas drilling or the demand for oil country tubular goods. Without such analysis, the USITC could not have ensured that injury caused by these other factors was not attributed to increased imports, the assertions on page I–30 of the report notwithstanding.

5.2   The allowable extent of a safeguard measure

On the question of the permissible extent of a safeguard measure, the AB ruled that the words "only to the extent necessary to prevent or remedy serious injury and to facilitate adjustment" in the first sentence of Article 5.1 of the SGA should be read as limiting the extent of a safeguard measure so that it addresses only the serious injury suffered by the industry that can be attributed to increased imports. To reach this conclusion, the AB reflected on whether the "serious injury" referred to in Article 4.2 of the SGA is necessarily the same "serious injury" mentioned in Article 5.1 of the SGA. The AB noted that the Agreement provides only one definition of "serious injury" and does not draw any distinctions in the two references to this term. It inferred from this that the two mentions of "serious injury" must refer to the same underlying concept. The AB reasoned that, inasmuch as the non-attribution clause modifies the serious injury described in Article 4.2 of the SGA, the same modification must apply to the usage of the term in Article 5.1 of the SGA. The AB concluded that

> [i]t would be illogical to require an investigating authority to ensure that the 'causal link' between increased imports and serious injury not be based on the share of injury attributed to factors other than increased imports while, at the same time, permitting a Member to apply a safeguard measure addressing injury caused by all factors.
>
> (para. 252)

We do not agree that such a requirement would somehow be "illogical." As we noted in Section 3, the obligation that injury be linked to external events might reasonably be included as a pre-requisite for safeguard measures in order to address the moral-hazard problem that otherwise would exist if firms could generate protection by their own actions. Once a Member can demonstrate, however, that the poor health of its industry is not (entirely) of its own doing, it might be desirable to allow that Member to counteract the full extent of the injury suffered by the industry *from all sources*. In other words, the reason for insisting on a causal link between increased imports and serious injury can be quite different from the considerations that determine the optimal extent of the consequent remedy.

While we cannot exclude the possibility that the Members intended to allow safeguard measures to offset the full extent of injury by applying *logic* to the wording of the first sentence of Article 5.1 of the SGA, neither do we see an obvious textual argument to conclude otherwise. If anything, the wording of Article XIX.1a of the GATT would seem to support the interpretation offered by the AB of Article 5.1 of the SGA. In particular, Article XIX.1a of the GATT allows safeguard measures when a product is being imported "in such increased quantities and such conditions as to cause or threaten serious injury," but only "to the extent and for such time as may be necessary to prevent or remedy *such* injury . . ." (emphasis added). The use of the word "such" in the latter clause would seem to refer the interpreter back to the injury attributable to increased imports.

As a matter of economics, there is little we can say about rules regarding the size of safeguard measures without knowing more about the object-ives of the Agreement. For example, if the purpose of the SGA is to compensate the losers from trade liberalization, then the applicable safe-guard measure should be limited in size to whatever would restore competitive conditions to what they would be but for the relevant changes in trade policy. But if the purpose of the Agreement instead is to encour-age restructuring of the domestic industry or to facilitate efficient adjust-ment, arguably it is the entirety of the injury suffered by the domestic industry that should be used as the basis for tailoring a temporary palliative. An industry that has suffered some injury due to foreign competition and more injury due to other causes will face greater needs for reinvestment and/or adjustment than one that has only suffered from trade competition. If the argument can be made that temporary protec-tion contributes to a more efficient adjustment process, the indicated safeguard measure in the former case may be larger than in the latter. In short, we cannot judge the appropriate size of a safeguard measure from an economic standpoint without knowing what distributive or efficiency-enhancing purpose the measure is intended to serve.

6   Conclusions

To conclude, we have argued that the text of the SGA suffers from two serious deficiencies: Article 4.2b of the SGA calls for a causality test that is economically incoherent and therefore not operational; and the agreement fails to express explicit objectives of the safeguard provisions. With an incoherent text and an absence of clear objectives, it is impossible for the adjudicator to determine when the conditions for a safeguard measure have been satisfied and what is the permissible extent of such a measure.

In the *Line Pipe* dispute, Korea claimed that the United States had not properly attributed injury to its various causes and that its safeguard measures exceeded in scope what is permitted under the treaty. The AB ruled against the United States essentially on procedural grounds. It is difficult for us to disagree with the AB ruling in view of the causal analysis contained in the USITC investigatory report. However, where the AB embraced the non-attribution requirement in Article 4.2b of the SGA, it lent operational significance to an incoherent requirement. To our mind, the AB ruling in this respect is flawed. The AB could instead have ruled that after exhausting the interpretative elements proscribed by Articles 31 and 32 of the Vienna Convention on the Law of Treaties, it had reached the conclusion that the legal text lacks an internally consistent interpretation.

Such a ruling would have left the AB with a dilemma: either it must refrain from ruling in the particular dispute and instead demand of the WTO members that they address, through legislative action, the shortcomings of the text (namely, that imports cannot be a cause of injury inasmuch as they are endogenously determined along with the health of the domestic injury, and so the causality test for a safeguard measure logically can never be met); or it must interpret the text imaginatively so as to render it internally consistent and operational. The first of these alternatives has the merit of respecting the institutional balance between the organs of the WTO, inasmuch as the AB as adjudicator should not be in a position of usurping legislative authority. The disadvantage of this approach, of course, is that until such a time as the WTO Members take corrective action with respect to the incoherent text, the AB would not be in a position to admit the legality of any safeguard measures. Clearly, the Members intended to permit the use of safeguards in some conditions; without them, the Members might well resort to the use of other instruments of contingent protection in situations that do not fit the "distortions" that the founding fathers meant to address with the SGA.

To avoid such an outcome, we believe that some judicial activism is warranted in the current jurisprudential environment. Our preferred interpretation of the treaty text is the "import supply curve" approach.

With this approach, the potential cause of injury to a domestic industry is not the increase in the quantity of imports per se (which would be impossible), but rather a shift in the import supply curve that both causes imports to surge and the domestic import-competing industry to suffer. By adopting such an interpretation, the AB undeniably would be adding words to the SGA that do not exist in the text. However, by doing so, the AB would be making sense of a conditions test that is *poorly described* in the SGA but not *wholly absent* from the SGA. It is clear that the treaty negotiators intended to permit application of safeguards in some but not all circumstances; and the circumstances had to do with the proximate cause of the deterioration of industry conditions. The import supply curve approach is faithful to these intentions.

We emphasize that we do not recommend judicial activism lightly. The *Line Pipe* dispute and other recent disputes arising from the SGA have two distinctive features. First, the text does indicate that the authors of the agreement intended some limits on the application of safeguard measures and some test for causality. Our interpretation certainly is not contradicted by the text of the agreement. Second, in the absence of some sort of judicial activism, the balance of rights and obligations that was intended by the signatories will be severely undermined. Our preferred approach allows the agreement to be operational, and provides for legal application of safeguard measures, during the period before the text of the SGA is improved.

References

Baldwin, Richard E. and Robert-Nicoud, Frédéric. 2001. Entry and Asymmetric Lobbying: Why Governments Pick Losers. Manuscript, Graduate Institute for International Studies, Geneva.

Burtless, Gary, Lawrence, Robert Z., Litan, Robert E. and Shapiro, Robert J. 1998. *Globaphobia: Confronting Fears About Open Trade*. The Brookings Institution: Washington.

Cassing, James H. and Ochs, Jack. 1978. International Trade, Factor Market Distortions, and the Optimal Dynamic Subsidy: Comment. *American Economic Review* 68, 950–955.

Davidson, Carl and Matusz, Stephen J. 2001. On Adjustment Costs. Manuscript, Michigan State University.

Davidson, Carl and Matusz, Stephen J. 2002. An Overlapping Generations Model of Escape Clause Protection. Manuscript, Michigan State University.

Deardorff, Alan V. 1987. Safeguards Policy and the Conservative Social Welfare Function. pp. 22–40 in H. Kierzkowski, ed., *Protection and Competition in*

International Trade: Essay in Honor of W. Max Corden. Blackwell Publishers: Oxford.

Feenstra, Robert C. 1992. How Costly is Protection? *Journal of Economic Perspectives* 12, 159–178.

Grossman, Gene M. 1986. Imports as a Cause of Injury: The Case of the U.S. Steel Industry. *Journal of International Economics* 121, 201–223.

Grossman, Gene M. and Helpman, Elhanan. 1994. Protection for Sale. *American Economic Review* 84, 833–850.

Grossman, Gene M. and Mavroidis, Petros C. 2003. Here Today, Gone Tomorrow? Privatization and the Injury Caused by Non-Recurring Subsidies. A Discussion of the Appellate Body Report on *United States – Imposition of Countervailing Duties on Certain Hot-Rolled Lead and Bismuth Carbon Steel Products Originating in the United Kingdom* in H. Horn and P.C. Mavroidis, eds., *The WTO Case Law of 2001.* Cambridge University Press: Cambridge UK.

Horn, Henrik and Mavroidis, Petros C. 2003. What Should be Required of a Safeguard Investigation? A Discussion of the Appellate Body Report On *United States – Safeguard Measures on Imports of Fresh, Chilled or Frozen Lamb Meat from New Zealand and Australia* in H. Horn and P.C. Mavroidis, eds., *The WTO Case Law of 2001.* Cambridge University Press: Cambridge UK.

Hufbauer, Gary Clyde and Elliot, Kimberly Ann. 1994. *Measuring the Costs of Protection in the United States.* Institute of International Economics: Washington DC.

Irwin, Douglas A. 2002. Causing Problems? The WTO Review of Causation and Injury Attribution in U.S. Section 201 Cases. NBER Working Paper No. 9815, Cambridge MA.

Kelly, Kenneth. 1988. The Analysis of Causality in Escape Clause Cases. *Journal of Industrial Economics,* 37, 187–207.

Lapan, Harvey. 1976. International Trade, Factor Market Distortions, and the Optimal Dynamic Subsidy. *American Economic Review,* 66, 335–346.

Messerlin, Patrick A. 2001. *Measuring the Costs of Protection in Europe: European Commercial Policy in the 2000s.* Institute of International Economics: Washington DC.

Mussa, Michael. 1982. Government Policy and the Adjustment Process. pp. 73–120 in Jagdish Bhagwati, ed., *Import Competition and Response.* University of Chicago Press: Chicago.

Mussa, Michael. 1984. The Adjustment Process and the Timing of Trade Liberalization. NBER Working Paper No. 1458, Cambridge MA.

Neary, J. Peter. 1982. Intersectoral Capital Mobility, Wage Stickiness, and the Case for Adjustment Assistance. pp. 39–67 in Jagdish Bhagwati, ed., *Import Competition and Response.* University of Chicago Press: Chicago.

Rousslang, Donald J. 1988. Import Injury in U.S. Trade Law: An Economic View. *International Review of Law and Economics* 8, 177–182.

Sazanami, Yoko, Urata, Shujiro, and Kawai, Hiroki. 1995. *Measuring the Costs of Protection in Japan*. Institute of International Economics: Washington DC.

Sykes, Alan O. 1991. Protectionism as a 'Safeguard': A Positive Analysis of GATT Escape Clause with Normative Speculations. *University of Chicago Law Review*, 58, 255–307.

Sykes, Alan O. 2003. The Safeguards Mess: A Critique of WTO Jurisprudence. John M. Olin Law & Economics Working Paper No. 187 (2D Series), University of Chicago Law School.

8

Chile – Price Band System and Safeguard Measures Relating to Certain Agricultural Products*

BY

KYLE BAGWELL
Columbia University

AND

ALAN O. SYKES
University of Chicago

1 Introduction

This study addresses the dispute brought to the World Trade Organization (WTO) by Argentina concerning certain Chilean measures affecting the importation of wheat, wheat flour, oil seeds, edible vegetable oils and sugar. The complaint by Argentina challenged two types of policies – a "price band system" that was applicable to four of those product categories, and safeguards measures that were applicable to three of them. The WTO panel ruled in favor of Argentina on both sets of measures.[1] It found that the price band system violated Article IV of the Agriculture Agreement and Article II of GATT 1994. The safeguards measures, according to the panel, violated various provisions of the Safeguards Agreement, as well as Article XIX of GATT 1994. Chile elected not to appeal the panel ruling regarding the safeguards measures, but did appeal the adverse finding as to the price band system. The Appellate Body subsequently affirmed in substantial part the finding that the price band system violated Article 4 of the Agriculture

* We wish to thank Alberto Martin for valuable assistance, and to thank the other reporters and conference participants of the American Law Institute for many valuable ideas and suggestions.
[1] *Chile – Price Band System and Safeguard Measures Relating to Certain Agricultural Products*, Report of the Panel, WT/DS207/R (May 3, 2002) (hereafter Panel Rep.).

Agreement, but reversed the finding of a violation under Article II of GATT 1994.[2] Chile has since indicated an intention to comply with the ruling, and an arbitration pursuant to Article 21.3 of the DSU has determined that the reasonable period of time for compliance will expire on December 23, 2003.

Because the issues raised by Argentina regarding the safeguards measures have for the most part surfaced in other cases that deal with them in greater detail, and because Chile did not appeal the panel's findings on these issues, we will not address them here. Instead, we focus on the issues before the Appellate Body, devoting careful attention to the treatment of the price band system, and very brief attention to some general procedural issues.

The price band issue has reasonably broad significance for three reasons. First, price band systems, which aim to reduce the volatility of agricultural prices, are maintained by a number of WTO members (some also maintain seasonal tariffs, which might also be subject to challenge in the future). Indeed, the complaining nation in the case – Argentina – maintains a price band system of its own for sugar imports.[3] Second, a resolution of the question as to the legality of the price band system implicates the broader question of what agricultural measures were required to be "tariffied" under the Uruguay Round Agreements. As shall be seen below, Chile's ultimate defeat before the Appellate Body rested on the proposition that its price band system should have been converted into an "ordinary customs duty" at the end of the Uruguay Round. Third, and perhaps most interesting from an economic perspective, the case raises the question of what constraints apply to WTO Members that wish to vary their tariff rates over time below their bound levels. The Chilean price band system, as amended, ensured that any additional tariffs required by the price band would not cause the total tariff on any imported good to exceed the applicable tariff binding. Nevertheless, the system was condemned because the way in which it was administered made it sufficiently "similar" to measures that had been required to be "tariffied."

We lay out the legal issues and arguments in Section 2. Section 3 offers a critical analysis of the case from a law and economics perspective.

---

[2] *Chile – Price Band System and Safeguard Measures Relating to Certain Agricultural Products*, Report of the Appellate Body, AB-2002–2, WT/DS207/R (September 22, 2002) (hereafter AB Rep.).

[3] See Raj Bhala and David Gantz, WTO Case Review 2002, 20 Ariz. J. Int'l L. 143, 255 (2003).

2 Factual and Legal Issues

2.1 Description of the price band system

The stated objective of the price band system was to "ensure a reasonable margin of fluctuation of domestic wheat, oil-seed, edible vegetable oil and sugar prices in relation to the international prices for such products."[4] To this end, Chile employed a somewhat convoluted procedure.

The price band itself was established annually. Depending on the product, either five or ten years of data would be gathered on the monthly average prices of the product in the "most relevant markets" abroad.[5] The edible vegetable oil price was apparently FOB Chicago Exchange, for example, while the wheat price was that of Hard Red Winter No. 2 FOB Gulf (Kansas Exchange).[6] These prices were adjusted for inflation, and then arrayed in ascending order. The highest 25 percent and lowest 25 percent of these average prices (35 percent in the case of sugar) were then discarded. From the remaining prices, the highest and the lowest for each product would be selected. Ordinary tariffs, transport, insurance and related costs were then added to these high and low prices, thus yielding a delivered price to Chile. These adjusted prices then became the annual price band for each product.

The process of establishing the price band was not transparent. There was apparently no published information indicating which foreign markets were the "relevant" ones or how they were selected. Likewise, no published information specified exactly which product prices would be used (soybean oil prices or sunflowerseed oil prices in the case of edible vegetable oils, for example), and no published source provided the basis for the various adjustments used to convert from FOB to delivered prices.[7]

Once the price band was established, it remained to compute the applicable duty on each shipment at the border. Interestingly, the actual transaction prices of products entering Chile were not employed, Rather, for each product, Chile would select a weekly "reference price." That price would be the *lowest* FOB price observed in any foreign "market of concern" during the week in which the shipment left its home market. Once again, it was not clear how the "markets of concern" were selected, or

---

[4] AB Rep. ¶11.
[5] AB Rep. n. 15.
[6] AB ¶18.
[7] See Panel Rep ¶7.44.

precisely which prices in those markets would be used.[8] The reference price was *not* adjusted for the costs of delivering the product to Chile from the market in question.

To determine the total tariff liability for each import shipment under this system, Chile would first apply its ordinary *ad valorem* tariff. In addition, Chile would ascertain when the shipment left its home market, and identify the reference price for that week for the product category in question. It would compare this reference price to the annual price band. If the reference price fell below the lower threshold of the price band, an additional specific duty would be applied to the shipment in an amount equal to the difference between the reference price and the low threshold price. By contrast, if the reference price fell outside the upper threshold of the price band, the importer would receive a rebate equal to the difference between the reference price and the upper threshold price. Finally, whenever the reference price fell within the price band, only the ordinary *ad valorem* duty would be collected, regardless of the actual transaction price of the shipment in question.

To illustrate, imagine a shipment of one ton of wheat arriving in Chile during the third week of September, and assume that its delivered price for tariff purposes is $100. Assume further that Chile's *ad valorem* tariff on wheat is 10 percent. The shipment originated in the United States during the first week of September. Assume further that the annual price band for wheat is $130–$180 per ton. Lastly, assume that the reference price for wheat during the first week of September was $90 per ton. Then, total tariff liability on the shipment would equal $50: $10 resulting from the 10 percent *ad valorem* tariff, and another $40 resulting from the difference between the lower threshold of the price band ($130) and the reference price ($90). If the shipment had instead had a delivered price of $200 and the pertinent reference price had been $190, tariff liability would have been only $10: $20 based on the *ad valorem* rate, less a $10 rebate due to the fact that the reference price exceeded the upper threshold of the price band by $10.

It is plain from the design of the system that it will tend to produce positive additional tariffs (above the *ad valorem* duty) on average (that is, the additional duties due to reference prices below the price band will not on average be offset by rebates due to reference prices above the price band). One reason is that the reference prices are FOB foreign markets, while the price band is based on delivered prices to Chile. Further, the reference price is always the lowest FOB price observed during the week in

---

[8] AB Rep. ¶¶23–25.

question in some foreign market of relevance. The average duty can be further inflated (or not) depending on precisely which foreign markets are used as the basis for the reference price, and which product prices are used. Finally, the rebates would never exceed the ordinary *ad valorem* tariff (there was never a "negative" duty), but the additional duties could well exceed it.

The reader may wonder how the total duty computed under this system related to Chile's tariff bindings. Chile had bound its tariffs under Article II of GATT 1994 at 31.5 percent for all of the products at issue in the price band system. In practice, however, Chile applied only a 7 or 8 percent tariff rate[9] to these products. Thus, as long as the additional duties under the price band system did not exceed each shipment's delivered value for tariff purposes multiplied by 31.5 percent less the applied *ad valorem* rate, the total tariff remained within the binding. But the total duty had on occasion exceeded the binding.[10] After the dispute began, however, Chile enacted an amendment to its price band system providing that in no event should the total duty applied to any product covered by the price band system exceed 31.5 percent of its value.

2.2   *Argentina's challenge and Chile's response*

2.2.1   Article II of GATT 1994

Article II(1)(b) of GATT 1994 provides:

> The products described in . . . the Schedule relating to any contracting party, which are the products of territories of other contracting parties, shall, on their importation into the territory to which the Schedule relates . . . be exempt from ordinary customs duties in excess of those set forth and provided for therein. Such products shall also be exempt from all other duties or charges of any kind imposed on or in connection with importation in excess of those imposed on the date of this Agreement or those directly and mandatorily required to be imposed thereafter by legislation in force in the importing territory on that date.

Argentina argued that the price band system violated Article II in two ways. First, as noted, the total duties imposed by Chile on products covered by the system had at times exceeded the applicable tariff binding. Each such instance, said Argentina, was a clear violation of sentence one of Article

---

[9] At one point the applied rate is said to be 7 percent on all products in question, and at another point it is said to be 8 percent. See AB Rep. ¶¶14, 128.

[10] AB Rep. ¶10.

II(1)(b) in that it represented the application of "ordinary customs duties" in excess of those set forth in Chile's Schedule of bindings.

Second, Argentina argued that Chile's price band legislation was "mandatory," in the sense that it afforded customs officials no discretion to avoid imposing the requisite duties in cases where the total duty would exceed the binding. Relying on past precedent regarding such mandatory legislation in the GATT and WTO, Argentina then suggested that the mere possibility that such legislation could compel a violation of WTO obligations was enough to condemn it, regardless of whether it had yet been applied in a manner that resulted in a violation.

Chile made a number of arguments in response, most of which were of little avail on their face. But it did have one argument with considerable force – the price band law had been amended to ensure that the total duties applied would never exceed the allowable duty under the binding. Whatever had happened in past practice, and even if the potential for violations under this "mandatory" legislation was evident prior to its amendment, the price band system as amended could no longer result in a violation of the Article II bindings.

2.2.2   Article 4 of the Agriculture Agreement

By way of background, one of the principal objectives of the Uruguay Round negotiations was the reduction of barriers to trade in agricultural products. The negotiators undertook to improve the transparency of such barriers as well as to reduce them, and an important part of this process involved the "tariffication" of nontariff barriers, i.e., the conversion of nontariff barriers into conventional tariffs. This process was to be completed by the end of the Round. Nations with substantial nontariff barriers would have the opportunity to convert them into tariffs and schedule them even if the resulting tariffs exceeded their prior tariff bindings under GATT.

Perhaps because it was contemplated that tariffication would be completed during the Round, the Agriculture Agreement does not contain specific text indicating what must be "tariffied" in prospective terms. Instead, Article 4.2 pertaining to "market access" simply provides:

> Members shall not maintain, resort to, or revert to any measures of the kind which have been required to be converted into ordinary customs duties,* except as otherwise provided for in Article 5 and Annex 5.
>
> * These measures include quantitative import restrictions, variable import levies, minimum import prices . . . and similar border measures other than ordinary customs duties.

Argentina contended that the price band system was either a "variable import levy" or "minimum import price" within the terms of the footnote, or at least a "similar measure" that had been required to be tariffed. According to this theory, Chile could have availed itself of the opportunity to convert the price band system into an equivalent conventional tariff, and to adjust its binding if necessary before the conclusion of the Uruguay Round. Once the Round ended, however, Chile could no longer "maintain" the price band system, whether or not it had taken the opportunity to tariffy it.

Chile responded in a number of ways. It suggested that the duties associated with the price band system had not been required to be converted into "ordinary customs duties" because they were ordinary customs duties already. Indeed, said Chile, Argentina's argument under Article II of GATT 1994, discussed above, was that the price band system imposed tariffs in excess of the binding on "ordinary customs duties," and thus implicitly conceded that the price band duties fell into that category. Chile argued further that the price band system was not a "variable import levy" or "similar measure," pointing to the conventional characteristics of such measures and to various distinctions between them and the Chilean price band system. Finally, Chile argued that given the vagueness of the footnote to Article 4.2 and its precise coverage, the question of which measures "have been required" to be converted should be answered based on the experience of the WTO membership during the Uruguay Round as to which types of measures had in fact been converted, or had been requested to be converted by other Members. In this regard, Chile noted that price band systems in general had not been converted, and that no Member had asked Chile to convert its price band system on any of the covered products.

2.3   The Panel decision

The panel began by rejecting Chile's suggestion that the amendment of the price band system mooted the dispute. Citing precedent, it held that the amendment of a measure should not prevent the dispute process from examining it, and suggested that it could not determine whether the amendment resolved the dispute without first determining how, if at all, the original measure violated WTO law.[11]

---

[11] Panel Rep. ¶¶7.3–7.8.

2.3.1 Analysis under the Agriculture Agreement

Beginning with Article 4.2 of the Agriculture Agreement, the panel rejected Chile's suggestion that the measures that "have been required" to be converted were limited to those that had actually been converted in practice, or that had been the subject of a request for conversion by another Member state. In so doing, it emphasized that Article 4.2 prohibits Members from maintaining any measures "*of the kind* which have been required to be converted," and argued that the phrase "of the kind" would have no purpose were the obligation limited to measures that had actually been required to be converted.[12] Thus, whether or not any nation had asked Chile to convert its price band system and whether or not other price band systems had in fact been converted, the issue for the panel was whether the price band system was among the "measures" covered by the footnote to Article 4.2.[13]

To fall within the footnote, the price band system would have to constitute one of the enumerated devices such as "variable import levies" or "minimum import prices," or at least be among the "similar border measures other than ordinary customs duties." The panel noted that the specifically enumerated devices were not defined in the Agreement. With reference to the footnote as a whole, the panel noted that "all the measures listed there are instruments which are characterized either by a lack of transparency and predictability, or impede the transmission of world prices to the domestic market, or both."[14] It then examined various reports prepared by GATT agriculture committees through the years, and on the basis of those reports set forth the "fundamental characteristics" of variable import levies and "minimum import prices."

The panel concluded that variable levies typically operate on the basis of two prices: a minimum threshold price linked to internal market prices or to a government target price, and a border price for imports usually based on the lowest world market offer price. The variable levy generally equals the difference between the second of these prices and the first. Thus, the variable levy has the quality that when world market prices fall, the variable levy rises. Likewise, variable levies tend to insulate domestic prices from international price variations.

---

[12] Panel Rep. ¶7.18.
[13] We note that Annex 5 to the Agriculture Agreement affords some exceptions to the tariffication requirements of Article 4.2, but they were not at issue in this case. See AB Rep. ¶198.
[14] Panel Rep. ¶7.34.

A minimum import price is similar to a variable levy in many respects, except that it usually operates on the basis of the actual transaction price of each import shipment. Whenever that price falls below the import price target, an additional duty is levied equal to the difference.[15]

The panel then noted that the Chilean price band system was not quite the same as either a variable import levy or a minimum import price as it defined them. The price band system did not rely on actual transaction prices like a minimum import price system, but instead on a reference price based on world market prices, a fact that made it more akin to a variable import levy. But unlike traditional variable import levies, the threshold target price was not based on domestic prices or a government target, but on average international prices from preceding years. And neither variable levies nor minimum import prices were generally accompanied by the possibility of a rebate when prices are high. Nevertheless, the panel found that the price band system was "similar" to variable levies and minimum import prices. It insulated the Chilean market from international price fluctuations to a significant extent, imposing a duty that rose as reference prices fell. Likewise, the system was marked by a lack of transparency and predictability regarding the selection of reference prices and markets, and the measurement of movement charges.[16]

It remained to consider the argument that the price band system was not a "similar measure other than ordinary customs duties" – as noted, Chile claimed that the duties under the price band system were indeed "ordinary customs duties." On this point, the panel rejected the suggestion that all duties made subject to an Article II tariff binding were "ordinary." Instead, it concluded that "ordinary" duties are either specific or *ad valorem* tariffs that depend exclusively on the volume or value of the goods in question and not on other "exogenous factors." The amount of such duties is predictable and transparent in accordance with the objectives of the tariffication process, and in contrast to duties under the price band system. Thus, the price band duties were within the footnote to Article 4.2, and because they did not fit any of the enumerated exceptions, Chile had violated Article 4.2 by maintaining them after the close of the Uruguay Round.[17]

---

[15] Panel Rep. ¶7.36.
[16] Panel Rep. ¶¶7.38–7.47.
[17] Panel Rep. ¶¶7.48–7.65.

2.3.2   Analysis under Article II of GATT 1994

On their face, the Article II bindings apply to "ordinary customs duties."
In its analysis under the Agriculture Agreement, the panel concluded that
the price band duties were not "ordinary customs duties." On the
assumption that this phrase has the same meaning in both the
Agriculture Agreement and in Article II – a proposition that no one
contested – the panel held that the price band duties could not be assessed
under the first sentence of Article II(1)(b), which requires that "ordinary
customs duties" not exceed the applicable binding.

The second sentence of Article II(1)(b), however, requires that "other
duties and charges" not exceed the amounts imposed on the date of the
agreement, or thereafter required by mandatory legislation in effect on
that date. Further, the Uruguay Round Understanding on the
Interpretation of Article II(1)(b) requires that "the nature and level of
any 'other duties and charges' levied on bound tariff items... shall be
recorded in the Schedules..." Chile had not listed its price band duties
among the "other duties or charges" in its WTO tariff schedules, and on
this basis the panel found that the price band system was a violation of
Article II(1)(b), second sentence.[18] It is noteworthy that this argument
had not been advanced by Argentina, which instead rested its Article II
claim on the proposition that the price band system, prior to its amendment, could result in total duties in excess of Chile's bindings.

2.4   The Appellate Body decision

The Appellate Body addressed some procedural points that we note only
in passing. It held that the amendment of the price band system during
the course of the dispute did not preclude the panel from considering it,
and further concluded that the panel could evaluate the price band system
as amended as well as in its original form because the amendment did not
change the "essence" of the system.[19] This principle allows the dispute
process to proceed in the face of amendments or other changes to a
challenged scheme without the need for a new round of consultations,
request for panel, and so on. It thus allows dispute resolution to proceed
more quickly and avoids the possibility of strategic behavior that could
delay it, a policy which strikes us as quite sensible.

[18]   Panel Rep. ¶¶7.104–7.108.
[19]   AB Rep. ¶¶134–144.

The Appellate Body also spent considerable time on the proper "order of analysis" in the case – whether the panel should have addressed the Agriculture Agreement first or the Article II issue first. It ultimately approved of the panel's decision to consider the Agriculture Agreement first on the ground that its provisions more "specifically" addressed the dispute. Chile apparently believed that had the Article II issue been considered first, the panel might have ruled that the price band system imposed "ordinary customs duties," and was thus outside the footnote to Article 4.2 of the Agriculture Agreement. The Appellate Body saw no merit in this contention, however, noting that the two provisions create separate and distinct obligations and that the outcome of the dispute would be the same regardless of the order of analysis.[20] As the issue seems quite unimportant for this reason, we do not address it further.

2.4.1   Analysis of the Agriculture Agreement

The Appellate Body began by considering Chile's argument, rejected below, that the reference in Article 4.2 to measures that "have been required" to be converted limits the obligation to measures that were in fact converted or had been requested to be converted. The Appellate Body agreed with the panel that the use of the present perfect tense refers to the obligation to convert measures at the conclusion of the Uruguay Round – the phrase "have been required" merely refers back to the point in time when the obligation arose, and does not limit the scope of the obligation to measures that were actually converted or discussed. It further emphasized that the footnote to Article 4.2 contains an illustrative and not exhaustive list of measures, thus suggesting that not all measures covered by the obligation had been specifically identified by the end of the Round.

It then proceeded to review the question whether the price band system was among the enumerated "measures" in the footnote, or at least "similar" to them. It quibbled with the panel's notion of similarity, which had rested on the proposition that measures should share some "fundamental characteristics." The Appellate Body thought that such a test unnecessarily embroiled the decisionmaker in assessing what is "fundamental" and what is not, and preferred merely to search for "likeness or resemblance sufficient to be similar."[21] It also quibbled with the panel's resort to extrinsic materials, such as the reports of old GATT agricultural

---

[20] AB Rep. ¶¶178–191.
[21] AB Rep. ¶226.

committees, for the purpose of defining the concepts of "variable import levy" and "minimum import price," preferring instead to rely on the ordinary meaning of the words in their treaty context and in light of their object and purpose, the familiar approach to treaty interpretation under the Vienna Convention.[22]

Following this approach, it found that a "variable levy" was a measure whereunder the amount of the duty was variable, and the variability was attributable to the terms of the measure itself (to differentiate it from an ordinary tariff, which could vary over time due to legislative amendment). In addition, a variable levy had to be at odds with the "object and purpose" of Article 4, which meant that it must lack the "transparency and predictability" of ordinary customs duties.[23] As to the concept of "minimum import price," the Appellate Body accepted the panel's definition in terms of a target threshold price and a levy that was based on the difference between the actual transaction price and the target price.

Having defined the terms in the footnote, the Appellate Body proceeded to the question of "similarity." Chile again emphasized the differences between traditional variable levies as described by the panel, but the Appellate Body was unpersuaded. It found that Chile's system could still have had the effect of insulating domestic prices from international price movements. Further, many aspects of the system – such as the selection of reference prices and the addition of movement charges to construct the price band – were not transparent and produced unpredictable results.[24]

Chile contended that the amendment to the law, which capped duties in accordance with the Article II binding, distinguished the price band system from the "measures" that had been required to be converted. But the Appellate Body found that the amendment to the law did not alter the essential nature of the price band measure, its trade distorting effects, or its lack of transparency and predictability.[25] The Appellate Body made note of the fact that the reference price in the Chilean system was chosen in such a way that it might "overcompensate" for downward price fluctuations in international markets,[26] and also noted that the failure to add movement expenses to the reference price tended to inflate the

---

[22] AB Rep. ¶¶230–231.
[23] AB Rep. ¶234.
[24] AB Rep. §246.
[25] AB Rep. ¶¶254–262.
[26] AB Rep. ¶260.

amount of the duty,[27] without explaining clearly why these facts were important. The Appellate Body further argued that if the presence of a cap on measures such as variable levies was enough to insulate them from the obligations of Article 4.2, there would have been no need to require conversion of any measure – the negotiators could simply have required that all agricultural tariffs be bound.[28]

Finally, the Appellate Body turned to the way that the panel had defined "ordinary customs duties" as duties that depend only on the value or volume of the goods and not on other "exogenous factors." It noted that nations may well choose to set their "ordinary" duties based in part on "exogenous" considerations, and that the text of Article II is quite unclear as to what constitutes an "ordinary" duty or "other duties or charges." The fact that most Member duties in most tariff schedules are simple *ad valorem* or specific duties is not relevant as to what is "ordinary" in the language of the treaty – Member state practice is only relevant if it is "subsequent practice" under the Vienna Convention, and the panel had provided no support for the conclusion here.[29] The Appellate Body accordingly reversed the panel in so far as it had defined "ordinary" duties as duties that did not depend on "exogenous" factors. But that did not change the fact that the price band system was "similar" to variable import levies and minimum import prices, and thus a violation of Article 4.2.

2.4.2   Analysis under Article II of GATT 1994

Chile argued on appeal that the panel erred when it found an inconsistency between the price band measure and Article II(1)(b), second sentence, because Argentina had not made such an argument during the course of the panel proceedings. The Appellate Body concurred. Although Argentina's request for a panel was phrased broadly enough to cover all aspects of Article II, the fact that Argentina did not subsequently advance the particular claim that the panel embraced meant that the panel had gone beyond an "assessment of the matter before it" under Article 11 of the DSU. To do so deprived Chile of "due process," as it was not on notice of the need to present a defense as to the consistency of the price band system with Article II(1)(b), second sentence.[30]

---

[27] AB Rep. ¶250.
[28] AB Rep. ¶256.
[29] AB Rep. ¶273.
[30] AB Rep. ¶¶145–177.

The Appellate Body thus overruled the finding against Chile under Article II(1)(b), second sentence, because the issue was not properly before the panel. Because it had also overruled the panel on the definition of "ordinary customs duties," it left open the issue whether the price band system created "ordinary customs duties" or "other duties or charges" for purposes of Article II. As it had already affirmed the finding that the price band system violated Article 4.2 of the Agriculture Agreement, the Appellate Body found no need to address its consistency with Article II(1)(b), first sentence.

3   Critical Analysis

3.1   Legal commentary

3.1.1   The Agriculture Agreement

Article 4.2 is an odd provision in many respects, and there is certainly some force to the position put forward by Chile. As indicated, Article 4.2 states that Members shall not "maintain, resort to or revert to" any measures that "have been required to be converted into ordinary customs duties," and lists some examples of such measures in the footnote. But nowhere in the Agriculture Agreement or in any other treaty text can one find a complete listing of measures which "have been required" to be converted, and no text contains any general criteria for the identification of such measures. The panel and the Appellate Body are no doubt right that many of the illustrative measures lack transparency and predictability, but those criteria are not to be found in the text either.

In the face of a text that refers to measures that "have been required" to be converted, but that lacks any comprehensive listing of them or any general criteria for identifying them, Chile's suggestion that the phrase refers back to a shared understanding among WTO members developed during the Uruguay Round has considerable plausibility. On this reading, the measures that "have been required" to be converted would be the sorts of measures actually converted as a result of Uruguay Round negotiations. Members could not maintain or revert to measures of that "kind," but could maintain other measures of a kind that had not been converted. The fact that a number of nations had price band systems, that apparently none were converted, and that no nation was asked to convert a price band system, then offers considerable evidence that price bands were considered to be different from the measures that were converted, and that they had not been "required" to be converted. The Appellate Body's observation that the footnote is illustrative and not exhaustive is of little moment on this view, as it merely lists some examples of measures that were in fact converted and was not intended to impose obligations with respect to other measures. To be sure, such a reading of Article 4.2 would leave open the question of what sort of measures are of the "kind" that had been converted, but shared practice would at least provide a clearer guide as to the types of measures that the negotiators had in mind.

We do not mean to say that the panel and Appellate Body were necessarily wrong in their legal disposition of the matter,[31] but we do think it somewhat peculiar that WTO Members should have structured a binding obligation in such a loose way as the case imagines – a non-exhaustive list of covered measures with no written set of unifying criteria, coupled with a rather open-ended "similarity" inquiry to determine what other types of measures were condemned. Such an approach is doubly peculiar in that the opportunity to convert to "ordinary customs duties" was lost as soon as the Uruguay Round ended. Members would thus have been forced at the end of the Round to guess what measures were covered and to convert all of those that might be covered lest they be lost and replaced with nothing.

Perhaps further reinforcing Chile's view is the fact that both parties to the dispute apparently thought that the duties under the price band system were covered by the Article II bindings, which by their terms apply only to "ordinary customs duties." That is why Argentina originally framed a claim under Article II(1)(b), sentence one, and ignored sentence two. But as Chile argued, if the price band system yielded "ordinary customs duties" subject to the binding, then what is meant by a requirement that they be *converted* into ordinary customs duties?

Lastly, we note the obvious difficulties inherent in "converting" the price band system into conventional tariffs. Conventional tariffs would not have the moderating effect on price fluctuations of the price band system, and to the extent that such moderation was a goal of the Chilean system it could not be achieved using conventional duties. A conventional tariff does not rise when international prices fall, or generate a rebate

---

[31] Indeed, we take note of a NAFTA decision in which the position of the parties accords with that of Argentina in this case – in the course of a dispute over Canadian tariff changes, both Canada and the United States apparently agreed that Article 4.2 required the tariffication of all non-tariff measures (save those protected by Annex 5). See *In the Matter of Tariffs Applied by Canada to Certain U.S.-Origin Agricultural Products*, Panel No. CDA-95–2008–01, *1996 FTAPD LEXIS 10* (1996).

when they are high. Moreover, it is hardly clear how one would have determined the conventional "tariff equivalent" of the price band system (though, to be sure, the same issue would have arisen for some of the other "measures" clearly covered by the footnote to Article 4.2).

In sum, we see considerable basis to think that Chile's interpretation of the system is a plausible one, though we hesitate to say which interpretation is right. Article 4.2 is no model of clarity, and it comes as little surprise that it should be subject to controversy.

Given the Appellate Body's approach to the question of "similarity," the case also leaves open a number of issues for the future. Are all price band systems "similar," or do some remain permissible? What of other conceivable mechanisms involving border measures to stabilize domestic agricultural prices? Are seasonal tariffs distinguishable because of a lesser degree of similarity to variable levies and minimum import prices? How crucial to the finding of "similarity" were the various factors that tended to inflate the duty under Chile's system, along with its non-transparency and unpredictability?

3.1.2   Article II

We have no quarrel with the principle that a panel should not rule *sua sponte* on matters that neither party has raised, for as the Appellate Body indicated, basic issues of fairness and due process are implicated when a party loses on grounds that it was not given an opportunity to address. The decision to reverse the panel finding against Chile under Article II(1)(b), second sentence, thus seems the right one.

But the Appellate Body also avoided the issue under Article II(1)(b), first sentence, even though it seemed to endorse the proposition that "ordinary customs duties" has the same meaning in both Article II and the Agriculture Agreement. By holding that the price band system had been required to be *converted* into ordinary customs duties, the immediate implication is that the duties under the price band system are *not* ordinary customs duties. If that is right, then the panel's conclusion that the duties are outside the purview of Article II(1)(b), sentence one, would seem to follow inexorably. But because the Appellate Body ducked the matter, the question whether a measure such as a price band system is subject to the bindings of sentence one or to the scheduling obligation of sentence two, and the broader question of what constitutes an "ordinary customs duty," remain quite muddled. This last question obviously has potential implications that extend beyond the agricultural sector, although we are not in a position to assess its significance in other areas.

3.2   Economic commentary

From an economic point of view, the wisdom of the ruling that (some? all?) price band systems must be replaced with ordinary tariffs is rather difficult to assess because it turns on competing factors. We first identify these factors, and then summarize their implications.

3.2.1   Factor one: the benefits of tariffication

The tariffication process envisioned by the Agriculture Agreement facilitates the negotiation between governments of mutually beneficial and reciprocal reductions in trade barriers. To develop this point, we identify two prominent reasons that governments may impose import barriers, and their implications for the role of reciprocal trade agreements in world trade.[32] With this foundation in place, we next make the argument that tariffication can facilitate mutually beneficial and reciprocal trade-liberalization negotiations between governments.

We focus first on a political rationale for import barriers. To isolate this rationale, we consider the situation in which a government presides over a small country. As is well known, if such a government were to maximize the national income of its country, then its optimal unilateral trade policy would be free trade. Suppose, though, that the government is motivated by political considerations as well. In particular, as suggested by the theory of public choice, the government may be more sensitive to the impact of trade liberalization on import-competing industries than on consumers. The underlying idea is straightforward: import-competing industries are harmed by lower import prices and may be better organized and more politically efficacious than consumers, who are the beneficiaries of lower import prices. The government may therefore wish to impose import barriers. Accordingly, the government would then regard a reduction in import barriers as costly, and such a "concession" would be entertained only if it could be exchanged for some benefit that is offered by another nation.

This rationale on its own, however, does not give rise to an explanation for why governments seek reciprocal trade negotiations. If all countries are small with governments that use import barriers for political reasons, then no one government can adjust its trade policy and thereby confer a

---

[32] For further discussion of the theory of reciprocal trade agreements, see Chapter 2 of Kyle Bagwell and Robert W. Staiger, The Economics of the World Trading System, 2002, The MIT Press: Cambridge, MA.

benefit to another. For example, if the government of country A considers
the proposal that it incur the cost of a reduction in its own tariff in
exchange for the benefit of a tariff reduction by country B, then the
government will reject this proposal as being one that has real costs but
no benefits. This is because the trade policy of a small country (country B)
does not change world prices and therefore does not offer any benefit to
exporters in another country (country A).[33]

The second rationale is economic in nature and derives from the
possibility that the country may be large. To isolate this case, suppose
that the government of a large country seeks to maximize national
income. When the government of a large country imposes an import
barrier, some of the cost of the barrier is borne by foreign exporters, who
sell at a lower export price (i.e., lose access to the domestic market).
Thus, if the government of a large country imposes an import barrier,
then domestic import-competing firms win, domestic consumers lose,
and foreign exporters lose. The loss experienced by foreign exporters is
an international externality that is associated with the government's
trade policy. Since the government does not internalize the costs of
import barriers on foreign exporters, the optimal unilateral trade policy
is not free trade but rather entails import barriers (e.g., positive import
tariffs). In effect, with import barriers, the government shifts onto
foreign exporters some of the costs of helping its import-competing
firms.

This rationale has the added benefit of suggesting a theory of reciprocal
trade agreements. Suppose that countries A and B are both large with
governments that maximize national income. When the government of
country A reduces an import barrier below the optimal unilateral level, it
incurs a cost, and it is therefore willing to make such a concession only if it
expects a sufficient benefit from a reciprocal reduction in an import
barrier by the government of country B. Given that country B is large,
this expectation is now entirely rational: when the government of country
B reduces an import barrier, the exporters in country A absorb some of
the benefit since they sell at a higher export price (i.e., gain access to

---

[33] While the small-country assumption serves as a useful benchmark, it is not clear that
many countries are, in fact, small. It is possible that a country is small in some markets
but not others, and likewise a country may be larger with respect to some countries (e.g.,
neighboring countries) than others. Further, even if it is posited that several countries
are (approximately) small, if such countries all cut tariffs as part of a multilateral
agreement, then the combined impact of their tariff cuts could change world prices.

country B's market). Thus, while each government has a unilateral incentive to impose import barriers, the governments together have a collective incentive to negotiate a trade agreement in which these barriers are reduced in a reciprocal manner.

The two rationales may be usefully joined. If countries are large with governments that have economic and also political motivations, then, as the discussion above suggests, the unilateral trade policies of governments result in import barriers. Furthermore, given that an import barrier imposed by the government of any one country generates a negative international externality to the (political–economic) welfare of the government of its trading partner, the governments can negotiate mutually beneficial and reciprocal reductions in trade barriers.

We emphasize that this perspective does not require that governments possess a sophisticated understanding of the external ("terms-of-trade") effects of their respective trade policies, or that governments acting in isolation actually seek to raise national income through "optimal tariff" policies. Indeed, governments may have political motivations when imposing tariffs, and may evaluate prospective trade agreements from a political orientation as well, balancing the political cost of a reduction in support from import-competing interests against the political benefit of an increase in support from export interests. The important point is that such an orientation reflects a belief on the part of each government that a reduction in a trading partner's tariff would generate some external benefit to domestic exporters. If pressed, government officials may offer the specific explanation that the external benefit derives from the improved access that exporters would then have to the trading partner's market. From an economic perspective, however, this is just another way of saying that a reduction in a trading partner's tariff results in an increase in the price at which domestic exporters sell. This is precisely the international externality that underlies the theoretical foundation presented above.

Our discussion here suggests that the trade–policy relationship between governments has the characteristic of a Prisoners' Dilemma game: the governments recognize that they are each better off when they both liberalize than when they both impose import barriers, but liberalization is difficult to maintain since each government does better yet if it alone "cheats" and imposes import barriers. In light of this characterization, it is clear that a trade agreement must have adequate enforcement provisions, so as to dissuade any one government from cheating on an agreement to liberalize. The threat of retaliation is the natural means of enforcing a trade agreement. A patient government will not pursue the short-term benefit from cheating, if it recognizes that such behavior gives rise to a long-term cost that is associated with retaliation (e.g., a return to unilateral policies).

With this context in place, we now discuss how tariffication facilitates the negotiation between governments of mutually beneficial and reciprocal reductions in trade barriers. The tariffication process has four important, and related, benefits. It lowers the transactions costs of reciprocal trade negotiations, it increases the expected trade volume resulting from tariff concessions, it reduces the uncertainty about trade volumes following a trade agreement, and it makes easier the enforcement of a trade agreement.

The greater the number of protectionist policy instruments that affect trade in a given product, the more difficult (and costly) it is to evaluate a particular concession on exports of that product. It is much harder to estimate the gains in market access opportunities for a reduction in a foreign tariff, for example, if exports subject to the lower tariff would also be subject to quotas, discriminatory domestic regulations, and other sorts of protective measures. And if trade negotiators face greater costs in the evaluation of offers by other nations, it is likely that fewer deals will be finalized in a given negotiating window.

Similarly, if a number of protectionist policy instruments can affect exports of a particular product, it becomes harder to have a high degree of confidence about the increased trade volume that will result from a concession on a particular instrument. Negotiators must worry that the apparent benefits of a tariff concession, for example, will be wiped out by unexpected consequences of some other protectionist instrument. Such possibilities reduce the expected increase in trade volume associated with concessions on tariffs or any other policy instrument and make them less valuable.

A further point is that not all protectionist instruments are equally predictable as to their effects on trade volume. A conventional tariff is generally thought to have relatively more predictable effects than a quota, for example. With a tariff, exporters know exactly how much "tax" they must pay to enter a given market. They will still face uncertainty about that market due to the usual factors that affect market demand and supply, but at least the amount of protection is certain. By contrast, under a quota, exporters must worry that other supplier(s) will have the opportunity to fill the quota before them, or that the importing nation will allocate the quota in a way that disadvantages them. These uncertainties are added to the usual demand and supply uncertainties. When trade negotiators are averse to risk associated with the volume of trade under a trade agreement, they will offer less to secure a given *expected* volume of trade if the *uncertainty* about the volume of trade is greater.

Finally, if trade-policy instruments are non-transparent, then the enforcement of trade agreements is particularly difficult. Our discussion above emphasizes that trade-policy interactions between governments share characteristics with the Prisoners' Dilemma game. Each government makes a costly concession in order to enjoy the benefits of a reciprocal concession by the other. If governments' trade policies were difficult to observe, then each government would be tempted to (secretly) withdraw its concession. Cheating of this kind can undermine a mutually beneficial trade agreement between governments. Tariffication thus facilitates such agreements, since tariffs are transparent and cheating is accordingly more difficult.

For these reasons, it is in the mutual interest of parties to reciprocal trade negotiations to limit the number of protectionist instruments in play as much as possible, and to channel protection into instruments that produce the least uncertainty about trading volume and the least opportunity for cheating. Tariffs are generally regarded as relatively transparent and predictable, and so they are the natural choice as the favored protectionist instrument. These observations go far toward explaining some basic structural features of the original GATT – the fact that negotiations were focused on tariffs and the Article II bindings, the presence of a general prohibition on quantitative restrictions in Article XI, and the prohibition on discriminatory domestic regulations and taxes in Article III.

The tariffication process under the Agriculture Agreement follows the same logic. The agricultural sector, certainly more so than most, had seen a proliferation of trade barriers beyond conventional tariffs. These barriers often resulted from the prevalence of agricultural price support and stabilization policies, and the need to insulate domestic markets from foreign price fluctuations if domestic targets were to be achieved. The proliferation of these barriers – the quantitative restrictions, variable levies, minimum import price systems, and the like – complicated market access negotiations in agriculture because they made it difficult to evaluate conventional tariff concessions, lessened the expected benefits of concessions on other policy instruments, increased the uncertainty associated with agricultural trade, and made enforcement more difficult. Tariffication addressed all of these problems.

3.2.2   Factor two: the effect of a tariffication requirement on the average tariff level

If Chile's price band system was truly problematic, why did Chile's trading partners not complain about it or raise the issue of tariffication explicitly during the Uruguay Round? Why, for that matter, did other nations with price band systems not tariffy their price bands or have discussions about the matter? We can only speculate as to the answer, but it is possible that tariffication may have resulted in higher average protection, and this prospect may have led trading partners to prefer that price bands remain in place.

The logic here is straightforward. One effect of the price band system was to reduce the variability of Chile's internal prices by insulating them from international price fluctuations outside of the price band. The rationale for such a system may lie in the fact that Chile's agricultural producers care not only about the average price that they receive, but about its volatility – i.e., that they are risk averse and to some degree will sacrifice periods of high prices to avoid periods of low prices.

If that is correct, then agricultural producers will be happy to trade off some reduction in average prices received to reduce uncertainty about price. And if political opposition exists to higher agricultural prices, the resulting political equilibrium may well entail some sort of device to reduce volatility, for which agricultural producers will "pay" in the form of lower average prices. One way to see the point is to imagine two different protectionist regimes – one with a fixed conventional tariff, and one with a price band. Let the two regimes be designed so that agricultural producers are indifferent between them. Thus, assuming risk aversion on the part of the agricultural producers, the price band system will produce lower prices on average. The domestic opponents of high agricultural prices will likely prefer the price band option for that reason, even if they are indifferent to price volatility themselves. Put differently, a price band system – with its reduced price volatility – may be Pareto optimal from a domestic political standpoint.

If the government is subsequently prohibited from maintaining a price band system and forced to substitute a conventional fixed tariff, the new domestic political equilibrium will likely involve a higher tariff on average. Intuitively, as agricultural producers are confronted with the prospect of greater price variability, their demand for protection will intensify. Assuming that domestic opponents of high agricultural prices are not themselves significantly harmed by greater price variability, the domestic political process might be expected to achieve a new equilibrium in which the fixed tariff is positioned above the average tariff under the price band system.

If we are right to this point, then it is conceivable that trading partners would prefer to allow the price band system to persist rather than to be "tariffied," despite its disadvantages as noted earlier. Tariffication would raise the average degree of protection that they confront on their exports, and as a consequence tariffication would contribute to a lower expected export price (i.e., lower expected market access). But we also note that the price band system may amplify (exogenous) fluctuations in the prices that exporters receive.[34] For example, when the export (i.e., world) price for a product is low, the price band system may call for a higher tariff, which works to further depress the export price. The rebate under the price band system when prices are high also tends to increase the net price received by foreign sellers. Tariffication may thus diminish the variability of the price at which exporters sell. An argument that trading partners are hurt by tariffication thus turns on the proposition that the cost to exporters of any associated decrease in the average export price outweighs the benefit of any associated reduction in the variability of export prices. This is more likely to hold if Chilean import-competing firms are more risk averse than are foreign exporters.

3.2.3   Summary of implications

Our discussion in the preceding subsection raises the possibility that trading partners may be better off with the price band than without it. This possibility seems even more plausible when, as with the amended Chilean system, the importing nation makes clear that it will never exceed its Article II binding. Recall that Chile had bound its tariffs at 31.5 percent, but its applied *ad valorem* duty was only 7–8 percent. Even with the price band system, the total duty was usually less than 31.5 percent, and could never be higher after the law was amended. It seems somewhat odd to condemn Chile under these circumstances when it had the right to impose a fixed 31.5 percent tariff if it wished, and it is difficult to imagine that the lack of "transparency and predictability" in the price band system could have done more to limit trade than a fixed tariff set at the level of the binding. Indeed, regardless of risk preferences, foreign

---

[34] A related point is recognized in the literature on variable import levies. For a recent contribution, see H. Nordstrom, "Do Variable Levies Beggar Thy Neighbor?," *European Journal of Political Economy*, 2001, 17, 2: 420–430.

exporters are better off facing tariffs that are variable over some range than a tariff that is fixed and set equal to the top value (i.e., the binding) of that range.

We are cognizant of the fact that, to some extent, this argument proves too much. First, if we are right that the level of trade protection will be less on average if the price band system is allowed to remain in place, why did Argentina bring a case? It must have expected to gain from the proceeding. It is possible to speculate. Perhaps Argentine exporters are risk averse and expected that Chile would set a fixed tariff sufficiently below its binding to leave them better off, or perhaps Argentina expected to extract some settlement by filing a strategic suit. A further possibility is that Argentina objected to the design of this particular price band system – perhaps its linkage between the tariff and the date of shipment, or its general lack of transparency, effectively facilitated the application of discriminatory tariffs that disproportionately burdened Argentina. It is also possible that Argentina was motivated to challenge the law before its amendment clarified that the tariff would never exceed the binding, and for some reason felt obliged to continue the case even after the amendment was passed. But we do not know the answer to this question.

Second, the Chilean price band system is similar to classic variable levies, which were tariffied in at least some cases during the Uruguay Round. If devices for reducing price volatility were on balance useful to the trading system because they facilitated a reduction in the average level of protection, why were any of these devices made subject to tariffication? In thinking about this question, it is useful to distinguish between transparent and non-transparent devices. Following our discussion above on the benefits of tariffication, it may be argued that non-transparent devices impede effective negotiations. Tariffication of such devices may thus facilitate mutually beneficial trade liberalization. Is the Chilean price band system "non-transparent?" Again, it is useful to contrast this system with a transparent tariff that is set at the binding. As long as it can be verified that the import tariffs called for under the price band system do not exceed the binding, the system is transparent in the sense that it can be verified that the negotiated binding is not violated. From this perspective, a price band system that is capped at the negotiated binding captures the main benefits of tariffication while also providing trading partners with frequent "gifts" of import tariffs that are strictly below the binding. We may thus endorse the tariffication of non-transparent measures generally, yet still wonder about the wisdom of tariffying a price band system that includes a cap to ensure that the tariff binding is never exceeded.

4   Conclusion

The Chilean price band system raised a difficult case from a legal perspective, and an intriguing set of issues from an economic perspective. On the legal side, Chile's position had some appealing elements. No WTO Member had asked Chile to tariffy its price band system during the Uruguay Round, and other members had apparently retained their own price band systems. The lack of clear criteria in the Agriculture Agreement for determining which measures should be tariffied further buffered Chile's suggestion that shared understanding during the negotiation process should be the touchstone. Once Chile amended the system to ensure that total tariffs never exceeded its binding, it apparently brought itself into full compliance with what it fairly understood to be its obligations under the Agreement.

Argentina's position also had its strengths. The price band system surely bore considerable resemblance to enumerated measures in Article 4 of the Agriculture Agreement that were tariffied, and it is thus reasonable to deem it "similar." Chile's system also lacked transparency in many respects, and no doubt frustrated trading partners who were unable to predict the variable levy with confidence.

Accordingly, it seems to us that the dispute could plausibly have been resolved either way. It is difficult to say which resolution is the "right" one as a legal matter.

From an economic perspective, the case is also a hard one. We cannot confidently say whether the demise of Chile's price band system will be trade liberalizing or trade restricting. It will be most interesting to see what fixed tariff rate Chile sets when it eliminates the price band. It would be an interesting though no doubt challenging exercise to compare it with the average total tariffs during the price band system to see which is higher, and to compare trading volumes before and after to see if access to Chile's market has been enhanced or diminished.

References

Bagwell, Kyle and Robert W. Staiger (2002). The Economics of the World Trading System (MIT Press: Cambridge MA).

Nordstrom, H. (2001). Do Variable Levies Beggar Thy Neighbor?, *European Journal of Political Economy* **17**: 420–430.

9

India – Measures Affecting the Automotive Sector*

KYLE BAGWELL

Columbia University

AND

ALAN O. SYKES

University of Chicago

1 Introduction

This study addresses the disputes brought to the World Trade Organization (WTO) by the European Communities and the United States concerning certain Indian measures affecting the importation of automobiles and components in the form of "completely knocked down" (CKD) and "semi-knocked down" (SKD) kits. The measures in question originated during a time when India employed extensive import licensing requirements, ostensibly for balance of payments purposes. India's broad licensing regime was challenged in 1997 by the European Communities and the United States, resulting in a settlement with the European Communities and a ruling in favor of the United States pursuant to which India agreed to abolish its import licensing system. Some restrictions in the automotive sector remained, however, which became the subject of this proceeding.

The automotive restrictions resulted from a law known as Public Notice 60 (PN60), enacted in 1997, which provided that companies desiring to obtain import licenses for CKD or SKD kits must enter a contract with the government known as a "Memorandum of Understanding" (MOU). These MOUs, among other things, required companies to achieve stated local content percentages ("indigenization requirements") in their manufacturing operations, and to ensure that the value of their

* We wish to thank Alberto Martin for valuable assistance, and to thank the other reporters and conference participants of the American Law Institute for many valuable ideas and suggestions.

exports was equal to the value of their imports ("trade balancing requirements"). The contractual commitments to the government through the MOUs remained binding and enforceable even after the import licensing regime that had given rise to them was abolished. The European Communities and the United States claimed that the indigenization requirements and the trade balancing requirements constituted violations of Articles III and XI of GATT 1994 and Article 2 of TRIMs.

The proceedings were consolidated before a single dispute panel, which ruled in favor of the European Communities and the United States with respect to both measures.[1] India indicated that it would appeal, but later withdrew its appeal and thus the Appellate Body did not address the substance of the dispute.[2] In a communication dated November 6, 2002, India informed the Dispute Settlement Body that it had issued new Public Notices withdrawing the indigenization and trade balancing requirements contained in Public Notice 60, and by implication suggesting that any such requirements in surviving MOUs would be deprived of effect.

The dispute is an unremarkable one and of limited significance from a legal standpoint. The indigenization requirements and trade balancing requirements are clear violations of GATT 1994 and TRIMs in the absence of a valid defense. India's purported justification for them – a balance of payments justification under Article XVIII of GATT 1994 – had been found insufficient in the earlier proceeding regarding its import licensing system. The case does touch on some broader legal issues of systemic importance: the role of *res judicata* in WTO law, the question of what constitutes governmental action sufficient to constitute a "requirement" or "measure," and the boundary between border measures covered by Article XI and domestic measures covered by Article III. But the case breaks little new ground on any of these points.

From an economic perspective, the issues raised by the case are also quite straightforward. Local content requirements such as the "indigenization" requirement, and measures such as the trade balancing requirement, disadvantage imports and the companies that use them. They can be understood as protectionist measures that benefit the domestic producers of inputs. Such measures may harm foreign manufacturers and input suppliers, and it is thus appropriate that WTO law should condemn them.

---

[1] Report of the Panel in *India – Measures Affecting the Automotive Sector*, WT/DS146/R, WT/DS175/R, adopted April 5, 2002 (hereafter Panel Rep.).
[2] Report of the Appellate Body in *India – Measures Affecting the Automotive Sector*, WT/DS146/R, WT/DS175/R, adopted April 5, 2002.

We proceed in the conventional fashion, laying out the legal issues and arguments in Section 2. Section 3 offers a critical analysis of the case from a law and economics perspective.

2 Factual and Legal Issues

2.1   The history and nature of the measures at issue

For many years, India applied import restrictions that it justified on balance of payments grounds. The restrictions were administered through an import licensing system. In 1997, the European Communities requested consultations with respect to all import restrictions maintained by India, including those on the products at issue in the automotive dispute. India and the European Communities reached a settlement later that year, a "mutually agreed solution" in WTO parlance, which called for all of the restrictions to be eliminated by March 31, 2003.

Also in 1997, the US requested consultations with India regarding quantitative restrictions applied by India for balance of payments reasons on 2,714 agricultural and industrial product lines. That dispute proceeded to a panel, which ruled that the restrictions violated Article XI(1) of GATT 1994 and were not justified by Article XVIII:B of GATT 1994 (pertaining to balance of payments measures by developing countries).[3] The Appellate Body upheld these findings.[4] The United States and India subsequently agreed that India would comply with the recommendations and rulings of the DSB no later than April 1, 2001, by which time India would eliminate the system of non-automatic licenses for imports.

In 2000, when the panel in the automotive dispute was requested by the United States and the European Communities, India still applied discretionary import licensing to 715 tariff line items including cars imported in the form of CKD and SKD kits. Pursuant to the agreement reached in the earlier proceedings, however, India altogether abolished its licensing scheme on April 1, 2001.

The end of the import licensing system did not end European and American concerns about the automotive sector, however, because of PN60 and the MOUs that resulted from it. PN60 required any passenger

---

[3] Panel Report on *India – Quantitative Restrictions on Imports of Agricultural, Textile and Industrial Products*, (hereinafter "*India – Quantitative Restrictions*"), WT/DS/90/R, adopted September 22, 1999.

[4] Report of the Appellate Body in *India – Quantitative Restrictions*, WT/DS90/AB/R, adopted on September 22, 1999.

car manufacturer wishing to obtain a license to import CKD or SKD kits to covenant, through an MOU, to:

(i) "Establishment of actual production facilities for manufacture of cars, and not for mere assembly.
(ii) A minimum of foreign equity of US $50 million to be brought in by the foreign partner within the first three years of the start of operations, if the firm is a joint venture that involves majority foreign equity ownership.
(iii) Indigenization (i.e. local content) of components up to a minimum level of 50% in the third year or earlier from the date of first import consignment of CKD/SKD kits/components, and 70% in the fifth year or earlier.
(iv) broad trade balancing of foreign exchange over the entire period of the MOU, in terms of balancing between the actual CIF value of imports of CKD/SKD kits/components and the FOB value of exports of cars and auto components over that period . . . "[5]

The third and fourth of these requirements became the subject of the automotive dispute.

Much of India's defense in the case rested on the proposition that the matter had already been resolved through the challenges to India's broad import licensing regime, or that it was otherwise mooted by the abolition of the licensing regime in 2001. But the European Communities and the United States argued that even if the import licensing regime that had been used to extract the commitments in the MOUs had ended, PN60 remained on the books and the MOUs that had been negotiated under it remained binding on the companies that had signed them.

2.2   The Panel decision

2.2.1   Relevance of prior proceedings on India – Quantitative Restrictions

Much of the panel decision relates to India's claims that the claims brought by the European Communities and the United States had already been resolved or were moot. The panel disagreed.

India argued first that the measures in question were no longer in existence due to developments subsequent to the initiation of the dispute. The panel responded by noting that the indigenization and

[5] Panel Rep. 2.5.

trade balancing requirements, as embodied in the MOUs, remained in effect after the licensing system was abolished.[6]

India also made a rather novel *res judicata* argument. Ordinarily, a party to litigation invoking the concept of *res judicata* does so to avoid relitigating an issue that it prevailed on in a prior proceeding. Here, by contrast, India invoked *res judicata* with respect to the issues that it had *lost* in the *India – Quantitative Restrictions* dispute. India's theory was that the United States and the European Communities could not seek a new ruling on the legality of measures that a previous dispute had addressed. The panel seemed to accept that in principle it was improper to relitigate the same issues, but concluded that the measures at issue in the automotive sector had not been before the prior dispute panel. The prior dispute had concerned the legality of the broad import licensing regime, but had not considered the indigenization and trade balancing requirements in the MOUs.[7]

The panel gave a similar response to India's argument that the measures in question could not be adjudicated because they were covered by the "mutually agreed solution" reached with the European Communities after its prior complaint. That agreement contained a promise by the European Communities to refrain from bringing further proceedings relating to the challenged measures, in exchange for India's promise to remove them over time. The panel accepted the proposition that Europe would be bound by its promise, but found once again that it did not encompass the specific measures at issue in the automotive sector.[8]

2.2.2   Analysis of challenged measures under GATT 1994 and TRIMs

Regarding the order of analysis, the panel saw little difference in the "specificity" of GATT 1994 and TRIMs with respect to the challenged measures. Accordingly, it decided to address the claims in the order that they were argued by the parties.

2.2.2.1   The indigenization requirement   As noted, the indigenization requirement committed the companies signing MOUs to procure

---

[6] Panel Rep. 7.28.
[7] Panel Rep. 7.103.
[8] Panel Rep. 7.132–734.

50–70 percent of their automobile parts and components from local sources, and was a classic local content requirement in WTO parlance. Both the European Communities and the United States claimed that the indigenization requirement was inconsistent with GATT Article III(4), which provides:

> The products of the territory of any contracting party imported into the territory of any other contracting party shall be accorded treatment no less favorable than that accorded to like products of national origin in respect of all laws, regulations and requirements affecting their internal sale, offering for sale, purchase, transportation, distribution or use.

To evaluate the indigenization measure against this standard, the panel believed that four issues must be addressed: "whether (1) imported products and domestic products are like products; (2) the measures constitute a "law, regulation or requirement"; (3) they affect the internal sale, offering for sale, purchase, transportation, distribution or use; and (4) imported products are accorded less favourable treatment than the treatment accorded to like domestic products."[9]

Regarding the first issue, the dispute involved imported and domestic parts and components of automobiles, distinguished only by their origin. The panel saw no basis for treating imported and domestic products as other than "like," and India did not dispute the point.[10]

Regarding the second issue, both the European Communities and the United States argued that the indigenization requirement in PN60 and embodied in the MOUs was a "requirement" under Article III(4). Companies were not compelled to subject themselves to it, but they had to do so if they wished to obtain a government benefit (an import license). Citing GATT precedent, the panel accepted the proposition that the term "requirement" includes "those which an enterprise voluntarily accepts in order to obtain an advantage from the government."[11]

But India argued that once the import licensing regime was abolished, any "requirement" ceased to exist – no longer would any company have to agree to the indigenization requirement to obtain an import license. The panel gave a twofold response. First, its terms of reference required it to assess the legality of the measures in place at the time the panel was constituted, and on that date the licensing regime was still in place. Second, even after the

---

[9] Panel Rep. 7.172.
[10] Panel Rep. 7.174.
[11] Panel Rep. 7.183.

licensing regime was abolished, the MOUs remained enforceable as private contracts with the government and could be expected to affect commercial behavior regardless of the government's enforcement policy.[12]

India's final argument was that even if the MOUs remained enforceable, private contracts with the government were analogous to "discretionary" legislation. It pointed to the distinction under the old GATT system between mandatory legislation, which left administering officials with no discretion to avoid violations if certain circumstances arose, and discretionary legislation, which might result in a violation but always be administered in a way that avoided violations. Only the former type of legislation could be challenged "on its face" in the GATT system; the latter could be challenged only if was *applied* in a manner that resulted in a violation. To this line of argument, the panel suggested that binding contractual obligations might be expected to affect companies' behavior, even if the government did not actively enforce them.[13] Further, India had apparently conceded that it had not released companies from their MOUs and had no plans to do so in the future.[14]

The third and fourth issues under Article III(4) were easily resolved. The indigenization requirement "affected" internal sale, and accorded imported products less favorable treatment, because it modified conditions of competition between imported and domestic like products and encouraged companies to buy domestic over imported products.[15]

The United States also argued that the indigenization requirement was inconsistent with Article XI(1), and both complainants challenged the requirement under TRIMs. Having ruled that it was inconsistent with Article III(4), however, the panel declined to examine its consistency with Article XI or with TRIMs.

2.2.2.2 The trade balancing requirement   Both the European Communities and the United States argued that aspects of the trade balancing requirement were inconsistent with Articles III and XI of GATT 1994, although their positions differed in certain details. The panel saw greater common ground in their discussion of Article XI, and decided to address issues under Article XI first.

[12] Panel Rep. 7.190–7.193.
[13] Panel Rep. 8.42–8.44.
[14] Panel Rep. 8.46.
[15] Panel Rep. 7.196–7.202.

Article XI(1) provides:

> No prohibition or restriction other than duties, taxes or other charges, whether made effective through quotas, import or export licenses or other measures, shall be instituted or maintained by any contracting party on the importation of any product of the territory of any other contracting party or on the exportation or sale for export of any product destined for the territory of any other contracting party.

The trade balancing requirement was not in itself a "quota, import or export license," and so the initial question was whether it is among the 'other measures' covered by Article XI(1). The panel had little difficulty concluding that it was. It reasoned that the balancing requirements, embedded in the MOUs, resulted directly from the legislative enactment PN60 and thus represented "measures" by the Indian government.

The next question was whether the "measure" amounted to a "restriction . . . on the importation" of goods. India contended that the measure did not relate directly to the entry of goods into Indian customs territory, and thus was not a "restriction on importation." The panel disagreed, relying on the plain meaning of "restriction." It simply noted that the balancing requirement prohibited imports in excess of stipulated amounts determined by each company's exports. It was further "comforted" by the following language to be found in the Illustrative List of TRIMs:

> TRIMS that are inconsistent with the obligation of general elimination of quantitative restrictions provided for in paragraph 1 of Article XI of GATT 1994 include those which are mandatory or enforceable under domestic law or under administrative rulings, or compliance with which is necessary to obtain an advantage, and which restrict:
>
> (a) the importation by an enterprise of products used in or related to its local production, generally or to an amount related to the volume or value of local production that it exports.[16]

The trade balancing requirement thus came within Article XI(1), and violates GATT 1994 in the absence of an effective defense. India claimed a balance of payments defense as in the earlier proceeding, but presented no evidence on the matter. The panel ruled, following prior decisions, that India had the burden of proof when asserting an affirmative defense under Article XVIII:B, and that its failure to come forward with evidence meant that its defense necessarily failed.

---

[16] Panel Rep. 7.279.

Having found an inconsistency with Article XI, the panel again appealed to judicial economy to avoid a full discussion of the trade balancing measure in relation to Article III and TRIMs. The panel did address one specific feature of the trade balancing requirement in relation to Article III(4). It noted that any company subject to an MOU buying a *previously imported* CKD or SKD kit in the Indian domestic market would have that purchase counted as an "import" for purposes of the trade balancing requirement. Thus, previously imported kits were disadvantaged on domestic resale relative to domestically produced like products. The panel was of the view that, whatever the proper boundary between the measures covered by Article III and XI in general, a measure disadvantaging imported goods on domestic resale was a potential violation of Article III(4). Proceeding through the four issues laid out above in the discussion of the indigenization requirement in relation to Article III(4), the panel again found that the trade balancing requirement incorporated a "requirement affecting internal sale" that afforded less favorable treatment to imported like products.[17]

2.3   The Appellate Body decision

As noted in the introduction, India ultimately withdrew its notice of appeal and rescinded PN60 without further proceedings. Accordingly, the Appellate Body did not consider the substantive issues in the case.

3   Critical analysis

3.1   Legal commentary

The automotive dispute was largely a "mopping up" operation aimed at eliminating some remaining vestiges of the import licensing regime that had been found to violate WTO law in *India – Quantitative Restrictions.* During that regime, the indigenization and trade balancing requirements in the automotive sector had been made effective through contracts (MOUs) with the government that companies executed to obtain import licenses. The contracts remained in force even after the licensing scheme was abolished, and the government gave no indication of an intention to release companies from them (indeed, it indicated to the contrary before the dispute panel).

---

[17] Panel Rep. 7.295–7.309.

The indigenization requirement was a classic "local content" requirement, a paradigm example of the sort of measure that was the target of the TRIMs agreement and that had been held to violate Article III(4) of GATT 1994 in the past.[18] The trade balancing requirement, in so far as it limited the value of goods imported by a company to the value of its exports, was likewise a clear target of TRIMs and was well understood to violate Article XI of GATT 1994.[19] Finally, the aspect of the trade balancing requirement that limited the capacity of companies to purchase products imported by others, and thus affected their domestic resale, was also a target of TRIMs and a clear violation of GATT Article III(4).[20] India's balance of payments defense for such measures had been rejected previously, and India's reassertion of that defense in this case was at best half-hearted.

The case touches on a few broader issues, but in the end does not say much about them. India's peculiar invocation of *res judicata* as to issues that it had lost in *India – Quantitative Restrictions* raises a general question about the place of doctrines like *res judicata* and collateral estoppel in the WTO system. The panel seemed willing to accept that it was inappropriate to relitigate identical issues between the same parties that had been resolved in prior disputes, but avoided any definitive statement on the matter simply by noting that the issues raised by PN60 and the MOUs were new and had not been previously considered.

The differences in the positions of the United States and Europe as to the applicability of GATT Articles III and XI to the various measures highlights another issue that has perplexed WTO/GATT scholars through the years, namely, the precise boundary between the measures covered by Article III and the measures covered by Article XI. The same issue confronted an old GATT panel faced with a challenge to the Canadian Foreign Investment Review Act, which stated in the course of its opinion:

> The Panel shares the view of Canada that the General Agreement distinguishes between measures affecting the 'importation' of products, which are regulated in Article XI:1, and those affecting 'imported products', which are dealt with in Article III. If Article XI:1 were interpreted broadly to cover also internal requirements, Article III would be partly superfluous.[21]

[18] See TRIMs Annex, Illustrative List 1(a).
[19] See TRIMs Annex, Illustrative List 2(a).
[20] See TRIMs Annex, Illustrative List 1(b).
[21] GATT Panel Report, L/5504, adopted on 7 February 1987, 5.14.

The potentially elusive distinction between measures affecting "importation" and those affecting "imported products" is to a considerable degree
unimportant. Complaining nations will usually care little whether a
measure is found illegal under Article III or Article XI as long as it is
found illegal under one of them, and there is no obstacle under WTO law
to alternative pleading. But whatever its importance, the panel's treatment of the issues here sheds no new light on the distinction. The panel
does not broach the general question of how to draw the line, but instead
maneuvers its order of analysis to follow the classification scheme in the
TRIMs Annex:[22] Based on the illustrative list in the Annex, the indigenization requirement and the part of the trade balancing requirement that
applies to previously imported goods are measures affecting "imported
products" subject to Article III. But the trade balancing requirement
affects "importation" when it restricts what a company may import
directly. It will be recalled that the panel analyzed the indigenization
requirement under Article III and invoked judicial economy to avoid
considering it under Article XI. It did the opposite with the trade balancing requirement, save for the part of it that applied to previously
imported goods which was analyzed under Article III. The panel thus
applied the pertinent GATT articles as TRIMs suggests they should be
without actually ruling on the dividing line between them.

One of the more interesting issues in the case relates to the distinction
in old GATT jurisprudence between "mandatory" and "discretionary"
legislation. The continued vitality of that distinction in WTO law remains
an open question, to be sure, and one unappealed WTO panel decision
concerning Section 301 of the U.S. Trade Act of 1974 questions its
utility.[23] Nonetheless, WTO Members continue to raise the distinction
in various contexts, and it surfaced in an interesting way in the automotive dispute. India argued that the measures contained in the MOUs
were in the nature of contractual provisions that the government could
elect not to enforce. As such, they were analogous to "discretionary
legislation" – legislation that might be administered in such a way as to
violate WTO law, but that affords sufficient discretion to administrators
to avoid any violations. Under GATT jurisprudence, such legislation
could not be challenged "on its face," but only if it resulted in a violation

---

[22] See text accompanying notes 18–20 supra.
[23] See Panel Report in *United States – Sections 301–310 of the Trade Act of 1974*,
WT/DS152/R, adopted January 27, 2000, 7.51–7.53.

as applied. Thus, India reasoned, the measures embodied in the MOUs could be challenged only if India took some steps to enforce them.

As noted, the panel rejected this line of reasoning by noting that India had not stated an intention to release companies from their MOUs, and that a mere possibility of enforcement action might encourage companies to follow their MOU commitments. Both observations are no doubt correct, but they may prove too much. It is perhaps often the case that legislation deemed "discretionary" under the old GATT system has some chilling effect at odds with GATT obligations because of the possibility of enforcement in a way that violates GATT. Only when a government unequivocally and credibly commits itself to administer the legislation in a way that complies with GATT might any such "chilling effect" be avoided. Thus, the analogy between the MOUs and discretionary legislation is stronger than the panel allowed. Its resolution of the matter perhaps hints at a new principle that also resonates with the panel decision in *United States – Section 301*: It is not enough that a measure affords administrative "discretion" to avoid violations of WTO law. To avoid challenges to such a measure on its face, a country must also provide credible assurances that administrative discretion will in fact be exercised in a way that averts any violations.

3.2 Economic commentary

We turn now to consider the economic aspects of local content requirements. A common form of a local content requirement specifies that a certain physical proportion of domestic inputs be embodied in the final good. We focus here on the economic implications of such local content requirements under different market structures.

A local content requirement is a protectionist instrument that is logically distinct from both import tariffs and import quotas. Unlike tariffs and quota licenses, a local content requirement does not generate government revenue. Such a requirement does, however, create a wedge between the prices of domestic and foreign inputs. When an effective local content requirement is in place, a foreign final good producer with a domestic plant is induced to increase the demand for domestic inputs, thereby raising the price of the domestic input relative to that of the foreign input. The domestic government then balances the consequent benefit to domestic input suppliers against the associated cost to domestic consumers, where the latter cost is experienced if the higher domestic input price leads to a higher domestic price for the final good.

The local content requirement also generates an international externality, if it reduces the profits of the foreign final good manufacturers
and/or foreign input suppliers. When setting its preferred unilateral policy,
the domestic government does not internalize such an effect. Thus, when a
local content rule changes prices in such a way as to create an international externality, a role may arise for an international trade agreement
that imposes restrictions upon local content requirements.

Using three models, we explore here the domestic effects of a local
content requirement and also the circumstances under which such a
requirement generates an international externality. The models share
a common foundation. In each case, a final good (autos) is produced,
where each unit of the final good requires one unit of the input (kits). The
final good manufacturers are foreign (US). The input is supplied by
a competitive market in the foreign country (US) and also by a competitive market in the domestic country (India). The domestic and foreign
inputs are perfect substitutes, and the final good requires no other input.
The models differ in terms of the market power that the foreign final good
manufacturers and the domestic government are assumed to possess.

Model 1: competitive final good market, small domestic country

We consider first a setting in which the final good is produced by a
competitive industry comprised (for simplicity) of foreign firms. Final
good manufacturers then earn zero profit, and so the domestic government is unable to use a local content requirement as a means to extract
profit from foreign manufacturers. Furthermore, we assume that the
domestic country is small, in the sense that the reduction in demand for
foreign inputs caused by the local content requirement does not depress
the (world) price of foreign inputs. This means that the profits of foreign
input suppliers are also unaffected by the local content requirement. Our
first setting is thus a benchmark case in which no international externality
arises.[24]

To examine the domestic consequences of a local content requirement,
we introduce the following notation. Let Q and P denote the output and
price of the final good in the domestic market, respectively. This output is
produced by a competitive final good market according to the technology
$Q = X + X^*$, where X is the quantity of input purchased from domestic

---

[24] For further discussion of related models, see Corden (1971), Grossman (1981) and
Vousden (1990, Chapter 2).

suppliers and X^* is the quantity of input purchased from foreign suppliers. The local content requirement specifies that a fraction k of inputs be purchased from domestic suppliers; thus, when this requirement is (exactly) met, $X = k(X + X^*) = kQ$. Let r and r^* denote the respective prices of the domestic and foreign inputs. In the present model, r^* is fixed and independent of any local content requirement, but the local content requirement may affect r and thus the average price of the input, $r_a = kr + (1 - k)r^*$. Since the final good industry is competitive and uses only a single input, the price of the final good is equal to the average price of the input: $P = r_a$

As illustrated in Figure 1, the domestic supply of the input is described by an upward-sloping supply function, $X(r)$, while the supply of the foreign input is perfectly elastic at the price r^*. We assume that the domestic supply function initially lies below the foreign supply function (i.e., the first unit of domestic supply is offered at a price below r^*) and then crosses the foreign supply curve at some quantity X_f. The demand for the final good is represented by the downward-sloping demand function, $D(P)$. Under free trade, all inputs trade at the price r^* and the total quantity of inputs that is demanded (and thus the quantity of the final good that is produced) is given by $Q_f = D(r^*)$. Accordingly, X_f units of the domestic input are employed, and $X_f^* = Q_f - X_f$ units of the foreign input are employed. Let $k_f = X_f/Q_f$ denote the fraction of the domestic input used under free trade.

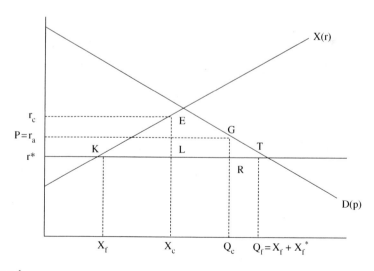

Figure 1.

Consider now the imposition of a local content requirement under which $k > k_f$. Such a policy must elicit a greater supply of the domestic input and so requires an increase in the domestic input price, r. The equilibrium outcome is illustrated by point E. At this point, the price of the domestic input is $r_c > r^*$ and the quantity of the domestic input used is $X_c > X_f$. Thus, the domestic input is now used at a higher volume and commands a higher price. The local content requirement also induces an increase in the average input price, with $r_a = kr_c + (1 - k)r^* > r^*$. This means that the total quantity of input that is demanded (and thus the quantity of the final good that is produced) is reduced by the local content requirement: $Q_c = D(r_a) < D(r^*) = Q_f$.

What are the domestic welfare consequences of the local content requirement? To answer this question, it is easiest to imagine that the first X_c units of final good output are sold at the price r_c while the next $Q_c - X_c$ units are sold at the price r^*. (The average price is then r_a.) We begin with the first X_c units. The area r^*r_c EL represents consumer surplus that is enjoyed under free trade and lost under the local content requirement. Some of this surplus is transferred to domestic input suppliers, who now enjoy additional producer surplus corresponding to the area r^*r_c EK. The remaining area of lost consumer surplus, KLE, is deadweight loss that is attributable to a production inefficiency that occurs when efficient foreign supply of inputs is displaced by domestic input supply. Now consider the next $Q_c - X_c$ units that are sold at the price r^*. For these units, the local content requirement has no effect on the final good price or welfare. Finally, we note that the local content requirement results in a reduction in the total output of the final good (from Q_f to Q_c). The corresponding area, RTG, represents a second source of deadweight loss associated with the local content requirement.

In total, then, the local content requirement reduces domestic national income, due to the creation of deadweight loss as captured by the areas KLE and RTG. Of course, if the domestic government has political objectives such that it values the benefits to input suppliers (i.e., the area r^*r_c EK) more heavily than the costs to consumers (i.e. the areas r^*r_c EL and RGT), then a local content requirement may be attractive.[25]

In this model, all of the costs and benefits of the local content requirement reside within the domestic economy. Since the foreign final good

---

[25] A local content requirement may also be attractive to the domestic government if the domestic input industry is subject to learning by doing. The analysis of this effect, however, requires a dynamic model.

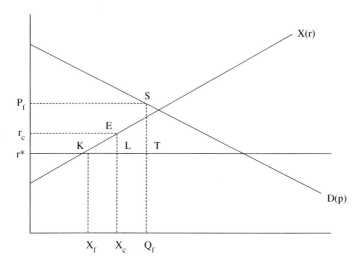

Figure 2.

manufacturers earn zero profit and the price at which foreign inputs sell on world markets is fixed, the local content requirement has no international externality. When the assumptions of this model hold, no obvious role for the WTO arises, since the local content requirement is a domestic policy that does not affect the welfare of any other Member government.[26]

Model 2: monopoly final good market, small domestic country

Maintaining the assumption that the domestic country is small, we now posit that the final good is produced by a foreign monopoly. The wrinkle here is that the foreign final good industry generates profit, and so a local content requirement may be entertained as a means through which to extract profit from the foreign final good monopoly and shift it to the domestic input suppliers.[27] An international externality is thus suggested.

As above, we consider a local content requirement that requires the monopolist to use a greater fraction of domestic input than it would

---

[26] Thus, when the assumptions of this model apply, if the foreign government challenges the domestic local content policy, then the domestic government has a solid economic basis from which to rebut a charge of nullification or impairment. We note, however, that these assumptions represent an instructive but extreme benchmark, in which all market power is absent.

[27] Brander and Spencer (1981) explore a related model, in which tariffs may be used to extract profit from a foreign monopolist.

under free trade. An important issue concerns the manner in which the monopolist adjusts its output in response to this requirement. To illustrate the issues involved, we first imagine that the foreign monopolist does not change its output following the imposition of the local content policy. The local content requirement then amounts to a transfer from the final good monopolist to the domestic input supply industry, since the monopolist must offer a higher domestic input price in order to elicit the increased domestic input supply. This strategic policy is attractive to the domestic government, even when the government has no political objective and simply maximizes national income, but the policy lowers world welfare, since it creates a productive inefficiency: on the margin, foreign input suppliers are replaced by less efficient domestic input suppliers.

These effects are illustrated in Figure 2. Under free trade, the foreign monopolist sets the price P_f and produces the output Q_f, and X_f units of the inputs are domestically supplied. The profit earned by the foreign monopolist is given by the area r^*P_fST. When the local content requirement is imposed, a greater proportion of the (fixed) output must embody the domestic input. Thus, the domestic input price rises to $r_c > r^*$, and the use of the domestic input rises to $X_c > X_f$. The area r^*r_c EK then represents profit that is extracted from the monopolist and shifted to the domestic input supply industry. The triangle KEL is lost profit that becomes deadweight loss. Thus, if the output of the foreign monopoly is held fixed, a local content policy is attractive to the domestic government as a means of shifting foreign monopoly profit to the domestic input supply industry. Such a policy imposes a negative international externality on the foreign monopolist (and thus the foreign government) and results in a loss in world welfare.

But of course the foreign monopolist is unlikely to keep its final good output constant. At the free-trade quantity, the local content policy induces a higher input price on all units of the domestic input without changing the input price of any units of the foreign input. The local content policy thus raises the costs of production, and as a consequence the foreign monopolist will respond by *lowering* its output.[28] In turn, this

---

[28] This raises the possibility that the local content rule might result in less overall use of the domestic input. While this possibility cannot be dismissed, plausible conditions can be identified under which a small local content requirement (i.e., a policy that requires that a slightly larger fraction of the domestic input be used than would be used under free trade) results in an overall increase in the use of the domestic input, and we will proceed on that assumption. For a general analysis and further discussion, see Grossman (1981).

means that a local content requirement induces a loss in consumer surplus for the domestic country. Accordingly, the domestic government must balance the benefit of profit shifting (from the foreign monopolist to the domestic input industry) against the cost of a decline in consumer surplus in the final good market. As a general matter, it is unclear whether a national-income maximizing government would seek to impose a local content policy. It is clear, though, that such a policy is attractive to the domestic government, if this government has political objectives such that it values sufficiently the profit of input suppliers relative to the surplus of final good consumers.

In this second model, not all of the costs and benefits of the local content requirement reside within the domestic country. If the domestic government chooses to impose a local content requirement (for whatever reason), then the welfare of the foreign government is reduced, since its monopolist suffers a reduction in profit. Thus, when market power in the final good industry exists, a local content policy is associated with an international externality, and a rationale for WTO rules that prohibit local content policies is provided.

Model 3: monopoly final good market, large domestic country

In the previous model, we introduce market power with the assumption that the final good is produced by a foreign monopoly. Our next step is to add market power over the input market as well, with the assumption that the domestic country is large, in the sense that a reduction in the demand of the foreign input by the foreign monopolist when serving the domestic market results in a decline in the (world) price of the foreign input. In this third model, a local content requirement may extract profit from the foreign monopolist and affect as well the profit of foreign input suppliers.

The novel assumption here is that the foreign monopolist faces foreign and domestic input supply functions that are upward-sloping. We assume further the input supply functions are symmetric. Under free trade, an efficient foreign monopolist then uses the same volume of domestic and foreign inputs, and the input prices are thus equated in the two markets. To assess the impact of a local content requirement, we again first imagine that the foreign monopolist does not change its output in response to the local content policy. As before, at a given quantity of output, an effective local content requirement forces the monopolist to use more of the domestic input, and the supply of this input is forthcoming only when the domestic input price rises. The local content rule again extracts profit from the foreign monopolist and shifts it to the domestic input industry.

We next consider the possibility that the foreign monopolist adjusts its quantity of output following the imposition of the local content requirement. At the free-trade quantity, the local content policy induces a higher input price on all units of the domestic input but now also results in a reduction in the foreign input price on all units of the foreign input. The latter effect arises only in the third model, and reflects the fact that the monopolist's reduced demand for foreign inputs causes a decline in the price of the foreign input. Now, if the local content policy is small (i.e., if it calls for only a slight increase in the use of the domestic input, when the monopolist produces the free-trade output level), then the policy has essentially no effect on the monopolist's costs: as before, the monopolist pays a slightly higher input price on all units of the domestic input, but now it also pays a slightly lower input price on all units of the foreign input; furthermore, under our symmetry assumption, it uses approximately the same amount of domestic and foreign inputs, when the local content policy is small. This means that the monopoly output is essentially unchanged after the imposition of a small local content policy. Such a policy thus generates a profit-shifting advantage for the domestic country without causing a loss in consumer surplus. Hence, a small local content policy is sure to be attractive to the domestic government, even if the domestic government maximizes national income.

The case for WTO restrictions against local content requirements is now quite clear. The domestic government has an unambiguous incentive to impose a small local content policy, but such a policy is unambiguously bad for the foreign monopolist and thus the foreign government, and indeed lowers global welfare overall. In other words, the rationale for WTO involvement with respect to local content policies is now the same as the rationale for WTO involvement with respect to tariffs by large countries. In each case, a small amount of the policy is unambiguously beneficial to the party that uses the policy, and unambiguously harmful to the trading partner and world welfare, with all of these implications holding even when benefits are measured in national-income terms.

Summary

Our analysis here reveals that local content requirements may be attractive as a unilateral policy in some circumstances. When markets are competitive and the domestic country is small, such policies may cause a redistribution of surplus from domestic consumers to the domestic input supply industry, with no associated international externality. The situation changes, however, when market power is present. If a foreign monopolist supplies the final good, then a local content policy may extract profit from the foreign monopolist and redistribute this surplus to the domestic input supply industry. Such a policy is more attractive to the domestic government if the foreign monopolist does not respond with a significant reduction in output. This is in turn more likely when the domestic country is large, in the sense that the associated reduction in demand for the foreign input results in a decline in the price of the foreign input. Accordingly, we conclude the local content policies may be attractive to the domestic government and harmful to the trading partner when market power is present. WTO rules that restrict the application of local content policies then rest on a firm economic foundation.

While the models developed above abstract from a number of features that characterize the market for automobile manufacturing in India, we believe that they nevertheless provide useful lessons. In particular, we speculate that US and European automobile manufacturers in India possess some market power. Our analysis thus suggests that local content requirements may be designed to shift the associated profit from foreign automobile manufacturers to domestic input suppliers. Consequently, our analysis provides support for WTO prohibitions against such requirements as they arise within the automotive sector in India.

We conclude with some brief remarks concerning the economics of the trade balancing requirement. Like a local content policy, a trade balancing requirement can limit the imports of the foreign input and thereby increase the price of the domestic input relative to that of the foreign input. When some market power is present, a trade balancing requirement may thus shift profit from the foreign final good industry to the domestic input industry. An international externality is then created and a role for WTO involvement is thus implied. A novel aspect of the trade balancing requirement, however, is that the foreign final good industry may increase exports in order to loosen the restrictions on its imports. The possibility of an induced expansion in exports suggests a more complex pattern of international externalities across trading partners.

References

Brander, James and Barbara Spencer (1981), "Tariffs and the Extraction of Foreign Monopoly Rents under Potential Entry," *Canadian Journal of Economics*, vol. 14, 371–389.

Corden, W. M. (1971), *The Theory of Protection*, Oxford: Oxford University Press.

Grossman, Gene M. (1981), "The Theory of Domestic Content Protection and Content Preference," *The Quarterly Journal of Economics*, Vol. 96, No. 4, November, 583–603.

Vousden, Neil (1990), *The Economics of Trade Protection*, Cambridge: Cambridge University Press.

10

United States – Section 211 Omnibus Appropriations Act of 1998 (WT/DS176/AB/R) A Comment

BY

ROBERT HOWSE
(*University of Michigan Law School*)

AND

DAMIEN J. NEVEN
(*Graduate Institute of International Studies, Geneva and CEPR*)

As usual the authors have divided their labor, based on expertise. In particular, the economic analysis in section 4 was the responsibility of Damien Neven; Robert Howse's own understanding of the costs and benefits of international trade law rules with respect to intellectual property protection *in general* depends on a rather different framework for analysing the problem. However, in so far as the legal and economic analysis of the *Havana Club* case itself is concerned, which deals only with trademarks as a form of IP protection, the authors are in agreement.

1   Introduction

The first part of the chapter (section 2) summarizes the facts of the case and the decision taken by the Appellate Body (AB). We emphasize two issues that the AB dealt with, namely the extent to which the TRIPs may contain a substantive obligation to grant protection to a trademark registered in another country and National Treatment. Section 3 discusses the notion of trademarks, the trade-offs involved in protecting trademarks and the extent to which trademark protection should be coordinated across jurisdictions. We observe that there is a strong case in favor of trademark protection in terms of alleviating moral hazard and adverse selection in product choices but we also identify instances where trademark protection can be abused. We also observe that the case for coordination across jurisdictions is less compelling for trademarks than other forms of intellectual property. We find that the international law of trademark protection is generally reflective of this insight, achieving only a minimum of harmonization and imposing constraints mainly when there is a significant external effect that would not be otherwise internalized, namely where the interests of foreigners are at stake.

Section 4 highlights and discusses the extent to which the AB has limited the scope for harmonization of trademark provisions across WTO Members and in particular has rejected the positive integration that would be induced by some mutual recognition of trademark provisions across countries. Section 4 takes a broader perspective and discusses how national treatment affects firms' incentive to set intellectual property rights and the outcome that arises when national treatment applies. This outcome is compared with that which arises under alternative policy regimes and in particular under independent setting of IP rights for domestic and foreign holders and under mutual recognition. It is found that National Treatment is not as attractive as in other areas (like those covered by Art. III) and that mutual recognition, which has been rejected by the AB even in a limited form, has attractive features.

2   Facts and procedure

After initial consultations in 1999, the European Communities requested in 2002 the establishment of a panel to consider its complaint that a particular section (Section 211) of a US law, the "Omnibus Appropriation Act of 1998", was inconsistent with certain obligations of the US under the Agreement on Trade-Related Aspects of Intellectual Property Rights (the TRIPs agreement).

Section 211 deals with trademarks, trade names, and commercial names that are the same as or substantially similar to trademarks, trade names, or commercial names that were used in connection with businesses or assets that were confiscated by the Cuban Government on or after 1 January 1959 (see panel report, § 2.1).

In the US, all transactions involving property in which a Cuban national has an interest require a license from the "Office of Foreign Assets Control" (OFAC). This office implements a specific regulation on the control of Cuban assets (the Cuban Asset Control Regulation, or

CACR). The office can provide "general licenses" which effectively allow transactions that are specified in the regulation on Cuban assets.

Up until the promulgation of the law under dispute, a general license was available for the registration and renewal of trademarks previously owned by Cuban nationals, independently of whether trademarks had been confiscated. In other words, Cuban nationals could obtain trademark protection in the US.

The new law (Section 211) stipulates that no payment should be made with respect to trademarks that were used in connection with confiscated assets (part (a1)) and that no US court should grant rights to a Cuban national with respect to these trademarks (section (a2)). The CACR was then changed to reflect these new provisions and effectively prohibited the registration of and renewal of trademarks or trade names that were used in connection with confiscated assets unless the original owner of the mark has explicitly consented.

Hence, the effect of the new law, and subsequent changes in the CACR, is to deny to trademarks used in connection with confiscated assets the protection that is normally granted under US law.

Since in the US trademark protection is effected through common law (when associated with use) as well as statutes, Section 211 also contained a provision (b) which prevented US courts from enforcing protection of a trademark used in connection with confiscated assets on the basis of common law (the *Trademark Act of 1946* – also known as the *Lanham Act*).

The (numerous) claims put forward by the EU can be sorted out broadly in four categories. The first category relates to the obligations that Members have under the TRIPS to grant protection to trademarks held by foreigners. The EU found three interpretations of TRIPS provisions which would contain such obligation.

First, the European Communities claimed that the Paris Convention (incorporated into TRIPs in this respect) contained an obligation to register and protect trademarks in the same condition ("as is") as in the original country of registration and hence that Section 211, which did not allow for the registration in the US of some trademarks as they are in Cuba, was inconsistent with this obligation. Much of the discussion by the panel focused on what should be understood by the same condition ("as is"). The panel found that it only referred to the form of the trademark. The EU appealed this finding.

Second, the European Communities claimed that Article 15 of the TRIPS stipulates a right to have a trademark protected, unless the decision not to protect falls within the scope of the exceptions and hence that Section 211 is in breach of this obligation (as it does not fall within the exceptions). The panel disagreed with the EU's reading of Article 15 and found that Section 211 was not inconsistent with Art. 15. The EU appealed this finding.

Third, the EU claimed that Section 211 was inconsistent with Article 16 of the TRIPs, which confers a substantive right to the owner of a mark to exclude third parties from using it when there is a substantial risk of confusion for consumers, because under Section 211, US courts cannot protect trademarks owned by Cuban nationals. The panel found that the EU had not met its burden of proof on this issue. The EU appealed this finding.

The second broad issue covered by the claims of the EU relates to national treatment and most favored nation clauses. The EU claimed that Section 211 was inconsistent with the national treatment obligation contained in Article 3 of the TRIPs and the most favored nation clause found in Article 4. The panel disagreed and the EU appealed those findings.

The third broad issue has to do with procedural rights. The EU claimed that Section 211 is inconsistent with Article 42 of the TRIPs, which requires WTO Members to establish fair judicial procedures concerning the enforcement of intellectual property rights. The panel accepted this claim.

Finally, the EU cast its claims both with respect to trademarks and trade names. The panel ruled that trade names were excluded from the TRIPs. The EU appealed.

Overall, this case thus raises essential issues of interpretation of the TRIPs and the AB ruling has diverged from the panel on important aspects. Broadly speaking, the AB has affirmed the panel on the first issue, namely the extent to which WTO Members have the obligation to register trademarks. The AB limited the scope of these obligations and effectively ruled out mutual recognition. However, the AB reversed the panel findings with respect to national treatment and MFN – emphasizing their importance. Finally, the AB made it clear that trade names were covered by the TRIPs.

3   Background

This section discusses the social and economic functions of trademark law (section 3.1) and international trademark rules (section 3.2).

Section 3.3 then considers the positive international law of trademark protection.

3.1 Social and economic functions of trademarks

The economic literature of trademarks is relatively limited. Landes and Posner (2003) emphasize the role of trademarks in reducing search cost for consumers.[1] They define a trademark as a "word, symbol or other signifier used to distinguish a good or service produced by one firm from the goods and services of other firms." They emphasize that a trademark allows for easier recognition and communication – effectively a short-hand way of recognizing a particular product (such that for instance, it is simpler to refer to "Sanka" than describe "the instant coffee which is produced by General Foods," to use their own example). These authors also point to the interplay between trademarks and the incentive to provide (or increase) quality, suggesting that "the benefit of trademarks in reducing consumer search costs requires that the producer of a trade-marked good maintain a consistent quality over time and across consumers. Hence, trademark protection encourages expenditures on quality."

This argument can possibly be made a little more precise by referring to explicit models of quality choice[2] with asymmetric information, and in particular the literature on experience goods.[3] Experience goods are such that consumers only know the characteristics (or quality) of a product after they have consumed it. In those circumstances, repeat purchases will play an important role, as long as consumers can recognize the product that they have already bought when they contemplate additional pur-chases. Repeat purchase will help alleviate problems of moral hazard and adverse selection. Consider first the latter: firms selling high quality products may be able to induce consumers to try out their products by offering a low price for initial purchases, and charge a higher price when consumers have learned the quality of the product. This strategy will work (at a, so called, separating equilibrium) as long as firms selling low quality product do not have an incentive to mimic the behavior of the high

---

[1] See also Landes and Posner (1987).
[2] Landes and Posner ((1987) and (2003)) do provide a model which is however not best suited to tackle the issue of the role of trademarks as it is a static model, and hence does not account for consumers' learning about product attributes.
[3] The models and results that we will use in the following paragraphs are standard in the IO literature. A detailed description can be found in any graduate textbook.

quality firms. Whether this condition holds depends on the relative cost of providing low and high qualities and the margin that can be earned from selling high quality products at high prices when consumers have ascertained quality. However, for the mechanism to operate at all, it is necessary that consumers should recognize in later purchases the products that they have initially bought[4] (something which is taken for granted by the literature). Trademarks will of course be instrumental in ensuring easy recognition. Trademark protection will also be necessary because firms selling low quality products will have an incentive to disguise their products to make them look like the high quality item that consumers have experienced. Consumers anticipating this will not try the products in the first place and the separation between low and high quality products will collapse.

Repeat purchases will also play an important role in the presence of moral hazard, such that firms have an incentive to pretend selling a high quality product but to deteriorate quality (after the purchase has been agreed). Firms might resist the temptation of selling a low quality item if this induces the consumers to make additional purchases (on which some margin will be earned). Similarly, if consumers entertain the possibility that the firm is somehow "honest" and would sell a high quality product in all instances, it might want to confirm these beliefs and establish the reputation of being an "honest" seller. In both instances, repeat purchases and the ability to recognize in later purchases the products that have been bought initially are essential. Trademark protection will also be necessary because competitors might have an incentive to take advantage of the reputation established by others firms (for instance, competitors with a higher discount rate).

To sum up, trademark protection seems important to ensure that repeat purchases help alleviate problems of moral hazard and adverse selection. The operation of mechanisms based on repeat purchases will also tend to increase welfare and bring benefits to consumers.

There are some striking differences between the role of trademarks and that of patents. Patents provide a stream of revenues to innovators and this, in turn, provides incentive to incur the fixed cost associated with

---

[4] Economides (1984) develops an argument along similar lines. He makes a distinction between frequently and infrequently purchased goods, suggesting that if trademarks are particularly useful for the former, they may also be useful in the latter case, in particular when a company sells both frequently and infrequently purchased goods (so the reputation spills over products).

development of innovations. A key feature of intellectual property is precisely the fact that the cost of dissemination is typically negligible.[5] In those circumstances, unrestricted use of the intellectual property by other firms would also lead to a net benefit ex post (the loss of profit for the innovator would be more than compensated by the increase in profit for the imitator and the increase in consumer surplus). Intellectual content thus has the feature of a public good and in a second best world where patents are the only instrument, the design of patents will balance the benefits that accrue from marginal innovations with the deadweight loss on infra-marginal ones.

In the case of trademarks, the matter would appear to be somewhat different. In the context of the models discussed above, the firm which establishes a trademark incurs a cost (it foregoes profit in the short term) in the hope of reaping profits in the long term. However, unlike what happens with innovations, unrestricted use of trademarks would actually lead to a net cost ex post; the imitator would appropriate some of the surplus that would accrue (ex post) to the firm which induces repeat purchases and consumer surplus would fall (repeat purchases would no longer take place). The improved communication which is sanctioned by trademark protection does not seem to have the feature of a public good. Unlike patents, whose extension imposes a deadweight loss, trademark protection would thus appear to confer benefits such that they should be unrestricted, at least in the framework that we have considered so far.

Special features of trademark laws and in particular the dependency of the entitlement to a trademark on use, not simply invention, are also best understood in terms of this framework. Only if a trademark is in use is there a danger that consumers will be misled by someone other than the original holder attaching it to their products or services. In addition, traditionally, it has been a requirement in establishing a trademark violation, to show the possibility of consumers being misled.

The case for trademark protection should however not be generalized beyond the confines of the particular models that we have referred to. Indeed, there are clearly some circumstances where it may be attractive to restrict trademark protection. Consider for instance a small variation of the models above in which entry by a more efficient producer is feasible at a later stage. This producer may have the same incentive as the original

---

[5] That is also to say that there is no rivalry in the consumption of intellectual content (a good whose production only requires to incur a fixed cost is effectively a public good).

producer with respect to the provision of high quality goods and repeated purchases. Trademark protection will however bar entry and might impose a net cost.

More generally, it would appear that trademarks can play an additional economic role, beyond that of securing repeated purchases and allowing for the operation of mechanisms which solve moral hazard and adverse selection. Consider for instance an environment where there is no asymmetric information regarding the characteristics of the products but in which a consumer's willingness to pay for the product can be increased through advertising.[6] The natural reference here is a model with endogenous sunk cost à la Sutton and the Rolex watch may provide a suitable illustration; the mechanical features of such watch can arguably be observed by consumers and can be imitated by other producers. Assume that advertising conveys no information about the product and has solely the effect of raising consumers' willingness to pay for the watch (because it conveys a signal of a particular life style). The welfare consequences of trademark protection in this case are not as clear-cut as those discussed above. In particular, the effect on consumer surplus of allowing for imitation ex post is less clear, as consumers who enjoy the mechanical features of a Rolex watch but do not value the signal would benefit at the expense of those who consider it as highly valuable.[7] In other words, the rationale for protecting the effect of advertising does not seem as compelling as protecting the operation of repeat purchases.

There are also some circumstances where trademark protection will be clearly unattractive. For instance, trademark protection could possibly be used in order to raise entry barriers and protect rents. This will arise if the trademark covers some generic product – for which asymmetric information is unimportant (imagine that the expression "pain killer" is given trademark protection). This could be the result of trademark protection being captured by producers' interests. The legal doctrines in some jurisdictions that allow the curtailment of trademark protection once the mark is deemed to take on a "generic" meaning may actually reflect the concern of not protecting producer rents.

---

[6] Economides (1984) discusses this as an instance where a "mental image" is associated with the product, so that the product acquires a new characteristic.

[7] Economides (1984) refers to this as a form of allocative inefficiency which arises from the fact that particular characteristics (the mental image and the mechanical features) are tied in fixed proportions.

Finally, it is worth noticing that in some circumstances, trademarks might have a public good aspect. This arises because, as symbols or communicative signs, trademarks become important features of the "Lebenswelt", as it were – they represent a significant part of the language of human social and even political communication. Protecting the trademarks could then lead to suppression of freedom of expression, and welfare reducing declines in human creativity. Consider Warhol's Campbell's Soup can, and the use and distortion of marks as a form of political parody or satire by anti-globalization activists (see Rosemary Coombe (1998); Beebe (2003)).

To sum up, if there is a presumption in favor of trademark protection when it contributes to mechanisms which solve problems of moral hazard and adverse selection, there are also some circumstances where trademark protection is less attractive.

The trade-off between the benefits from additional trademarks and the cost of trademark protection on infra-marginal ones is also such that extensive trademark protection is probably desirable. The terms of the trade-off are different from what is normally found for innovations, given that the cost of trademark protection on infra-marginal products is likely to be much less than the cost of patent protection on infra-marginal innovations. Trademark protection may be costly only when trademarks have a public good aspect as a means of fostering communication.

3.2   International trademark rules

How do these welfare trade-offs play out when we move from the domestic context to the international one: what do they imply about the justification or lack thereof for global trademark protection?

The external effects that patent protection induces across jurisdiction will be discussed later. In this section, we will emphasize that in defining patent protection in the domestic market for domestic (or foreign) firms, a domestic government will not consider the benefit that accrues to foreign consumers from additional innovations. In addition, in defining its policy towards foreign firms, a domestic government will not consider the benefit that accrues to foreign firms.

When it comes to trademarks, the matter is a little different because the external effect to foreign consumers may not be important. If we confine ourselves to the most favorable case for trademarks (as protecting repeated purchases), a trademark policy towards firms operating in the domestic market will mostly affect the range of products sold to domestic customers and not that sold to foreign customers. Indeed, one expects, as a first approximation, that the range of product sold in the foreign market will be determined by the protection that can be obtained abroad (of course, to the extent that foreign consumers may be exposed to domestic trademarks through distance media like the internet, there will still be a spillover effect across countries). As in the case of patents however, a domestic government will not consider the profit accruing to foreign firms in deciding whether to grant trademark protection in the domestic market. Still, the benefit to domestic consumers may be enough to justify a decision to grant trademark protection to the foreign firms (independently of the rents accruing to the firms).[8]

Overall, external effects across jurisdictions in the case of trademarks are less of a concern than in the case of patents. They only arise to the extent that foreign profits are not taken into account and may thus lead to insufficient protection to foreign firms.

The issue still arises whether in those circumstances, the foreign government might be able to invoke the interest of domestic consumers in order to obtain trademark protection. There is nothing as such illegitimate in a country making a claim to care for the welfare of consumers in another country (international human rights and labor law are illustrations of the principle that human concern does not stop at national boundaries).

Still, the external effect that we have identified would be best addressed by an international trademark law concerned with fair treatment of foreigners, in other words, with preventing abusive or discriminatory application of trademark law to aliens. Thus, it could be considered to be a *lex specialis* of general international law on the protection of aliens. In this environment, one would expect to see little substantive harmonization of domestic trademark laws, but rather the exclusion of certain kinds of grounds or pretexts for disposing of trademark applications by aliens, grounds or pretexts that sound in arbitrariness or discrimination. While formally appearing as a kind of at least "negative" harmonization, this kind of international trademark law might better be understood as a set of specialized rules for the protection of aliens.

Our discussion of external effects has so far focused on circumstances where trademark protection is most likely to be attractive in terms of

---

[8] For instance, if trademark protection is a discrete instrument. With a continuous instrument, the degree of protection to foreign firms will be less.

welfare. If trademarks are used in order to raise entry barriers, or protect advertising aimed at raising consumers' willingness to pay, the external effects will be different and may be closer to those normally associated with non-tariff barriers which shifts rents between domestic and foreign producers.

Finally, note that besides the internalization of external effects, international trademark law could be fundamentally concerned simply with reducing those enforcement costs of trademark law that arise from trans-boundary economic activity. In such cases, each jurisdiction would preserve its sovereignty to make such choices for its own consumers.

3.3 Positive international law of trademark protection

With these conceptual considerations in mind, we now turn to the positive international law of trademark protection. The *locus classicus* for such law is the *Paris Convention*.

The trademark provisions of the *Paris Convention* are not preceded or prefaced by any preamble or statement of objectives (nor does the Paris Convention itself have Preamble). Instead, the trademark provisions in the Convention begin with the assertion of a default rule in favor of domestic sovereignty: "The conditions for the filing and registration of trademarks shall be determined in each country of the Union by its domestic legislation." (6.1). Article 6 then goes on to state some specific limitations on this default rule, listing a limited number of grounds on which it is impermissible to refuse to register and protect a trademark held by an alien. These impermissible grounds include: that the mark was not registered originally in the alien's own country (6.2); that the mark differs from the mark registered in the country of origin "only in respect of elements that do not alter its distinctive character and do not affect its identity in the form in which it has been registered in the said country of origin"; grounds that relate to "the nature of the goods"(7).

In addition, there is a general obligation to "refuse and to cancel the registration, and to prohibit the use, of a trademark which constitutes a reproduction, an imitation, or a translation, liable to create confusion, of a mark considered by the competent authority of the country of registration or use to be well known in that country as being already the mark of a person entitled to the benefits of this Convention and used for identical or similar goods."(6bis(1)).

Considered individually and in relation to each other, these various obligations suggest a quite limited degree of positive harmonization of domestic trademark law. There is a default rule in favor of domestic sovereignty, and the only general substantive norm, reflected in 6(bis)(1) is that of avoidance of consumer confusion.

The limited harmonization implied by these obligations is in line with the absence of strong external effects discussed above. The emphasis on consumer confusion is also consistent with the main motivation for trademark protection discussed above. From that perspective, it should be noted that the language "liable to create confusion" would probably exclude from the obligation in 6(bis)(1) uses of trademarks in general social and political communication (parody etc.), since such uses do not confuse consumers searching for goods, almost by definition. Nor would it require the protection of "generic" names, since in such instances most consumers may be simply expecting that the similar or identical product has certain generic characteristics, rather than a particular quality associated with it being manufactured by the original user of the mark.

Apart from 6(bis)(1), which introduces an element of positive harmonization, the other trademark rules in the *Paris Convention*, do not really go beyond the objectives of fair and non-discriminatory treatment that characterize a *lex specialis* on protection of aliens. They seem to aim at insuring aliens' demands for recognition and registration of their marks are not denied or frustrated on grounds that could invite arbitrary or discriminatory behavior by governmental authorities in other states.

Apart from the *Paris Convention* there are a range of other international legal instruments that relate to trademark protection, such as the *Trademark Law Treaty* (1994) and the *Madrid Agreement Concerning the International Regulation of Marks*. These Agreements seem aimed primarily at the reduction of transboundary enforcement costs of trademark law. They deal with many technical aspects of registration of marks outside the jurisdiction, and related matters. To some extent, by specifying procedures to be used by national authorities in dealing with aliens, these Agreements could also, in certain aspects, be considered *lex specialis* of the law of protection of aliens.

This brings us to the trademark provisions of the WTO TRIPs Agreement, the relevant provisions in the *Havana Club* dispute.

The Preamble to TRIPs recognizes "underlying public policy objectives" for the protection of intellectual property in domestic legal systems. It does not single out any particular purpose or objective as far as trademark law is concerned. Article 7 of TRIPs acknowledges that complex welfare trade-offs may be implicated in the way and extent to which intellectual property is protected, and states the principle that "The protection and enforcement of intellectual property rights should contribute to the promotion of technological innovation and the transfer of technology . . . in a manner conducive to social and economic welfare, and to a balance of rights and obligations." Article 8.1 states that Members have a general police power to adopt health and nutrition measures and promote the public interest in sectors of vital importance to their socioeconomic and technological development subject only to any specific constraints contained in the textual provisions of TRIPs. Taken together, these various provisions suggest that interpretations of TRIPs should not be based upon a *presumption* of the intent to *harmonize* intellectual property laws, especially beyond the extent to which it would be clearly "conducive to social and economic welfare," but instead a presumption that TRIPs preserves domestic regulatory autonomy and diversity subject to certain precisely specified textual constraints.

The provisions of TRIPs that apply to trademarks largely follow the Paris Convention, discussed above; and the general TRIPs obligations of National Treatment and MFN also apply to trademarks. A WTO Member may deny registration to a trademark on any ground that does not "derogate from the provisions of the Paris Convention" or is explicitly prohibited by TRIPs provisions themselves.

The only clear instance of substantive harmonization of trademark law to be found in TRIPs is the requirement that anyone other than the original holder be excluded from using the mark, where there the consumer is liable to be confused (16(1)). However, TRIPs is slightly more harmonizing than the Paris Convention, by virtue of establishing a *presumption* of confusion in the case of identical goods and services. Also TRIPs 16(1) does not require that the mark be well known in order to benefit from this general norm of protection. On the other hand, unlike Paris Convention 6bis, which refers to "interested party", only the "owner" of a trademark may assert exclusive use, under 16(1) of TRIPs (an aspect of that provision which as we shall see will be quite crucial to the AB's disposition of the appeal). Finally, 16.1, and *all* the other provisions of TRIPs on trademarks, are however subject to a general exceptions provision, which states: "Members may provide limited exceptions to the rights conferred by a trademark, such as fair use of descriptive terms, provided that such exception take account of the legitimate interests of the owner of the trademark and of third parties" (Article 17). TRIPs explicitly acknowledges that a WTO Member may make trademark protection contingent on use, and that trademark protection may be cancelled due to non-use, subject to certain conditions. The TRIPs obligations on enforcement of intellectual property rights apply mutatis mutandis to trademarks. The provisions can be understood as a *lex specialis* of the law of protection of aliens, as well as going to the reduction of enforcement costs across national boundaries.

In sum, none of the provisions of TRIPs related to trademarks evidence any intent to substantially harmonize trademark law beyond the minimal extent evidenced in the Paris Convention. The minimum harmonization which is contemplated by the international law of patent protection is also broadly consistent with the economic analysis discussed above which has emphasized that external effects across jurisdictions may not be as important for trademark protection as for other instruments. The emphasis given by international law to the protection of aliens is also appropriate given that the main external effects in patent protection which would not otherwise be internalized arise with respect to the profits accruing to foreign producers.

4   The AB ruling

Article 6 *quinquies* of the Paris Convention

The EC appealed the panel's finding that the United States legislation did not violate Article 6quinquies of the Paris Convention, incorporated into the TRIPs agreement through TRIPs 2.1. This provision reads, in part: "Every trademark duly registered in the country of origin shall be accepted for filing and protected *as is* in the other countries of the union, subject to the reservations indicated in this article . . ."(emphasis added).

These reservations include situations where the trademark may "be of such a nature as to infringe rights acquired by third parties in the country where protection is claimed"; where the mark "is devoid of distinctive character" or has become essentially generic; and where the mark is "contrary to morality or public order, and in particular, of such a nature as to deceive the public."

Placing considerable emphasis on the expression "as is" in the first paragraph of Article 6quinquies, the panel found that Article 6quinquies did not create a self-standing obligation to register a trademark, subject to a limited number of reservations or exceptions, but rather only required that, if domestic law *otherwise* permitted registration of the mark, it must be registered "as is", i.e. in exactly the form presented to the authority upon registration. Thus, Article 6quinquies did not derogate from a Member's general right under Paris Convention 6.1 to determine the conditions for the filing and registration of trademarks by its domestic legislation", except as regards the *form* of the mark. In consequence, the challenged US legislation did not violate Article 6quinquies, in as much as the restrictions it placed on registration were not related to the form of the mark.

The grammar of 6quinquies is logically consistent with either the broader meaning asserted by the EC ("You must register this trademark, and not only that, you have to register it as is unless one of the exceptions applies") and the narrower meaning discerned by the panel ("if your domestic law otherwise permits the registration of this trademark, you are obliged to register it in exactly the form that it is presented, subject to the exceptions).

Thus, the Appellate Body rightly found that the "ordinary meaning" of the words in 6quinquies was not sufficient to resolve the issue, and went on to explore the "context" of 6quinquies. The Appellate Body then determined that the "context" supported the narrower interpretation made by the panel.

The first contextual consideration that the Appellate Body adduced was Paris Convention Article 6.1, the general default rule of domestic sovereignty: the AB suggested that "if Article 6quinquies A(1) were interpreted too broadly, the legislative discretion reserved for Members under Article 6(1) would be significantly undermined." This is an important interpretive move by the Appellate Body. In effect, the AB uses 6.1 as evidence of the limited or modest aspiration of the Paris Convention with respect to the substantive harmonization of trademark laws. Some might criticize the AB here, since 6.1 explicitly limits the default rule of domestic sovereignty, by stating it is subject to the obligations in the Paris Convention itself, and therefore, 6.1 merely begs the question of how narrow or broad those obligations might be, i.e. how much they cut into the default rule of domestic sovereignty. Yet such an alternative reading of 6.1 would reduce the provision to a triviality: "you are permitted to do what is not prohibited to you." That would simply restate what is already obvious, at least since the *Lotus* case, namely that the sovereignty of states is presumed to be unlimited, unless bounded by specific rules of law.

Thus, to give 6.1 an effective meaning, it must be interpreted as signaling that, in fact, such derogations from domestic sovereignty *as are provided for in the Paris Convention,* will be narrow, bounded, and clearly expressed.

It is to be noted that there are provisions in other WTO Agreements with a rather analogous structure to that of Paris Convention 6.1. For example, the Preamble of the TBT Agreement states that "no country should be prevented from taking measures necessary to ensure the quality of its exports, or for the protection of human, animal or plant life or health or for the prevention of deceptive practices, *at the levels it considers appropriate,* subject to the requirement that they are not applied in a manner which would constitute a means of arbitrary or unjustifiable discrimination between countries where the same conditions prevail or a disguised restriction on international trade, and *are otherwise in accordance with the provisions of this Agreement."* (emphasis added). A reading of this provision analogous to that which the AB makes of Paris Convention 6.1 would have the result that the treaty interpreter should be very reluctant to read the provisions of TBT in such a way as to limit a Member's right to choose the appropriate level of regulatory protection or intervention, unless the text cannot be read any other way. This would defeat expansive readings of certain provisions of TBT, which suggest a proportionality test, for example, even though such a test is not explicitly specified in the language in question (see Howse and Tuerk, 2001 on TBT Article 2.2, footnote 91, p. 317, criticizing the expansive interpretation of the late Bob Hudec).

Similarly, according to SPS 2.1, "Members have the right to take sanitary and phytosanitary measures necessary for the protection of human, animal or plant life or health, *provided that such measures are not inconsistent with the provisions of this Agreement."* By stipulating domestic regulatory autonomy as a general right, SPS 2.1 implies that any limit to that right must be clearly established by the textual provisions of SPS, and that the treaty interpreter must avoid interpretations of SPS provisions that would result in largely uncircumscribed or unbounded interferences with the general right.

To return to *Havana Club,* the AB went on to illustrate the wisdom of a narrower reading of 6quinquies by reference to the jurisdiction-shopping effects if the broader EC reading were adopted. As the AB noted, there are two means by which a holder of a trademark from a Member of the WTO/ Paris Union can seek trademark protection in the territory of another Member. Pursuant to Article 6 of the Paris Convention, it can seek directly to register the mark with the authorities of that other Member, in which case such registration is, on account of 6.1, subject to such conditions as exist in the domestic law of that other Member.[9] Alternately, the AB noted, a trademark holder of a Member could first register the mark with that Member's authorities, and *then* seek registration from the authorities of the other Member, pursuant to Article 6quinquies. If the EC interpretation were correct, the AB conjectured, then a mark holder could do an end run around the domestic legal requirements of the other Member, by going the route of Article 6quinquies, which, on the EC reading, *requires* registration and protection of the mark, subject to the limited exceptions in that Article itself. The AB suggested that thus "a national of a Paris Union country could circumvent the "use" requirements of a particular regime by registering in the jurisdiction that does not impose "use" requirements.

The problem with the AB reasoning here is that Article 6quinquies itself states that "In determining whether a mark is *eligible* for protection, all the factual circumstances must be taken into consideration, particularly the length of time the mark has been in use."(C.1) (emphasis added). This clearly implies that whatever else Article 6quinquies means, it *does* allow for the possibility that a Member could make a decision that a trademark is not *eligible* because of lack of use. Thus, the AB is wrong that, on the EC reading of Article 6quinquies, the mark holder of a Member could avoid the use requirement of another Member, through resorting to Article 6quinquies. Moreover, whatever reading is adopted of Article 6quinquies, this Article, *as incorporated into TRIPs*, is subject to the explicit acknowledgement in Article 19 of TRIPs that use may be required to maintain a registration, subject to the conditions stated in that Article.

We emphasize however that the error of interpretation in this particular step in the AB's reasoning does not really mar the compelling logic of its general view that interpreting 6quinquies in the way proposed by the EC would introduce a requirement of minimum positive harmonization, or mutual recognition, not warranted by the context of 6quinquies and the overall structure of the TRIPs trademark regime. Once having interpreted 6quinquies in context, the AB felt it necessary to address one particular argument of the EC in favor of its alternative, broader reading, namely that the exceptions listed in 6quinquies would only make sense if its application were broader than to just the *form* of the mark. The

---

[9] It should be added, a Member could also, quite apart from registration, simply demand the substantive minimum of protection afforded by the Convention Article 6bis/TRIPs Article 16/1, namely exclusion of other users where the consumer is likely to be confused, provided it could otherwise establish in some way that it is "owner" of the mark.

AB, in reply, simply asserted: "The *form* of a trademark may be devoid of distinctive character within the meaning of paragraph 2 . . . Equally the *form* of a trademark may be contrary to morality or public order, or of such a nature as to deceive the public within the meaning of paragraph 3."

Finally, the AB introduced an additional contextual consideration, namely an agreed interpretation of Article 6quinquies as it appeared in the original Paris Convention of 1883, which made clear that the provision in question only prohibits exclusion from registration based on the form of the mark, leaving Members free to deny registration, based on other conditions or criteria in their domestic laws. However, this agreed interpretation was omitted in subsequent versions of the Paris Convention.

The AB was clearly unsure about relying on the agreed interpretation in these circumstances, so it states ". . . [W]e simply observe that our interpretation . . . is not inconsistent with this interpretation." Was it correct, under the Vienna Convention rules, to avert to the 1883 agreed interpretation as part of the "context" of the Paris Convention as incorporated into TRIPs? We believe so. According to VCLT 31(2)(a), "context" includes "any agreement relating to the treaty which was made between all the parties in connection with the conclusion of the treaty." VCLT 31(2)(a) applies not only to agreements that are explicitly made an integral part of the main treaty, but to any agreement *connected* with the conclusion of the treaty. The fact that the instrument incorporating the agreed interpretation was not made an *integral part* of subsequent versions of the treaty, does not as such defeat its status as an "agreement . . . made in connection with the conclusion of the treaty." And, as the AB notes, there was no attempt at any time to explicitly revoke or repudiate the agreed interpretation, or to alter it. In our view, the VCLT would have allowed the AB to rely to a greater extent than it did on the agreed interpretation, which it appeared to treat almost as supplementary means, like *travaux*, which could normally only be used to confirm an interpretation based on primary sources.

There is a way in which the AB could have acted with greater judicial economy in its consideration of the meaning of Article 6quinquies. It could have held that even if, *arguendo*, the expansive interpretation by the EC of the Article were correct, the US legislation would nevertheless have fallen within the "third party rights" exception, which allows a Member to exclude registration and protection where the trademark is of such a nature as to infringe rights acquired by third parties in the country where protection is claimed.[10] Under the US legislation at issue, clearly, rights have been acquired by the original owners of confiscated assets, and their heirs and assigns. It is in the name of these third party rights that the US was excluding registration under the challenged legislative provisions. This is reinforced by the fact that should the third parties *waive* their rights the legislation would permit registration and protection to proceed.

Why then did the AB decide to venture an interpretation of a complex legal provision that it wasn't required to make, and indeed one based in part on what seems to be an incomplete and erroneous reading of aspects of the Paris Convention? The AB seems to have thought it important to shut the door to the use of TRIPs to expand the scope of legally mandated intellectual property protection, beyond that strictly and clearly mandated by the treaty language. Here one cannot wonder if there was a broader policy context at least in part influencing (if sub-consciously) the judges: the context of debates over globalization and intellectual property, where many aspects of TRIPs have been criticized as the product of industry capture, extending IP protections at the global level beyond what could be justified on the basis of either domestic welfare in all WTO Member states, or global economic welfare).

Importantly, the defeat of the EC's broad reading of Article 6quinquies also helps to close the door to the use of TRIPs to grant trademark protection in other circumstances than those where they reduce consumer search cost.

To see this, it is important to compare carefully Paris Convention 6bis and 6quinquies as interpreted by the EC. 6bis, as already discussed, does create a substantive right for an "interested party" to insist that the authorities of a Member country prohibit on their territory the use of a mark well known in the country of origin, where that use is liable to confuse consumers. Moreover, it is *this* substantive right to a certain level of trademark protection in other Member countries that is, in a slightly modified form, restated in Article 16(1) of TRIPs. If, as the EC proposed, 6quinquies were to be read as creating a right to registration and protection, subject to a set of exhaustively listed exceptions, a new substantive right would be created that would rival and exceed that in Paris 6bis/ TRIPS 16(1). Since 6quinquies does not limit the meaning of "protection" to the enforcement of exclusive use where other use might confuse

---

[10] This would be somewhat analogous to the way that the AB avoided deciding the question of territorial nexus under Article XX(g) in *Shrimp/Turtle* I.

consumers, and indeed does not define "protection" at all, the EC interpretation would allow the door to open at the WTO on expansive views of
trademark protection now being advanced by corporate interests in the
courts of various domestic jurisdictions, with varying degrees of success,
e.g. anti-dilution. These expansive views are widely questioned in the
economics literature as discussed above. The TRIPs Agreement itself
mandates readings of that Agreement that would make intellectual property protection "conducive to social and economic welfare." On the basis
of economic analysis, an expansion of trademark protection beyond what
is required to support the consumer search cost reduction function might
well not be "conducive to social and economic welfare."

TRIPs 15.1 and 15.2

TRIPs 15.1 states certain grounds on which a mark may *not* be denied
eligibility for trademark protection. Namely, WTO Members may not
exclude from eligibility for trademark protection a sign because of the
kind of sign that it is – thus whether the sign is constituted of words,
letters, numerals, figurative elements, combinations of colors, or a mix of
any of the above, it shall nevertheless be eligible for registration. There
thus seems to be some overlap between TRIPs 15.1 and Paris Convention
6quinquies, which requires that a trademark be registered as is.

TRIPs 15.2 provides that 15.1 "shall not be understood to prevent a
Member from denying registration of a trademark on other grounds,
provided that they do not derogate from the provisions of the Paris
Convention (1967)."

Much in the manner in which it sought to discern in Paris Convention
6quinquies a substantive right to trademark protection, the EC argued that
15.1 provided not merely for negative harmonization (stating certain discrete grounds on which Members were not permitted to distinguish
between trademarks as eligible or not eligible for protection), but rather
stated a right to have a trademark protected, unless the decision not to protect was well within one of the exceptions permitted by the Paris Convention.

Unlike the case with Paris Convention 6quinquies, the ordinary meaning of the words in 15.1 excluded the interpretation being urged by the
EC. As the Appellate Body noted (paragraph 155), Article 15.1 deals with
the question of when a mark may be "eligible" for or "capable of"
receiving trademark protection. The EC's reading would in effect eliminate those words from the treaty text, such that 15.1 would say not when
a mark must be *eligible* for protection, but rather when there is an
obligation to provide the protection.

However, the AB went further, and sought support for its (obvious) reading of 15.1 from the "context" of 15.2, which states that Members can nevertheless deny registration of a trademark on "other grounds", provided that they do not derogate from the Paris Convention. As the AB pointed out, the reference to "other grounds" suggests that all 15.1 does is to state *one* particular kind of grounds on which Members *cannot* refuse to consider a trademark eligible for registration and protection, namely what kind of signs or symbols it consists of. The AB further cited as "context" for its interpretation, TRIPs 15.4, which establishes that a trademark may not be denied registration simply because of the nature of goods or services that it designates. As the AB noted, if, as the EC suggested, 15.1 constituted a general obligation to register and protect trademarks, rather than stating a single prohibited ground for denying registration and protection, then 15.4 would be superfluous; there would be no need to state prohibited grounds one by one, since by virtue of 15.1 there is instead (on the EC theory) a general obligation to register and protect, subject to certain defined exceptions.

Even though this disposed of the EC's appeal on this issue, since no violation could be found (the US legislation in question having nothing to do with the kind of sign that composes the mark), the AB made a point of going on to consider and reject the EC's interpretation of 15.2. The EC's view of 15.2 was that it limited the legal right to refuse registration and protection to those situations explicated stated as *exceptions* in the Paris Convention (or TRIPs itself). The AB, however, regarded 15.2 as an affirmation of the default rule of domestic sovereignty in Paris Convention 6.1. In other words, Members are free to determine the conditions of trademark registration and protection, subject to certain explicit prohibited grounds, which they are forbidden to use to discriminate between trademarks with respect to eligibility for registration and protection.

Here, the AB made an explicit decision to jettison judicial economy, it would seem, in order to make clear as guidance for future panels the overall nature of TRIPs as far as trademarks are concerned; TRIPs is not an agreement for substantive harmonization, or mutual recognition, but merely reinforces or reaffirms the negative integration commitments of the Paris Convention.

TRIPs Article 16.1

If there *is* some element of positive harmonization or integration in the TRIPs trademark provisions, it would have to be found in Article 16.1, which as noted in an earlier section of this chapter, is similar to Paris Convention 6bis, in conferring a substantive right to exclude third parties from using the mark for identical or similar goods or services such that there is a likelihood of consumer confusion. Unlike Paris Convention 6bis, TRIPs 16.1 requires a presumption of likelihood of confusion where the sign being used is identical to the original mark.

There is, however, a crucial difference between Article 16.1 and Paris Convention 6bis. Paris Convention 6bis does not depend on the concept of *ownership*. Instead, it states that the mark "must be considered by the competent authority of the country of registration or use to be well known in that country as being already the mark of a person entitled to the benefits of the Convention . . ." Thus, *who* can exclude others from using a mark appears to depend on the decision of the authorities of the jurisdiction of initial registration and/or use.

By contrast, neither TRIPs 16.1, nor any other provision of TRIPs for that matter, defines *how*, or by *whom*, the question of ownership is to be determined. In the absence of any explicit provisions on these matters in either TRIPs or the Paris Convention, the panel had asked the Director General of the International Bureau of WIPO for an expert opinion on whether the Paris Convention contained an *implicit* definition of "ownership." The Director General answered in the negative.

The Appellate Body approved the panel's deference to this opinion from WIPO. This is an example of the kind of "institutional sensitivity" that Howse and Nicolaidis recommend in dispute settlement (Howse and Nicolaidis, 2003: Howse, 2000). The legitimacy of the dispute settlement organs is enhanced when they are prepared to defer to the judgment of non-WTO international institutions with expert competence in a specialized legal regime that intersects with the rules of the WTO. What is striking here, though, is the AB's endorsement of such deference not just with respect to factual matters, but also in legal interpretation; this qualifies what seemed in some earlier cases the AB's tendency to consider itself competent to interpret the relevant law of other regimes, including municipal law, as if it were interpreting WTO law itself (provided of course that the other law was properly before it as relevant to the application of a WTO Agreement; *India – Patents, EC – Bananas*).

On the other hand, the absence of an implicit definition of ownership in the Paris Convention, as determined by the official experts of that legal regime, does not excuse the Appellate Body from attempting a contextual definition of ownership as it relates, not to the obligations of the Paris Convention, but to those in *TRIPs itself.* The EC pointed to a number of provisions of TRIPs that, contextually, seemed to suggest that the owner of a trademark, at least presumptively, was the undertaking that had originally used or registered the mark, and anyone who had legally acquired the mark from that original "owner".

The very nature of 16.1 is that of an obligation that rights established in one jurisdiction (the home jurisdiction) be *recognized* by the authorities of *other* WTO jurisdictions; thus, there is arguably no need to define ownership. Ownership and other pre-conditions for the establishment of a trademark are naturally governed, in the logic of a recognition provision, by the laws of the home country, absent any explicit minimum international standards. Viewed in this way, the conclusion that the Appellate Body draws from the silence on ownership in TRIPs is perverse – namely, that the jurisdiction obliged to *recognize* a trademark right duly established in the home country gets to decide who is a *bona fide* owner of the right.

A recognition and enforcement regime such as that in 16.1 is of course appropriately subject to exceptions of a public policy nature; and in a case such as *Havana Club* the United States could arguably invoke such an exception, if the decision of the host country to recognize a certain individual or entity as an owner violated the public policy of the United States. But that is quite another matter than inferring a general default rule that the country of recognition and enforcement, not the country where the rights are established in the first place, has full latitude to determine who is a trademark "owner."

As was discussed earlier in this chapter, economic analysis questions whether positive harmonization of the substantive norms of trademark law can be justified on welfare grounds. The strongest economic case for positive harmonization is that global consumer welfare is likely to be enhanced if every country was required to take steps to avoid use of marks so as to confuse consumers. In interpreting TRIPs 16.1 the way it does, the AB seems to shrink from accepting even that degree of positive harmonization that would, broadly speaking, be supportable on the basis of economic analysis. But there are important reasons of democracy, reasons that relate to the legitimacy of WTO law and adjudication, for taking as seriously as the AB does a declared default rule of domestic sovereignty.

At the same time, by virtue of TRIPs Article 2.1, Article 6bis of the Paris Convention is incorporated into TRIPs. While substantially overlapping with TRIPs 16.1, there is nothing in 16.1 that explicitly states that it alters and surpasses Paris Convention 6bis. Since Paris Convention 6bis confers, not on the "owner" of the mark but rather on an "interested party" the right to demand that the authorities of a Member enforce exclusive use where the mark is "considered by the competent authority of the country of registration or use to be well known in that country as being already the mark of a person entitled to the benefits of the Convention . . .", the AB could have gone on to complete the analysis, as it were, applying to the facts Paris Convention 6bis, which contains a substantive right closely analogous to that in 16.1. Paris Convention 6bis appears to resolve the kind of situation where ownership of the mark is contested across different jurisdictions (here the US vs. Cuba) by deferring to the views of the authorities in the country of registration and use, assuming that that is a country where the authorities consider it to be well known that the mark is already the mark "of a person entitled to the benefits of the Convention . . ." (the panel below had rejected the EC claim that the US legislation violated Paris Convention 6bis, on rather unclear grounds, that seem related to a concession of the EC to the US position that 6bis in no way precluded each country's authorities from making their own decision about how confiscation might affect the determination of whether a mark was a "mark of a person entitled to the benefits of the Convention").

In any case, the AB's holding that domestic sovereignty to restrict the ownership of trademarks remains essentially unconstrained by TRIPs is of no small importance. On the AB's logic, through ownership measures, a government can impose a wide range of responsibilities on an entity that wishes to have the status of "owner" of a mark, including social responsibilities. If the US view of the Cuban revolution and the Castro regime is a legitimate basis to make a determination of who owns a trade mark, then denying a mark, for example, to an entity that manufactures marked goods in sweatshops that violate internationally recognized labor standards might equally be legitimate, if not more so. (See Katherine Van Wezel Stone, 1999).

Moreover, one may ask if the analysis of "ownership" by the AB in *Havana Club* might not have implications for the interpretation of TRIPs obligations in respect of *other* forms of intellectual property. Take the case of patents. Article 28.1 of TRIPs requires that certain exclusive rights on the "owner" of a patent. Article 27 of TRIPs lists *specific grounds* on which Members *may or may not* exclude patentability. But TRIPs says nothing about the determination of who is the "owner" of a patent and is therefore entitled to the exclusive rights named in TRIPs 28.1. Of course, the National Treatment and MFN obligations in TRIPs would apply to determinations of ownership under domestic law.

As for the Berne Convention, as incorporated into TRIPs, it appears to have a similar default rule in favor of domestic sovereignty over the conditions of substantive protection of intellectual property as does the Paris Convention in respect of trademarks. Thus Article 27.5 of the Berne Convention provides: "... any Contracting State is free to apply, when determining the patentability of an invention claimed in an international application, the criteria of its national law in respect of prior art and *other* conditions of patentability not constituting requirements as to the form and contents of applications."

If thus WTO Members are free (subject to the National Treatment and MFN obligations of TRIPs) to determine the criteria or conditions for someone to be an "owner" of a patent, this has major implications for the ability of developing countries, for instance, to insure that patent protection does not conflict with their development needs.[11] Technology transfer, acceptance of price controls, etc. could all be imposed as conditions for an entity to be recognized as an "owner" of a patent, and thereby the beneficiary of the rights enumerated in TRIPs 28.1.

In sum, the finding of the Appellate Body concerning the significance of ownership not being defined or specified in TRIPs with respect to trademarks has significant promise for rebalancing the TRIPs Agreement in a manner conducive to answering many of the critiques of TRIPs by developing country activists and governments. The problem is that the AB's approach reposes on an erroneous interpretation of TRIPs 16.1 – an interpretation that ignores the fundamental structure and nature of the obligation in 16.1 as an obligation of recognition and enforcement of substantive rights established before the authorities of *another* jurisdiction.

TRIPs Article 42

Article 42 requires that WTO Members afford to holders of intellectual property rights "civil judicial procedures concerning the enforcement of any intellectual property right covered by this agreement." Article 42 goes

---

[11] At the same time, depriving a foreign economic actor of the status of "owner" of certain intellectual property rights might constitute, for example, a violation of the customary international law of investor protection, and in some cases might violate provisions of trade or bilateral investment treaties, depending on how they are worded. There could be circumstances where a deprivation of "owner" status for example might be considered an "expropriation" or a denial of "full protection and security."

on to stipulate certain minimum level of due process to which "right holders" are entitled.

The EC argued that the US legislation in dispute took away this entitlement from Pernod, by essentially taking away from it the status of a "rights holder." Thus, the legislation, while not taking away the *standing* of someone *claiming* to be a "rights holder" to assert their substantive claim, would allow that claim to be defeated such that the court might never get to the application of the general provisions of trademark law, including those in TRIPs.

The AB rightly held that the legislation went to the *substantive* not *procedural* validity of trademark claims, and therefore did not violate the procedural rights in Article 42. While a US court might, as a matter of judicial economy, rule against the substantive claim of a trademark holder on the basis of the legislation in dispute, without going on to consider the merits of the claim otherwise, the AB held that to do so did not violate any of the procedural rights in Article 42; nothing in the legislation in dispute authorized or mandated the US courts **not** to apply the guarantees of fair procedure in the Rules of Evidence and federal civil procedure legislation. Only after determining, on the basis of rules of fair procedure, that a right holder did not "own" the mark in question, would a court, on the basis of the legislation in dispute, find its claim to be invalid.

Paris Convention Article 8

Article 8 of the Paris Convention provides that "A trade name shall be protected in all the countries of the Union without the obligation of filing or registration, whether or not it forms part of a trademark." Article 8 is one of the provisions of the Paris Convention incorporated into TRIPs by virtue of TRIPs Article 2.1. Article 2.1, however, states that this incorporation is "in respect of Parts II, III and IV of TRIPs." Since trade names are not dealt with as a separate kind of intellectual property from trademarks in Part II of TRIPs, the panel held that Paris Convention Article 8 was not incorporated into TRIPs; it interpreted the words "in respect of . . ." as limited or circumscribing the scope of the incorporation of the Paris Convention into TRIPs. Both the US and the EU appealed this finding, which the panel also sought to sustain by reference to the negotiating history of TRIPs.

The Appellate Body correctly observed that Article 8 – which deals with trade names *exclusively* – was explicitly chosen as among those articles mentioned in 2.1. If would be nonsensical to include Article 8 in the list of Articles of the Paris Convention incorporated in TRIPs, and then

completely nullify the incorporation by virtue of the language "in respect
of . . ." The AB found that the language "in respect of . . ." could be given
a meaning that would avoid this result.

Here, the AB was, we believe, on solid ground. The principle of effectiveness in treaty interpretation requires that the interpreter seek a meaning that gives effect to *all* of the relevant treaty provisions, and to do so
before claiming a contradiction or ambiguity that would justify recourse
to the negotiating history.

As the AB suggested, the language "in respect of . . ." need not mean
that a form of intellectual property protection dealt with in an incorporated provision of the Paris Convention need appear in the titles or
headings of Parts II, III or IV of TRIPs. As the AB observed, the Patents
section of TRIPs refers to a *sui generis* system of intellectual property as an
alternative to patentability in the case of plant varieties. Such an provision
could not be defeated just because there is no heading in Part II of TRIPs
on *sui generis* patent protection.

In the case of trade names, Article 16.1 of TRIPs makes it clear that a
mark may not be denied protection because it consists merely of words,
including personal names. To this extent, Part II of TRIPs does protect
trade names, either *as* marks or part of marks. The fact that none of
the substantive provisions in TRIPs Part II mentions trade names as a
distinct form of intellectual property may well be because the drafters
considered the protection provided to trade names *as distinct from marks*
in Article 8 of the Paris Convention to be sufficient. The incorporation of
Paris Convention Article 8 might well be the reason why it was not
necessary to deal with trade names independently of marks in Part II;
thus, to defeat the incorporation of Paris Convention Article 8 into TRIPs
on the grounds that trade names are not mentioned separately in Part II
would be utterly perverse. These considerations, in our view, provide
strong support for the Appellate Body's decision to reverse the panel, and
find that Article 8 of the Paris Convention is indeed incorporated into
TRIPs.

Having so decided, it should be noted, the AB chose not to exercise its
discretion to complete the analysis, the panel having not made any
findings of fact concerning the claims on trade names (since the panel
viewed them as excluded from TRIPs altogether). It is likely, based on its
interpretations of other provisions of TRIPs and the Paris Convention in
this ruling that the AB would have found Article 8 to be largely, if not
entirely, procedural in character, stating only that protection of trade
names may *not* depend on the prior formalities of filing and registration,

but without specifying when and at what level Members are required to provide substantive protection to trade names.

National Treatment and MFN

TRIPs incorporates the National Treatment obligation of the Paris Convention Article 2(1), which states: "Nationals of any country of the Union shall, as regards the protection of industrial property, enjoy in the other countries of the Union the advantages that their respective laws now grant, or may hereafter grant to nationals."

With respect to successors-in-interest, those who acquire a trademark from the original owner, the contested US legislation on *Havana Club* proved that US courts shall not recognize, enforce or validate any rights by a "designated national" (where of course the trademark was at one time the property of a confiscated entity); "designated national" is defined in the Regulations pursuant to the legislation not only as Cuba or any Cuban national of any foreign country (that is, non-United States nations) who are successors-in-interest to a designated national.

The United States persuaded the panel that although these provisions *explicitly* barred certain *foreign* nationals only from the assertion of trademark rights in the US Courts, in practice there was no denial of National Treatment, since it was also the consistent practice of the US authorities to deny recognition of these rights where held by US nationals, and since there were other statutory and international law bars to the recognition of rights acquired in connection with confiscated property, which would equally function as a bar to US nationals and foreign nationals attempting to assert such rights in the US courts, quite apart from the legislation being challenged in *Havana Club*.

The Appellate Body reversed, finding that the *Havana Club* legislation constituted an additional hurdle to the recognition of trademark rights that was imposed only on certain foreign nationals, but not on US nationals. While the AB recognized that there were serious obstacles faced by US nationals in the same situation, there remained a hypothetical possibility that these might be overcome in a given case, resulting in better treatment of the US national in question, in relation to the foreign national who would, in like circumstances, now face the additional obstacle in the *Havana Club* legislation.

The AB ruling seems to be a relatively straightforward application of the spirit and letter of the GATT *S. 337* panel ruling; there, the panel suggested that in cases of explicitly different, and *prima facie* less favorable, treatment of foreign products in a *particular* law, in order for the defendant to successfully claim that a full comparison of the *overall* treatment of the relevant foreign products shows that the latter are not discriminated against, there must be certainty that, in *every* instance, the factors extrinsic to the particular legal provisions being challenged would fully balance or neutralize any less favorable treatment that would result from those particular legal provisions. This seems a heavy burden to meet, but again it must be recognized that here, in *Havana Club*, as in *337*, foreigners were being singled out explicitly and categorically in the law itself.

With respect to original owners of trademarks attempting to assert their rights in the United States, the Appellate Body found that if there were "two separate owners who acquired rights, either at common law or based on registration, in two separate United States trademarks before the Cuban confiscation occurred" and these trademarks were the same as or similar to a Cuban trademark used in connection with a business that was confiscated, and the one owner was American and the other Cuban, only the Cuban national would be affected by the regime in the *Havana Club* legislation. Thus, again there was explicit discrimination against foreign, in this case Cuban, nationals.

The United States pointed out however that the *Havana Club* legislation did not *apply* to trademarks registered in the United States prior to the existence of Section 515.527 of the CACR. The AB responded that this "does not address the discrimination against Cuban nationals who are original owners of trademark rights in the United States *based on common law*."

Unlike with respect to successors-in-interest, where it is obvious that *all* designated foreign nationals face at least an additional formal hurdle under the *Havana Club* legislation, the discrimination discerned by the AB in the case of original owners seems to depend *entirely* upon a hypothetical, i.e. the existence of a class of persons, Cuban nationals who are original owners of trademarks rights in the United States based on common law, which trademarks are the same or similar to trademarks used by businesses then confiscated by Cuba. Finding less favorable treatment of foreigners based upon an entirely hypothetical situation of certain (possibly non-existent foreigners) in relation to US nationals, seems at odds with the AB ruling in *Canada – Periodicals*, where the AB faulted the panel for basing its analysis of National Treatment on comparisons based on purely hypothetical situations.

In addition, Cuba was not a party to the *Havana Club* litigation and the question arises as to the appropriateness of the AB's implicit conclusion that the obligation of National Treatment towards Cuban nationals is one that the United States owes to the EC or the entire WTO Membership not just to Cuba. The AB did not even address the question of whether or not National Treatment, in TRIPs or the Paris Convention, is an obligation of that nature, i.e. *erga omnes partes*. (See Pauwellyn, 2002). Certainly, if one were to view National Treatment in these instruments as a kind of *lex specialis* of the law on the treatment of aliens, there would be a strong presumption against *erga omnes partes*, because, traditionally under the law of protection of aliens, only the state of which the alien is a national can assert a claim against another state based on its treatment of that alien. Matters in *Havana Club* may not be that simple, however, because the meaning of "Cuban national" seems to extend to persons who were Cuban nationals and are currently residing outside of Cuba in third countries, including possibly the EC. From the perspective of the National Treatment obligation, these persons might well be properly considered EC "nationals" even if they might fall within the definition of "Cuban national" in the statute.

This brings us in fact to the MFN violation claimed by the EC. In the case of original owners, the *Havana Club* legislation, by singling out Cuban nationals (not other foreign nationals as is the case with the legislation as it applies to successors-in-interest) discriminates between Cuban nationals and original owners from other WTO Members. The United States responded that a Cuban original owner could be "unblocked" under different legislation; however, the AB pointed out that 1) only Cuban nationals resident in the US were automatically "unblocked"; 2) Cuban nationals resident in Cuba cannot be unblocked; 3) Cuban nationals resident in the EC may be "unblocked" but must go through an additional procedure. The difference in treatment between 2 and 3 does in fact show racial discrimination of a kind prohibited by the MFN obligation. But the worse treatment of Cuban nationals residing in the EC than Cuban nationals residing in the US, 1 and 3, arguably illustrates why it might have been reasonable for the AB to find a National Treatment violation in respect of treatment of original owners, even without Cuba being a litigant, or without directly addressing the issue of *erga omnes partes*.

National Treatment and mutual recognition   As discussed above, the AB ruling confirms the importance of National Treatment in the TRIPs. It also takes the view that mutual recognition of intellectual property rights should not go beyond the form in which it was filed.

This section discusses how National Treatment affects the incentive to set intellectual property rights and the extent to which it improves efficiency. We also consider the incentives that mutual recognition would trigger and compare the outcomes arising out of national treatment and mutual recognition.

In order to discuss this issue, we develop a framework that can deal with patents and copyrights as well as trademarks. As discussed above, trademarks, unlike patents, do not involve important public good aspects. In the context of the framework that we develop below, this will generally yield a higher level of protection for trademarks, relative to innovations. But the essential ingredients of the model remain the same. The case of trademark can thus be obtained as a special case, in which the balance between the marginal cost and the marginal benefit of extending IP protection yields a high level of protection.

As indicated above, the external effects across jurisdiction may also be less pronounced in the case of trademarks than in the case of patents. This arises because trademark protection in one country, which allows for the profitable sale of a particular product item, will not yield benefit to foreign consumers. Trademark protection in the foreign country will be necessary in order to trigger profitable sales abroad. In the case of innovation, once produced, it will be sold abroad even if there is no protection. In other words, benefits abroad are not contingent on the existence of IP protection abroad for domestic products.

However, the absence of one external effect across jurisdictions will not change qualitatively the results discussed below. Domestic governments will still have less of an incentive to grant IP protection to foreign firms than domestic firms and the effect of both national treatment and mutual recognition will be qualitatively unchanged. In what follows, we will refer to the broader framework, involving IP rights and innovations, keeping in mind that trademarks can be obtained as a special case.

We find that National Treatment effectively pools incentives with respect to domestic and foreign innovations. It prevents government from discriminating between IP rights with different perceived returns and as a consequence leads to a sharp fall on the IP rights granted to domestic firms. We find that National Treatment is unlikely to improve much over the uncoordinated outcome in which each government sets different IP rights for domestic and foreign innovation. By contrast, we find that mutual recognition has attractive features; in a symmetric environment (where countries have the same size), mutual recognition actually achieves the outcome that would be selected by a central government, which internalizes all external effects across countries. This arises because under mutual recognition, a domestic government induces the foreign government to select towards domestic firms the IP policy that it would have selected if it had internalized external effects across countries.

At first glance, the fact that National Treatment does not seem very efficient may come as a surprise, given that national treatment is often considered as a reference in the area of non-tariff barriers (Art. III). This may reinforce the extent to which National Treatment should be seen in the context of the Trademark provisions of TRIPs as part of a *lex specialis* with respect to the fair and non-discriminatory treatment of aliens, rather than a mechanism for insuring welfare maximizing levels of trademark protection.

Hence, before considering in detail how different regimes will affect IP rights, we briefly compare the effect of National Treatment in the area of non-tariff barriers (Art. III) and the area of intellectual property rights.

(i) National Treatment: NTBs versus IP rights

Let us first consider National Treatment in the area of NTBs, for instance a product regulation, which raises the costs of foreign firms, relative to those of domestic firms. Such barriers can be attractive for the domestic government to the extent that they affected the competition between domestic and foreign firms and reallocated rents in favor of domestic firms.

As is well known from the literature on strategic trade policy, the governments involved (assumed to maximize domestic welfare) face an incentive structure, which conforms to a prisoner's dilemma – in which the dominant strategy is to introduce product regulations which favor domestic firms. The outcome is inefficient, and both countries are worse off relative to the situation where neither country introduces non-tariff barriers.

In this instance, the source of the inefficiency is the (pecuniary) external effect that the introduction of a non-tariff barrier imposes on the profits of the foreign firms. This external effect is not internalized by the governments involved. A treaty between governments which bans the implementation of the non tariff barriers will also naturally remove the inefficiency but it will require a strong mechanism of compliance as the government will always have an incentive to introduce such non-tariff barriers, in the hope that they will remain unnoticed or fall through the cracks of the legal system.

Let us now consider the recognition of intellectual property rights. The recognition of intellectual property rights to foreign firms has two aspects: first, by granting intellectual property rights to foreign firms, the domestic government will again affect the allocation of rents between domestic and foreign firms, as long as domestic and foreign products associated with the intellectual property rights are not independent. If these products compete,[12] by granting intellectual property rights to foreign firms, domestic governments will make foreign products less attractive – as domestic users will have to pay some royalties. This will also increase the profits of domestic firms, so that the rents to both domestic and foreign firms will increase. Such a policy may thus only be attractive to the domestic government if it gives an important weight to profits – relative to consumer surplus. In what follows, we will mostly abstract from this first aspect of intellectual property rights.

The second aspect is associated with the design of an intellectual property policy. The design of intellectual property rights strikes a balance between the distortion that they involve with respect to existing products and the benefit that would accrue from additional innovations (see Nordhaus, 1969). In evaluating the distortion that intellectual property will impose on domestic products, a domestic government will only consider the deadweight loss. In other words, it will consider the profit to domestic firms as a transfer from consumers. However, with respect to the intellectual property rights granted to foreign firms, foreign profits will not be counted as part of the country's welfare and hence the cost of an increase in price associated with an intellectual property regime will include the entire reduction in consumer surplus. Hence, the domestic government will have less of an incentive to grant intellectual property rights to foreign firms relative to domestic firms. As in the case of non-tariff barriers, the external effect that the domestic policy has on foreign profits is not internalized.

With respect to the benefit of intellectual property rights, a national government considering new domestic innovation will only take into account the benefit accruing to domestic consumers (at the margin a new innovation will yield no profit). It will neglect the external effect to foreign consumers. Similarly, in considering the benefit that might

---

[12] The opposite would occur if products are complement.

accrue from extending intellectual property rights to foreign firms, a domestic government will only consider the benefit that will accrue to domestic consumers.

Overall, in designing an intellectual property regime for domestic firms, a domestic government will fail to consider benefits accruing to foreign consumers and hence will provide excessively low protection to domestic innovations. This bias in favour of excessively low protection will persist in designing intellectual property for foreign firms; in addition, when it comes to foreign firms, the cost of intellectual property will be biased upwards as foreign profits will not be considered. This will reinforce the bias in favor of excessively low protection towards foreign firms.

Let us now consider national treatment, whereby domestic governments commit to provide to foreign firms the treatment that they provide to domestic firms. As observed by Scotchmer (2002), national governments have little incentive to adopt this policy unilaterally: the additional profits that they would grant to foreign firms is unlikely to be compensated by the domestic benefit that would accrue from the development of new products abroad, at least if the domestic country is relatively small. This will also arise independently of whether foreign countries have themselves adopted a regime of national treatment. As in the case of non-tariff barriers, the uncoordinated outcome will thus involve insufficient protection of foreign firms and the implementation of a regime of national treatment will require a strong compliance mechanism.

The question of the extent to which National Treatment will improve efficiency is less clear-cut. National treatment effectively ensures that intellectual property rights are the same for domestic and foreign firms – despite the fact that underlying incentives are different for foreign and domestic firms. It does not directly address the underlying sources of inefficiencies either. A policy addressing the external effects would have to ensure that national governments consider the profit accruing to foreign firms when intellectual property rights are raised and consider the benefits to foreign consumers from new innovations. National Treatment does not do either of these. It imposes the same IP rights on both domestic and foreign firms.

These consequences will be discussed in more detail below. At this stage, it is worth emphasizing that the analysis of national treatment should not be imported from the area of non-tariff barriers (Art. III) to that of TRIPs. If the incentives faced by governments with respect to the imposition of non-tariff barriers and with respect to the extension of intellectual property rights to foreign firms are similar, the parallel should not be extended further. Whereas NTBs have to do with the allocation of rents between firms, the extension of intellectual property rights to foreign firms has to do with the provision of public goods (in a second best world). National treatment can be expected to have different consequences in these two environments.

(ii) A simple model of innovation and trade

In order to investigate some of the properties of the outcomes induced by national treatment and mutual recognition, we will develop a simple benchmark model of trade and innovation. This benchmark model will abstract from many issues and in particular will assume that products developed domestically and abroad are independent. More precisely, any product developed in one country will have a market in both domestic and foreign countries and will not compete with other existing or future innovation. In addition, countries will not "compete" with respect to the development of innovations. Each country can be thought of as being completely specialized in a particular innovation segment.[13] This model thus abstracts from all issues of rivalry between innovations (both within and across countries) to focus on the issue of coordination between countries in the provision of public goods.

Both Scotchmer (2002) and Grossman and Lai (2002) have analyzed the non-cooperative choice of IP policies under national treatment. They consider richer models in which innovations compete (Grossman and Lai (2002)) or in which countries face a coordination problem in the development of new innovations (Scotchmer (2002)). These authors however focus on the interplay between countries in defining their IP policies under national treatment and do not attempt to evaluate national treatment relative to other policy regimes.

There are two countries, 1 and 2. There is a technology, common to both countries such that new products can be designed at a cost k where k is uniformly distributed in the $[0, 1]$ interval and such that for each cost k there is a density $\gamma = 1$ of new products that can produced (the set of potential innovation is thus given by $[0, 1] \times [0, 1]$. If the

---

[13] Alternatively, one can think of this model as describing an environment where there are innovation races for each product across countries and in which each country has an intrinsic advantage in developing a range of innovations.

two countries develop innovations simultaneously in the same cost range, each country will obtain a share γ_i of the corresponding innovations (with $\gamma_1 + \gamma_2 = 1$). These shares might be thought of as reflecting the relative efficiency of the two countries in developing new products.

In each country, there is a demand for each new product which is denoted $P_i = a_i - Q_i$, all products are independent (neither substitute, nor complement) and once developed can be produced at constant (zero) marginal cost.

An IP policy towards innovators selling products in country i can then be modeled as a level of rent, Π_i. In turn, in the absence of rivalry between innovations, any level of rent can be determined by a price level P_i, where $\Pi_i = P_i(a_i - P_i)$, so that an IP policy can be seen as the choice of a particular price level for each new product. Note that profits can be seen as discounted flows over time so that the choice of a particular price level can also be interpreted as a patent length (an increase in the patent length will increase profits and the deadweight loss and reduce consumer surplus).

Each country's government will select at most two IP policies, one towards domestic innovations and one towards foreign innovations. We denote $\tilde{P}_i$ as the IP policy of country i, which applies to its domestic innovators, whereas y_i will denote the IP policy which applies to foreign innovators.

There is free entry in the production of innovation so that any innovation which is profitable is produced. The range of innovations which takes place is thus determined by the flow of profits which arise from IP rights in both countries (that is from IP rights granted to domestic firms by the domestic government and the IP rights granted to the same firms by the foreign government). Let us denote $k_i(\tilde{P}_i, y_j)$ as the marginal innovation in country i. This marginal innovation is determined by the level of profits accruing from both domestic and foreign IP rights, with $k_i(\tilde{P}_i, y_j) = \tilde{P}_i(a_i - \tilde{P}_i) + y_j(a_j - y_j)$.[14] The range of innovation which is produced in country i is thus given by $\left[0, k_i(\tilde{P}_i, y_j)\right]$.

Let $CS(\tilde{P}_i)$ and $DWL(\tilde{P}_i)$ denote respectively the consumer surplus and deadweight loss that accrue as a function of a domestic IP policy

---

[14] We assume that there is no arbitrage across countries so that the demands for any given products are independent across countries.

in country i. Standard calculation yields that

$$CS(\tilde{P}_i) = \frac{(a_i - \tilde{P}_i)^2}{2}, DWL(\tilde{P}_i)$$
$$= \frac{\tilde{P}_i^2}{2}, \text{ and } CS(\tilde{P}_i) + DWL(\tilde{P}_i) + \Pi_i(\tilde{P}_i) = \frac{a_i^2}{2}$$

The same expression applies, mutatis mutandis, for IP rights granted to foreign firms.

We consider four policy regimes: first, we derive the choice of an optimal IP policy by each country, with respect to domestic and foreign firms, in the absence of any coordination. Second, we consider the choice of an IP policy under national treatment (whereby domestic and foreign firms have to be treated alike). Third, we consider the choice of an IP policy under mutual recognition (whereby foreign firms have to be treated in the same way as in their domestic base). For reference, we also derive the policy that would be chosen by a central authority, which internalizes all external effects across countries.

(iii) Independent IP policies

As shown by Nordhaus (1969) (see also Grossman and Lai (2002)), the optimal choice of an IP policy (or patent length) will balance the benefit from new innovations with the distortions that the IP policy implies ex post on existing products, as long as profits are considered as transfer from consumer to firms. This condition will thus determine the IP policies towards domestic firms. Given the behavior of innovators (such that all innovations which yield a positive profit are undertaken), the benefit associated with new innovations is solely the consumer surplus that it will yield ex post.

By contrast, the optimal IP policy towards foreign innovators will balance the benefit from additional innovation abroad (for domestic consumers) with the fall in consumer surplus on existing foreign innovations. In this case, the profit, which accrues to foreign firms, is not counted as part of domestic welfare.

The condition for the optimal domestic IP policy in country i can then be written:

$$CS(\tilde{P}_i)\frac{\partial \tilde{k}_i}{\partial \tilde{P}_i} - \frac{\partial DWL(\tilde{P}_i)}{\partial \tilde{P}_i}k_i(\tilde{P}_i, y_j) = 0, \ i = 1, 2 \qquad (1)$$

The first term represents the benefit that is obtained from increasing IP rights in terms of additional consumer surplus. The second term

Table 1. *Independent IP policies*

	$a_1 = a_2 = 1$	$a_1 = 1.25, a_2 = 1$
P_1	0.301	0.401
y_1	0.129	0.215
P_2	0.301	0.276
y_2	0.129	0.067
k^*	0.323	
W	0.259	

represents the cost in terms of increasing the deadweight loss on existing products. Note that this formulation assumes that profits and consumer surplus are equally weighted by the government (so that the change in the sum of consumer surplus and profit is equal to the opposite of the change in the deadweight loss).

The condition for the optimal IP policy in country i toward foreign firms can be written;

$$CS(y_i) \frac{\partial k_j}{\partial y_i} - \frac{\partial CS(y_i)}{\partial y_i} k_j(\tilde{P}_j, y_i) = 0, \quad i = 1, 2 \qquad (2)$$

The uncoordinated outcome can then be derived by solving the four equations given in (1)–(2). It is easy to check that these conditions yield downward sloping reactions functions, such that the IP rights granted to domestic firms will fall as the IP rights that they obtain abroad increase. As one would expect, the IP rights granted to foreign firms are always less than those granted to domestic innovators. For the sake of illustration, table 1 reports the optimal IP rights, when markets are symmetric (with $a_i = 1, i = 1, 2$) and in the case where market 1 is larger, $a_1 = 1.25, a_2 = 1$.

The comparison between asymmetric and symmetric outcomes confirms that large countries have a stronger incentive to grant property rights to foreign firms – simply because they have a stronger effect in triggering marginal innovations.

Table 1 also reports the range of innovation that is undertaken in each country (k^*) in equilibrium, as well as the level of welfare, for further reference.

(iv) National Treatment

Under National Treatment, domestic and foreign firms have to be treated alike. In other words, we have that $\tilde{P}_i = y_i, i = 1, 2$. The optimal IP right in country i will then balance the benefit for domestic consumers of additional innovations at home plus the benefit for domestic customers of additional innovations induced abroad with the deadweight loss on existing innovations at home and the loss of (domestic) consumer surplus on existing innovations from abroad.

The condition for an optimal IP policy under national treatment is then written:

$$CS(\tilde{P}_i)\frac{\partial k_i}{\partial \tilde{P}_i} - \frac{\partial DWL(\tilde{P}_i)}{\partial \tilde{P}_i}\, k_i(\tilde{P}_i, \tilde{P}_j) + CS(\tilde{P}_i)\frac{\partial k_j}{\partial \tilde{P}_i}$$
$$-\frac{\partial CS(\tilde{P}_i)}{\partial \tilde{P}_i}k_j(\tilde{P}_j, \tilde{P}_i) = 0, \quad i = 1, 2$$

The reactions functions implicitly defined by these equations are downward sloping. One can also check that the equilibrium IP rights which solve these two equations are in between the domestic and foreign IP rights defined above under the assumption that IP policies are independent. To illustrate, assuming that countries are symmetric (with $a_i = 1, i = 1, 2$), one obtains that $\tilde{P}_i = 5/4 - \sqrt{17}/4 \simeq 0.219$. In the context of this example, the level of innovation which is undertaken and the welfare are given by : $k^* = 0.342, W = 0.267$.

The comparison between the outcomes under independent IP policies and national treatment is striking. Under national treatment, government has to offer the same rights to domestic and foreign innovators despite the fact that IP rights to the latter yield much lower perceived returns. As a consequence, the marginal returns from IP rights fall relative to marginal returns from domestic rights. The aggregate right increases only marginally and as a consequence, the range of innovation hardly increases. The level of welfare is also barely changed.

One should possibly not pay too much attention to the results that aggregate IP rights, the range of innovation and welfare do not change significantly with national treatment, relative to the independent solution, as these results are likely affected by the shape of the demand function. However, the observation that national treatment is ineffective because it prevents government from discriminating between IP rights with different perceived returns and as a consequence leads to a sharp fall on the IP rights granted to domestic firms deserves attention.

(v) Mutual recognition

In a regime of mutual recognition, the domestic government has to grant to foreign firms the same treatment that they receive at home. In the context of our model, this implies that $y_i = \tilde{P}_j, i = 1, 2$. In this environment, national government can effectively make sure that the same IP rights are granted to domestic innovators, irrespective of where the innovation is sold. Unlike what happens under national treatment, domestic government cannot affect the profitability of foreign innovations but rather raise contributions to domestic innovations from foreigners.

The optimal IP right will then balance the benefit of additional innovations at home with the deadweight loss on existing innovations, taking into account that an increase in domestic IP rights will be matched by an increase in foreign IP rights on domestic innovations. The condition for optimal IP rights is then written:

$$CS(\tilde{P}_i) \frac{\partial k_i(\tilde{P}_i, y_j)}{\partial \tilde{P}_i}\bigg|_{y_j = \tilde{P}_i} - \frac{\partial DWL(\tilde{P}_i)}{\partial \tilde{P}_i} k_i(\tilde{P}_i, y_j)\big|_{y_j = \tilde{P}_i} = 0$$

Interestingly, this condition is equivalent to the condition for optimal IP rights that would be chosen by a government which considers all external effects across markets, when the markets are symmetric. This condition can be written as:

$$2CS(\tilde{P}) \frac{\partial k(\tilde{P})}{\partial \tilde{P}} - 2 \frac{\partial DWL(\tilde{P})}{\partial \tilde{P}} k(\tilde{P}) = 0$$

When markets are symmetric, we have that $\partial k(\tilde{P})/\partial \tilde{P} = \partial k_i(\tilde{P}_i, y_j)/\partial \tilde{P}_i\big|_{y_j = \tilde{P}_i}$ and $k(\tilde{P}) = k_i(\tilde{P}_i, y_j)\big|_{y_j = \tilde{P}_i}$ so that the two conditions are equivalent.

To illustrate, assuming that countries are symmetric (with $a_i = 1, i = 1, 2$), one obtains that under mutual recognition (and the fully coordinated solution) $\tilde{P}_i = 1/3$. The level of innovation which is undertaken and the welfare are then given by: $k^* = 0.44, W = 0.296$.

The intuition behind the effectiveness of mutual recognition can be expressed as follows: mutual recognition forces the foreign country to adopt the same IP protection towards domestic firms. But in a symmetric world, the level of protection that the foreign country is "forced" to adopt is also the level of IP protection that foreigners should have adopted if they were taking external effects into account.

Hence, mutual recognition effectively mimics the outcome that would be chosen by a central authority.

One can also expect that in an asymmetric world, the equivalence will no longer hold. Presumably, large countries will induce smaller ones to choose an IP policy which is more extensive than what they would choose if they were taking external effects into account and vice versa. This could lead to excessively broad protection in large countries and excessively low protection in small ones.

References

Beebe, B. (2003), The semiotic analyis of trademark law, Mimeo, Benjamin Cardozo School of Law, Yeshiva University.

Coombe, R. (1998), *The Cultural Life of Intellectual Properties: Authorship, Appropriation, and the Law*. Durham, NC: Duke University Press.

Economides, N. (1984), The economics of trademarks, WP 21, Columbia.

Grossman, G. and E. Lai (2002), International protection of intellectual property, NBER Working Paper N° 8704.

Howse, R. (2000), Adjudicative Legitimacy and Treaty Interpretation in International Trade Law: The Early Years of WTO Jurisprudence, in *The EU, the WTO, and the NAFTA: Towards a Common Law of International Trade?* edited by J. H. H. Weiler, 35–69. The Collected Courses of the Academy of European Law, 9/1. Oxford: Oxford University Press.

Howse, R. and K. Nicolaidis (2003), Enhancing WTO Legitimacy: Constitutionalization or Global Subsidiarity? *Governance* 16, no. 1 (2003): 73–94.

Howse, R. and E. Tuerk (2001), The WTO Impact on Internal Regulations – A Case Study of the Canada-EC Asbestos Dispute, in *The EU and the WTO: Legal and Constitutional Issues*, edited by G. de Búrca and J. Scott, 283–328. Oxford: Hart Publishing.

Landes, W. and R. Posner (1987), Trademark law: an economic perspective, *The Journal of Law and Economics*, XXX (2), 265–310.

Landes, W. and R. Posner (2003), *The Economic Structure of Intellectual Property Law*. Cambridge, MA: The Belknap Press of Harvard University Press.

Maskus, K. (2000), *Intellectual Property Rights in the Gobal Economy*. Washington, DC: The Institute for International Economics.

Nordhaus, W. (1969), *Invention, Growth and Welfare: a Theoretical Treatment of Technological Change*. Cambridge, MA: MIT Press.

Scotchmer, S. (2002), The political economy of intellectual property treaties, NBER Working Paper N° 9114.

Van Wezel Stone, Katherine (1999), To the Yukon and Beyond: Local Laborers in a Global Labor Market. *Journal of Small and Emerging Business Law.*

11

United States – Preliminary Determination with Respect to Certain Softwood Lumber from Canada: What is a Subsidy?*

BY

HENRIK HORN

Institute for International Economic Studies, Stockholm University Centre for Economic Policy Research, London

AND

PETROS C. MAVROIDIS

University of Neuchâtel and Columbia University Centre for Economic Policy Research, London

1 Introduction

In August 2001, the United States Department of Commerce (USDOC) issued a preliminary determination that Canadian schemes for allocating standing timber to private harvesters – "stumpage" programs – provided countervailable subsidies to Canadian softwood lumber producers. It also preliminarily determined that critical circumstances existed in the US softwood lumber industry, caused by Canadian imports. Provisional measures were imposed on the basis of a preliminary subsidy rate of 19.31 percent, applicable to all producers/exporters, and applied to all entries of softwood lumber from Canada.

As an immediate response to the publication of the USDOC determination, Canada requested the establishment of a WTO panel. In its complaint, Canada argued that the USDOC Preliminary Countervailing Duty Determination (CDC), as well as the Preliminary Critical

* We are grateful to Gene Grossman, Johan Stennek and the other Reporters in the project for helpful exchanges. We have also benefited from editorial assistance by Michael Greenwald and Christina Lönnblad.

Circumstances Determination, violated various provisions in the Subsidies and Countervailing Measures (SCM) Agreement, as well as Art. VI:3 of GATT 1994. Canada also claimed that the US countervailing duty (CVD) law regarding expedited and administrative reviews, and the application of that law to the importation of Canadian softwood lumber, violated various provisions of the *SCM Agreement*.

Broadly speaking, the Panel found that the USDOC did not undertake an adequate countervailing duty determination, and that the CVDs imposed on the basis of this determination thus were illegal. The Panel also found that the *SCM Agreement* did not allow for the retroactive application of provisional measures, but that the US CVD law concerning expedited and administrative reviews was legal under the agreement.

The purpose of this chapter is to comment on some of the issues discussed in the Panel report that are of particular interest from an economic perspective.[1] The Panel in *US – Softwood Lumber* did not interpret its task as to make a *de novo* analysis of the degree of subsidization of Canadian lumber producers, but instead to determine whether the US had adequately demonstrated such subsidization. Similarly, this chapter will not seek to evaluate whether the Canadian stumpage programs actually subsidized their lumber producers, but whether the argumentation by the Panel seems to "make sense" from an economic angle, pointing to aspects of the *SCM Agreement* where there seems to be a conflict between the law, as interpreted by the Panel, and what makes good economic sense.[2]

The economics of this dispute is complicated for several reasons. A first reason is the market structure of the industry involved. Provincial governments own most, but not all, standing timber in Canada. The timber is harvested by private companies, which then sell the logs as inputs into

---

[1] WTO Panel Report *United States – Preliminary Determination with Respect to Certain Softwood Lumber from Canada* (WT/DS236/R, WT/DS178/AB/R, 27 September 2002); the dispute is here referred to as *US – Softwood Lumber*.

[2] This dispute concerned a preliminary determination by the USDOC. The final determination was also challenged by Canada, and a Panel and an Appellate Body report have been issued during the writing of this report. (*United States – Final Determination with Respect to Certain Softwood Lumber from Canada* (WT/DS257/R, 29 August 2003), and WT/DS257/AB/R, 19 January 2004). Those determinations will be discussed in next year's reports. We merely note that the determination by the AB in the latter dispute is inconsistent with some of the findings of the Panel in this dispute.

sawmills or pulp mills. Sawmills, in turn, produce softwood lumber, among other products. The lumber is partly sold outside the industry, but it may be bought by remanufacturing firms for further processing. The US countervailing duty determination concerned softwood lumber imported from Canada, whereas the measures alleged to give rise to subsidization were contracts between Canadian provincial governments and harvesters of standing timber. The nature of the vertical relationship in the industry therefore plays a central role in the dispute.

Another difficulty in this dispute is the complicated nature of the contractual terms under which standing timber is turned into logs. A party interested in harvesting timber must normally enter an agreement with a provincial government, even though (important for this dispute) there are also private suppliers of stumpage. This agreement – the stumpage contract – stipulates the conditions under which the standing timber can be harvested. The agreement typically involves a number of obligations on the part of the harvester, such as requirements to build and service roads and protect against fire, as well as possible minimum or maximum cut requirements. There are also charges levied on the harvested volumes, so-called stumpage fees. These contracts differ in structure among the Canadian provinces, and each province typically employs several contractual forms that differ in a number of ways. Hence, the dispute does not concern a single easily described measure, but a large number of complex and often different types of contracts.

The structure of the chapter is the following. The next section very briefly sketches the role of CVDs in trade agreements, from the point of view of economic theory. Section 3 examines whether Canadian provincial governments can be said to provide goods. Section 4 discusses the central issue of how to define the no-subsidy benchmark against which one is to compare the actual situation. It also points to problems with the benchmarks suggested by the US, and Canada and the Panel, respectively. Section 6 reflects on the link between benefits to Canadian lumber producers and injury to US competitors. Section 7 concludes.

2   The purpose of the CVD instrument in the *SCM Agreement*

Adjudicating bodies should interpret provisions in light of their purposes and context. The *SCM Agreement* forms part of a larger trade agreement, and we therefore need to set the stage by first identifying the role of the

SCM Agreement in this larger agreement, as seen from an economic perspective.[3]

Following the bulk of the formal literature on trade agreements, we will view governments as interacting strategically with trading partners, and the gains from a trade agreement stem from its influence on the outcome of this interaction.[4] Governments may possibly seek to maximize national social welfare, but much more plausibly they put more weight on the well-being of certain groups, such as import-competing industry, than on, say, consumer welfare. We therefore need to understand the role of an *SCM Agreement* among such governments, and how it should be interpreted for the governments to achieve their objectives as far as possible. This approach differs from a more conventional, positive economic approach, which assumes that governments seek to maximize welfare, possibly constrained by "political realities," or a conventional normative approach that evaluates outcomes with a social welfare yardstick.[5]

The basic rationale for trade agreements from such a perspective is that when national governments make policy decisions, they typically do not put the same weight on foreign interests as on domestic interests. As

---

[3] Fuller discussions of the rationale of CVDs and the *SCM Agreement* can be found in Bagwell and Staiger (2002), Grossman and Mavroidis (2003), Janow and Staiger (2003), and Sykes (2003).

[4] An alternative view of trade agreements is that they affect the interaction between governments and their respective private sectors. For instance, in an industry a government might prefer a situation with a low tariff and wages low enough to maintain a high level of employment to one in which the tariff is higher. But should unemployment threaten, it may be willing to impose a higher tariff. Wage setters may in such a case see that by driving up wages, they can trigger protection, thus increasing the surplus for firms and workers in the industry to share. A restriction on the government's possibility of bailing out – perhaps implemented through a trade agreement – might then be to the benefit of the government, since it may induce wage setters to set lower wages, knowing that they will not be bailed out even if unemployment threatens. (A very similar mechanism provides a main motive for central bank independence in monetary policy.)

[5] Sykes (2003) thoroughly discusses the appropriate role of subsidies and CVDs in trade agreements in general, and in the WTO in particular, from the point of view of social welfare maximization. Such an approach tends to lead to more skeptical conclusions with regard to the value of CVDs in trade agreements (and export subsidies) than the approach employed here. But Sykes (2003) draws very similar conclusions concerning for instance the inadequacy of the *SCM Agreement* to deal with subsidies of the type alleged to exist in *US – Softwood Lumber*. In our view, neither approach is more correct than the other. Instead they reflect different "mandates" for the analyst, our "mandate" being narrower, accepting the outcome of the domestic political process as reflecting the country's preferences.

a result, these policies give rise to international externalities, and these spillovers on other country governments are often negative. For instance, a tariff may benefit an importing country government by improving that country's terms of trade. But the improvement of one country's terms of trade is a worsening of someone else's, and the combined effect is often to reduce the (loosely speaking) combined welfare of the governments; the measure thus constitutes a *beggar-thy-neighbor* policy. The importing country government does not have an incentive to give up its protectionist policy unilaterally. But if its producers face similar treatment in their export markets, it might benefit from a reciprocal reduction in tariffs. A trade agreement codifies such a concerted move.

At stake in *US – Softwood Lumber* is an alleged subsidy to the production of logs that stimulate exports, and such subsidies in general have more ambiguous impact than tariffs. For the importing country, there is a presumption that a subsidy is beneficial in the aggregate by reducing the price at which a country can import. However, the consequences of the subsidy are likely to be unevenly distributed in the importing country: buyers of the imported product benefit from the discount the subsidy provides, while import-competing producers (and possibly also providers of inputs to the industry) are likely to lose. The combined effect on the importing country, as perceived by the government, depends on the magnitude of these counteracting effects, and how the government weighs them. Under certain conditions, such as when the government seeks to maximize social welfare and the industry at hand is perfectly competitive, the net effect is positive. But, depending on its preferences, the government may also see the losses to the import-competing industry as dominating the gains to consumers.

For the exporting country, a subsidy is costly since it provides a discount on the price at which the trading partner purchases its imports. But certain groups in the exporting country are likely to gain, and the exporting country government may find that these gains dominate the cost to other groups, such as, for instance, taxpayers. It is therefore possible that the subsidy may simultaneously benefit the exporting country government, and harm the importing country government.

Production subsidies are generally legal under the *SCM Agreement*, but can under certain conditions be countervailed by importing countries. There is a strong presumption that subsidization benefits the importing country government when it has access to CVDs.[6] The importing country government can set CVDs so as to restore the price prevailing absent the subsidy, thereby leaving domestic consumers and producers unaffected by the subsidy. But in the process, it collects tariff revenue, and is therefore better off than without the subsidy. In other words, the CVD instrument ensures that importing countries can neutralize negative externalities from the subsidy. Importing countries may also prefer to offset just part of the subsidization, letting the rest pass through to domestic buyers. If the exporter continues to subsidize in such a situation, such a subsidy will presumably be beneficial to both the importing and the exporting country government.[7]

As can be seen, the CVD instrument has certain virtues. However, there are reasons to suspect that due to the way it is implemented through the *SCM Agreement*, the level of CVDs will not be optimal from the point of view of the Membership as a whole. The decision to implement the CVD rests with the importing country only. When this country decides whether to countervail, it will probably not take into consideration the positive effects of the subsidy for the exporting country government. If so, the importing country may expose the exporting country to a negative externality in its choice of CVD. This suggests a reason why the *SCM Agreement* allows for too large CVDs.[8]

---

[6] Recall that we disregard domestic strategic interaction of the type mentioned above. In its presence, the CVD instrument may weaken an importing country government, since it presents a new tool for protectionism that the government has difficulty withstanding.

[7] When there are several exporting countries, they may end up in a Prisoners' Dilemma-type situation where they all subsidize too much, and thus would prefer an agreement that prevents subsidization.

[8] Consider the following simplistic illustration of the inefficiency that might arise. Country A produces a certain gadget in a remote region. The government (and people in general) in A puts great value on maintaining the traditional way of life in this region, which is based on the production of this gadget. The whole produce of gadgets is exported to country B, which also maintains a small local production thereof. This small industry also suffers economic problems. However, there is no special value attached to gadget production in B, and it would be easy for gadget producers and employees to find alternative sources of income. If country A were now to subsidize its production to help maintain this traditional lifestyle (subsidizing incomes would for some reason not be as effective), country B could offset this subsidy to the full extent of the benefit it yields to country A producers. This would clearly not be an efficient outcome for the two countries combined. For instance, it might well be the case that country A would be willing to fully compensate B for the minor harm it suffers from the subsidy, if it could be maintained. Again, we should recall the assumed absence of domestic strategic interaction. With such interaction the exporting country government may be better off, being better able to withstand domestic pressure for subsidies the government would prefer not to implement.

A second reason why the CVDs permitted by the *SCM Agreement* may be of inappropriate magnitude is the fact that they are to be calculated on the basis of the benefit to the exporter. As argued, the purpose of the *WTO Agreement* in general, and also the *SCM Agreement*, should reasonably be seen as to prevent harm to trading partner interests from nationally pursued policies. It seems highly unlikely that this will be achieved when the magnitude of the CVD is calculated solely on the basis of the benefit to the exporters.[9]

We now turn to the Panel's findings with regard to the claims by Canada concerning the USDOC's Preliminary CVD Determination. The first is the question of whether Canadian provincial governments can be said to be providing goods. If not, they could not from an economic point of view (nor legally) be subsidizing lumber production.

3   Do Canadian provincial governments "provide goods"?

According to Art. 1.1 *SCM Agreement* a subsidy to a good is deemed to exist if

> there is a financial contribution by a government or any public body . . . i.e., where:
>
> (i)   a government practice involves a direct transfer of funds . . .
> (ii) government revenue that is otherwise due is foregone or not collected . . .
> (iii) a government provides goods or services other than general infrastructure . . .
> (iv) a government makes payments to a funding mechanism . . .
>
> . . .
>
> and . . . a benefit is thereby conferred.

In its determination, the USDOC claimed that Canadian provincial governments had provided financial contributions in the sense of point (iii), that is, by providing goods rather than by making financial payments, which would occur in the situations exemplified in points (i), (ii) and (iv). A central issue therefore is whether the challenged measure involves provision of goods.

---

[9] The fact that Art. 19 *SCM Agreement* states that it is "desirable" that CVDs be not larger than what is adequate to remove the injury does not seem importantly to affect this conclusion.

Canada claimed that stumpage programs do not "provide goods" in the sense of the *SCM Agreement*, for several reasons. For instance, according to Canada, stumpage is not a "good" but a property right. And even if stumpage contracts are taken to provide standing timber, such timber is not a "good" since it cannot be traded (and thus lacks customs classification). It is not "provided" by the governments, since there is no positive action on the part of provincial governments, which only allows the harvesters to cut the timber.

The Panel refuted Canada's arguments, determining that stumpage programs provide standing timber, and that standing timber is indeed a "good," as argued by the US (7.16–7.18).

In our view, the Panel's determination makes good economic sense. The provincial governments initially own the standing timber. But by entering into a contract with such a government and fulfilling the associated obligations, a private party obtains the right to enter the land, cut trees, and remove the logs from the land, and it also obtains ownership over the logs. The contract specifies the volume that can (and sometimes must) be cut. There are financial payments related to the volume taken out. The harvester is also required to undertake various costly measures, such as silviculture, building and maintenance of roads, etc, which presumably benefit the government. It is hard not to see these costs as a partial payment by the harvester for the timber it is taking out; if the harvester did *not* have the right to harvest, the firms would not have any reason to enter into these contracts. The total "price" paid for the timber is, of course, not only the volume-dependent fee, but also includes the various forestry management measures stipulated in the contract. In economic jargon, the price is thus highly "non-linear," since the total payment is not proportional to the purchased volume.

Several comments are in order:

First, the conclusion that the costs borne by the harvester are to be seen as the price paid in order to transfer the ownership of the timber to the harvester, is unaffected by the fact that provincial governments may at least partly have other interests than raising revenue when designing these contracts, such as environmental concerns. Normally, the motives why a private entrepreneur provides a product do not have to be taken into account; whether it is to make a financial profit, to become famous, for enjoyment, or whatever, the entrepreneur is nevertheless providing the product. Similarly, governments' objectives are immaterial to the question of whether they are supplying standing timber, at least from an economic point of view.

Second, and contrary to what was argued by Canada, it is also immaterial whether the timber is "delivered" standing; a physical item is nevertheless transferred from one owner to another.[10] The government could cut the timber and just leave it where it falls. The timber would then be physically mobile, like any other product. Naturally, this would not be of importance for the economic question of whether the product is supplied or not. More generally, the fact that the purchaser must undertake certain actions before the product can be used lacks significance from this point of view. Most goods have to be picked up at a different location than where they will be consumed, and actions such as unwrapping are necessary before they can be used. Nevertheless, the products are supplied to the buyers.

Third, Nordhaus (2001) argues that timber-harvesting rights are essentially options and that stumpage charges are payments for exercising these options, and thus cannot be seen as "prices." It might indeed be useful to view these arrangements as options. This suggests that the whole agreement, and not just the variable charges, must be considered, and also that the extent to which the harvesters will use the option may be uncertain at the contracting date. But the fact that the contract allows the harvester to decide unilaterally at a later date whether to cut a specified amount of timber and then pay a certain fee per unit does not change the basic fact that this "option contract" specifies the terms under which timber that initially belongs to the government is cut and removed by the harvesters. Clearly, an option contract can have more or less favorable terms for the buyer, and can implicitly subsidize the buyer or someone else downstream if the buyer is an intermediary, relative to some benchmark.[11]

Fourth, Nordhaus (2001) suggests yet another reason why the terms of stumpage should not be seen as the price paid for the supply of timber: these contracts give governments the right to unilaterally decide on the volume-dependent charges. Therefore, they are more accurately seen as taxes on the rents accruing to the harvesters from the

---

[10] The claim that standing trees are immobile (or non-tradable) can also be challenged on factual grounds, considering the fact that there are forestry machines that effectively "pick" trees, including the roots.

[11] To illustrate, a railway or bus company might offer its customers a contract whereby it pays a fixed fee in order to travel at a reduced rate during a month or a year. This can be seen as an option contract, since at the time when it pays the fixed charge, the travelers do not know how much they will travel. But the company must still be said to be providing a product (a travel service) whenever the traveler uses the bus or train.

standing timber. However, these rents would not accrue to the harvester unless the ownership of the timber was transferred to the harvester, and stumpage fees are part of the terms of these transfers. They are therefore effectively part of the price the harvester pays for the timber. It might be argued that harvesters are uncertain about the level of these charges. This uncertainty may (depending on the way it affects the stumpage fees) weaken the impact of the stumpage fees on the incentives of tenure holders to log. But even if the total logged volume were perceived to have no impact on the total payment of stumpage fees, these fees would still be considered as part of the total cost of harvesting, even if uncertain at the contracting date.

Fifth, another special aspect of stumpage contracts is that they are often very long term. But, again, this does not fundamentally change the fact that these are the conditions under which the ownership of standing timber changes hands, and that the terms of these contracts may affect the incentives for logging. Also, and related to the previous observation, the long-term nature of these contracts should limit any uncertainty about the stumpage fees.

To conclude, the Panel's determination as well as its reasoning seem sensible from an economic point of view. From such a perspective, Canadian provincial governments must be said to supply timber, and stumpage contracts (including stumpage fees and other contractual obligations) specify the terms for the transfer of ownership of this timber. Consequently, the question of whether the terms of stumpage are such as to subsidize lumber production becomes meaningful.

4   Is "a benefit thereby conferred"?

For there to be a subsidy, Art. 1 *SCM Agreement* not only requires that there be a "financial contribution by a government" (which arises when a government provides a good), but also that "a benefit is thereby conferred." The USDOC claimed to have established that this was the case. But Canada argued that the USDOC employed an illegal, and economically inappropriate, no-subsidy benchmark when finding and measuring such a benefit.

In order to examine these issues, and the Panel's reaction to them, it is necessary to first determine how stumpage programs might benefit lumber producers and, in particular, stimulate an increased production of lumber.

4.1 How could stumpage programs benefit lumber producers?

Basic economic theory suggests that for stumpage programs to benefit lumber production (relative to some benchmark), they must reduce the marginal costs of production for lumber producers. This, in turn, requires that stumpage programs reduce the price of logs.[12] The most likely way for this to come about would be for stumpage programs to stimulate larger volumes of logging. Differently put, for there to be subsidization of lumber production, it must be the case that *absent the alleged subsidization, there would be less logging.*

There are two basic mechanisms through which governments may increase logging through the design of stumpage programs. The first is to encourage *more intensive logging per acre* under a stumpage contract. For stumpage programs to have this effect, they must reduce the marginal harvesting costs – among them the stumpage fees – relative to the benchmark situation. A subsidy reducing these costs would induce harvesters to cut trees that would otherwise be unprofitable to harvest. It should be noted that this consequence of a lower marginal cost is likely to show up for market structures among harvesting firms ranging from a monopoly to perfect competition.

The second mechanism through which stumpage contracts may tend to induce more production of logs is by *increasing the total acreage* used for stumpage. It is clear that the demand for stumpage contracts will be higher, the lower the variable costs in the contract. The demand will also be higher, the lower the fixed costs the contracts impose on harvesters in the form of obligations to construct and maintain roads, silviculture, etc. For this increased demand to result in increased logging, however, governments must be willing to respond by using more of their land for stumpage. If the governments supply a constant amount of land for harvesting, regardless of the terms of the stumpage, there will be no impact on the amount of logging working through the entry and exit of harvesters, and consequently there will be no benefit conferred to lumber producers from the subsidy to harvesters through this mechanism (any effects working through changes in the intensity of logging may still be at work, however).[13]

---

[12] The argument here does not critically hinge on whether harvesters are vertically integrated with lumber producers.

[13] A conventional demand and supply representation is only used for the sake of expositional simplicity, since provincial governments have significant market power, and

It can thus be concluded that the validity of the US claim concerning subsidization, when considered from an economic angle, critically hinges on the claim that *the design and supply of stumpage contracts are such as to increase logging* and thereby subsidize lumber production, relative to an appropriate benchmark. A critical issue is therefore the definition of this no-subsidy benchmark.

It can also be seen that when comparing two different contract types, it is not a trivial matter to determine whether one induces more production than the other. For instance, a contract with a lower variable fee, which through this mechanism would tend to induce more output per contract, may also be associated with higher fixed costs. The latter would reduce the general profitability of logging, and thus tend to reduce output. The combined consequence of these effects may result in less logging, despite the lower stumpage fee. On the other hand, it is possible that a contract that essentially transforms marginal costs to fixed costs will induce more production, even if the total cost per stumpage contract increases. It should be emphasized that these issues cannot simply be disregarded as details, but are central to the issue at stake in this dispute.

4.2   What should be the no-subsidy benchmark?

The concept of a "subsidy" implicitly or explicitly relies on a comparison between two situations, one in which the subsidy exists (which is normally the actual situation) and one in which it does not. The answer to the question of what should be the no-subsidy benchmark may seem obvious: use a situation in which the contested measure is revoked. However, this is not a well-defined benchmark, since there are innumerable situations without the subsidy with which to make the comparison. But why then not choose the situation without the subsidy, *ceteris paribus*? There are at least two reasons why this definition of the no-subsidy benchmark is also problematic.

The first, and normally less significant, problem is that all else *cannot* be constant even if the importing government wanted to keep it so.[14] The second reason why the *ceteris paribus* assumption is problematic is the fact

their behavior is therefore not readily illustrated with supply schedules (which assume price-taking behavior).

[14] To see why, consider the simplest possible case in which a government provides a monetary transfer per unit of output produced. Suppose the no-subsidy benchmark is taken to be a situation where there is no subsidy transfer scheme, all else being constant. However, it is normally not possible to change only the subsidy scheme and leave

that the government may not want to keep all else constant as the subsidy is removed, but may resort to *other measures* with a similar effect. Consider the following highly stylized illustration. A government has two instruments, an actionable specific subsidy of s and a non-actionable lawful instrument with effects equivalent to a smaller specific subsidy r. The government's preferred rate of subsidization is equal to s. Its first choice would therefore be to use the actionable subsidy, but when unable to do so, it uses the other instrument, and provides a subsidy equal to r. Now let the CVD equal the difference in price with and without the subsidy. How large will it be? If the no-subsidy benchmark were taken to be the situation where neither of the instruments is used, then the CVD would equal s, this being the difference in price between the two situations. But if instead the no-subsidy benchmark is meant to capture *the situation as it would be absent the actionable subsidy*, the difference in price would be $s - r$, which is potentially a much smaller number than s. Differently put, the *effect* of the actionable subsidy is not to change the subsidy with the amount s but with $s - r$.

The suggested benchmark "revoke measure, *ceteris paribus*" is hence associated with conceptual problems due to the *ceteris paribus* part. These problems may or may not be quantitatively important depending on the exact circumstances. But what appears to make this benchmark unsuitable in the case of *US – Softwood Lumber* is the fact that it would not be very interesting to employ a situation where the stumpage programs are simply abandoned as a benchmark. The governments own the standing timber, and in any relevant benchmark, there must be a supply of government timber to private harvesters, and this must be regulated through some form of contract that allows for the pursuit of legitimate forestry management policies. A fundamental difficulty in a case like *US – Softwood Lumber* is thus to identify the alternative no-subsidy type of contract.

---

everything else the same. For instance, without the subsidization and with all other measures unchanged, the government's accounts would not add up, since there would now be a surplus due to the unspent revenue. Consequently, some form of adjustment must take place. For instance, less revenue may be collected, the government may borrow less, or, if there is a government budget surplus, it might lend more or spend more on other goods, etc. The point is not to argue that these induced changes are likely to be quantitatively important in practice, but to illustrate the fact that the definition of the no-subsidy benchmark is conceptually unclear even in the simplest of settings.

4.2.1   A conceptually desirable, but impracticable, no-subsidy benchmark

At a general level, the conceptual problems with the suggested "revoke, *ceteris paribus*" definition of the no-subsidy benchmark stem from the fact that it is not derived from the purpose of the *SCM Agreement*, or the *WTO Agreement* more generally. As discussed above, economic theory suggests that a main purpose is to prevent Members from pursuing policies with negative externalities on trading partners, to the extent that these negative effects are larger in magnitude than the positive effects on the countries pursuing these policies. Following the approach of Bagwell and Staiger (2002), one could naturally define the no-subsidy benchmark as *a situation in which Canadian provincial governments when deciding the stumpage terms do not take into consideration the consequences for the terms of trade vis-à-vis the US, or for the market access of Canadian lumber exporters.* The question would thus be whether the provincial governments would induce a smaller supply of logs if terms-of-trade and/or market access considerations were not taken into account? If so, there would be an actionable subsidy, since they would then be exposing US producers to negative externalities for beggar-thy-neighbor purposes.

A main virtue of this definition is hence that it is intimately related to the assumed purpose of the agreement, in that it neither directs Members to choose particular policies, nor to maximize some notion of global welfare, but to refrain from behaving in a beggar-thy-neighbor fashion. Another advantage is that it does not focus on just one component of a complex contract – the stumpage fees – but takes into account the combined effect of the whole contract, and it would also include the induced changes in the supply of stumpage contracts.[15]

---

[15] It can be noted that this notion of a subsidy does not require a positive financial payment by the government to harvesters, since a regime with positive stumpage fees may also involve subsidization. In contrast, Nordhaus (2001, p. 44) argues that under "market principles," the stumpage fee would be zero, and that a zero stumpage fee is also a feature of an efficient regulation of the industry. The virtue of a zero fee is that it does not distort the amount of logging. A positive stumpage fee would thus provide a disincentive for logging relative to the "market principles" solution, or the efficient solution, and can therefore not be part of a subsidization of lumber production. This is thus a statement concerning the properties of the benchmark situation. However, for this discussion Nordhaus (2001) "... ignore[s] market failures, public goods, and the interaction of timber management with the other forest-use objectives," aspects that elsewhere in the Nordhaus (2001) report are seen as essential characteristics of the forest industry, and which presumably would make non-zero stumpage fees socially optimal.

Unfortunately, there are also certain drawbacks to this subsidy definition. First, it may include measures one would not want to denote as subsidies, even though they might have basically identical effects. For instance, a tax on other uses of logs than for lumber production has basically the same impact as a subsidy to lumber production, since it would reduce the price of logs for lumber producers. If this tax is set higher than it would be if the government disregarded the impact on lumber exports, then one would, according to the definition above, conclude that there is a subsidy. This subsidy would still be administered by the government, but it would come directly from the other users of logs, rather than from the subjects on which the tax would be normally levied. One may therefore want to further restrict the definition of a subsidy.[16]

The major drawback of this definition is, however, that it is likely to be very hard to employ in practice. For instance, it probably requires knowledge of the government's objective functions. The informational problem is exacerbated in *US – Softwood Lumber* by the fact that the contracts under consideration do not simply specify a single price, but establish a range of undertakings for the harvester. The no-subsidy benchmark situation is thus much harder to identify in the present case. We are thus led to conclude that a conceptually satisfactory subsidy definition is likely to be very difficult to implement in practice.

4.3   The solution in the SCM Agreement: a private sector benchmark

The *SCM Agreement* points to a very different no-subsidy benchmark; Art. 14 (d) *SCM Agreement* requires a benefit calculation to be made.

> . . . in relation to *prevailing market conditions* for the good or service in question *in the country of provision* . . .
>
> (emphasis added)

The idea behind this "private investor test" is hence that since the terms of the benchmark contract are strictly commercial, they will not be influenced by any incentive to subsidize.

A main issue in *US – Softwood Lumber* was the interpretation of this phrase. The US argued that while private sector contracts in the allegedly subsidizing country should ideally be used, this was not possible in the

---

[16] This is done in Art. 1.1 *SCM Agreement* through the requirement that there should not only be a benefit but also a financial contribution.

present case, since the Canadian private sector stumpage market was too distorted by the government subsidies to serve as a reasonable non-subsidy benchmark. Therefore, the USDOC compared stumpage fees, adjusted for various differences in costs, with private market prices in mainly neighboring US states.

Canada, for its part, maintained that there was no legal basis for the argument that distortions of the domestic private sector prices invalidated their use as a benchmark. Canada also claimed that there is no support in the *SCM Agreement* for the US method of cross-border comparisons. In addition, Canada argued that there were private sector stumpage contracts that the USDOC could have used for its comparison.

The US countered that its methodology was nevertheless consistent with the object and purpose of Art. 14 *SCM Agreement*. The US also pointed to the fact that the provision states "... *in relation to* prevailing market conditions in the country under investigation...," and does not merely refer to the market conditions in this country.

The Panel basically agreed with Canada, emphasizing that the term "prevailing market conditions" in Art. 14(d) *SCM Agreement* strongly suggests that the benchmark should be the *existing* private market. In particular, the relevant benchmark should not be a hypothetical undistorted market identified through a "but for" test. Instead, the Panel held that

> ... the text of Article 14 SCM Agreement leaves no choice to the investigating authority but to use as a benchmark the market ... *as it exists* in the country of provision ...
>
> (7.44, emphasis in original)

The Panel acknowledged that US prices could still be used if they could be said to be part of the prevailing market conditions *in Canada*. The Panel refuted this interpretation, however, stating that the US argument would imply that world market prices are part of the market conditions in the exporting country, an interpretation for which it found no support in the *SCM Agreement*. Such an interpretation would also effectively read out of the text the explicit reference to "the country of provision." The Panel also stated that

> ...[w]e note that the prices of *imported* goods in the market of provision can indeed form part of the prevailing market conditions ... But this is not the same as the price for those goods prevailing in the country of export....
>
> (7.48, emphasis in original)

Two alternative private sector benchmarks are thus suggested in this dispute. They are both beset with serious conceptual problems, however.

A first potential problem, common to both suggested benchmarks, is that private parties selling standing timber not only lack the incentive to subsidize that governments may have, but they are also likely *not to share the other objectives of governments.* For instance, in the case of *US – Softwood Lumber,* provincial governments may legitimately care more about other uses of the forests than would private owners. Indeed, this might at least partly explain why the forests are publicly owned. When comparing with private sector stumpage, it is therefore important to take into consideration the extent to which differences in contract terms reflect the generally different roles of governments and private parties, rather than differences in the desire to subsidize lumber production.

But there are also other problems with the suggested benchmarks, as seen from an economic perspective.

4.3.1   Problems with a domestic private sector benchmark

Insisting that the benchmark is the private market "as it exists," the Panel rejected the use of a "but for" test:

> ... We are thus of the view that Article 14 (d) SCM Agreement does not require that the authority constructs a market price that could have existed but for the government's involvement, nor does it allow the authority to decline to use in-country prices because they may be affected by the government's financial contribution.
>
> (7.51)

As discussed above, it is hard to see how the calculation of the benchmark can be made in a conceptually adequate fashion in any other way. The fact that such a test is likely to be very difficult to perform in practice is not a reason completely to reject its use, but rather to be cautious about the quality of any such test. Indeed, when claiming that the US had not demonstrated that prices of private stumpage contracts were distorted but only assumed this to be the case, Canada actually seemed to be arguing in favor of such a test: Canada was essentially requesting the US to calculate what Canadian private sector prices would be "but for" the intention to subsidize Canadian lumber producers.

The US argument against using existing Canadian stumpage contracts as a benchmark is correct from an economist's viewpoint, in that, if there is a subsidy, it *might* seriously distort the private sector benchmark. Whenever government stumpage contracts are designed so as to increase the supply of logs, the value of private stumpage is likely to be affected. In particular, the more government stumpage schemes increase harvesting, the lower will be the price of logs. The relationship between the price of logs and the price of private stumpage is not entirely clear, since this partly depends on how government stumpage contracts are allocated. But there is a presumption that the stronger the price-depressing effect of the subsidy for logs, the lower should be the willingness to pay for private stumpage, and the less informative should be private sector prices. Hence, the more pronounced the subsidization, the less useful are private sector contracts in demonstrating subsidization that harms US lumber producers.[17]

It should be stressed, however, that while the US argument is correct as a matter of principle, in the sense that private sector contracts *may* be affected by the terms of government stumpage programs, the USDOC did not show that Canadian prices *actually were* distorted. It is not clear however, how such a demonstration could be made.

To summarize, there are at least two serious problems with the domestic private sector benchmark. First, WTO Members have not promised each other to let their policies mimic private sector outcomes, but not to behave in a protectionist fashion. It is not self-evident that a private market would yield the same outcome as a government pursuing forestry policy in a non-protectionist manner. Hence, the benchmark against which to compare actual behavior should not be taken from the private sector, but should be what a government without protectionist motives would do. Second, the private sector benchmark would also be likely to be inadequate to measure subsidization for the reason advanced by the US.

Finally, although this may be a misunderstanding on our part, it seems as if the Panel had some sympathy for the US argument, but felt constrained by the *SCM Agreement* to reject it:

> [w]e wish to note that even if in certain exceptional circumstances it may prove difficult in practice to apply Article 14 (d) SCM Agreement, that would not justify reading words into the text of the Agreement that are not there or ignoring the plain meaning of the text. In our view, the text of

---

[17] It can also be noted that the outcome of a comparison with private sector contracts depends on the market structure in this industry. This implies that the outcome of the calculation of the subsidy that is to be countervailed will depend on the market structure of the Canadian private market for stumpage. This might not be a significant problem in the present case, but it does point to an additional conceptual problem with the private domestic (or foreign) market benchmark.

Article 14 SCM Agreement leaves no choice to the investigating authority but to use as a benchmark the market... *as it exists* in the country of provision.

(7.53, emphasis in original)

4.3.2 Problems with a foreign private sector benchmark

The US argument in favor of using US prices (which are said to equal world prices) seems based on the notion that differences in the price of stumpage across countries reflect differences in the degree of illegal subsidization, and that, in a world "undistorted" by government actions, the price of stumpage should generally be the same in Canada and the US. The strongest economic basis for this notion is probably the well-known "Factor Price Equalization Theorem." Very loosely, the Theorem establishes conditions under which goods trade alone suffices to equalize factor prices across countries, despite differences in countries' endowments of such factors. If in such a world factor prices nevertheless differ, for instance, standing timber being cheaper in one country than in another, a possible explanation might be a government subsidy.

This Theorem does not provide a strong foundation to build a case in favor of using foreign private sector prices, however, since it rests on far too restrictive assumptions. Indeed, in empirical tests, it normally does not perform well. For instance, it assumes perfect competition, constant returns to scale, and identical production technologies across countries. It would be violated if, in comparison to the US, Canada were sufficiently better endowed with standing timber relative to other factors. But since it is not clear what "sufficiently better" quantitatively means, it would be very hard to determine whether differences in stumpage prices between the US and Canada are due to differences in the relative endowments of factors of production, or to government policy.

The predictions of the Factor Price Equalization Theorem may be further obscured if governments in Canada and the US pursue different policies, since this will, of course, have implications for prices in the two countries, even if all these measures are "non-protectionist." In particular, if Canadian stumpage fees are lower than those in the US, this may reflect the fact that the fixed cost obligations in stumpage contracts are more onerous in Canada than in the US, due to different policy preferences. But differences in government policies in other areas and other industries are also likely to affect prices. For instance, if capital costs are higher in

Canada due to differences in macroeconomic policies, this will naturally affect other prices in the economy.

Yet another reason why one should not expect input prices to be equal among trading partners is the existence of trade costs, widely interpreted. There are obviously costs associated with physical transportation. However, recent empirical literature has highlighted the fact that physical distance (which should be a good proxy for physical transportation costs) is not the only barrier to international trade. National borders seem to have an important impact beyond what can be explained by distance. That is, comparing trade between two locations, A and B, in the US with trade between A and a location C in Canada, where the distance between A and B is the same as between A and C, one will typically find substantially less trade between A and C. The interpretation is that national borders are associated with trading costs beyond physical transportation, resulting, for instance, from differences in legal systems, cultural differences, the red tape involved in international trade, etc.[18] These findings suggest that when Canadian lumber producers export to the US market, they are likely to receive lower producer prices, not only because of the often (but not always) higher costs of physical transportation, but also because of these border effects. These effects will thus contribute, perhaps importantly, to a lower reward in the exporting country for the factors going into lumber production, such as logs and thereby stumpage. This is yet another reason why international price comparisons are fraught with practical problems.

It follows from the above that in case the standing timber in Canada is sold through stumpage at lower prices than in the US, this need not signal any form of subsidization, but could simply reflect various underlying differences in the economic structure of these countries.[19] Naturally, this argument is weaker, the more similar the two countries are in terms of economic structure. But as long as there *are* differences, there is no

---

[18] See Leamer (2001) for a discussion of implications of this literature for the question of whether Canadian export restrictions on logs subsidize lumber production.

[19] Another way of looking at this issue is to observe that with private ownership of forests, the remuneration received by forest owners is essentially a *rent* – an income bestowed on them through their ownership of a fixed amount of timber, rather than in return for some productive activity. The magnitude of this rent will depend on the profit opportunities of firms in possession of standing timber. The higher the costs for cutting the timber, for transporting it to lumber producers, for producing lumber and for transporting the resulting lumber to the US market, etc, the lower the value of the forest. Only under very special circumstances would the rents be the same in the two countries.

presumption from an economic point of view that the lower price of government stumpage in Canada necessarily indicates the existence of subsidization. It must therefore be demonstrated that even when accounting for all the underlying differences between countries, there remain differences in price that can only be due to subsidization. Such a demonstration seems almost impossible to perform in practice.

It can be noted that the problems with international price comparisons pointed out here already arise with vertically integrated firms. When harvesters and lumber producers are at arm's length, there are additional problems involved in international price comparisons. For instance, the linkage between the market for stumpage and the lumber market will now depend on the market structure for logs; we will return to this issue in the next section.

Finally, an argument advanced by the US in favor of the practice of using US prices as benchmarks was that many Canadian companies import US logs despite the stumpage program. According to the US, this shows that the US market is part of the market available in Canada. However, it rather seems to suggest that Canadian stumpage prices are *not* very attractive from the point of view of Canadian buyers of logs or, alternatively, that the supply of logs is insufficient to meet demand, given the terms of stumpage. If anything, this observation seem to suggest the absence of a subsidy.

To conclude, the conceptually desirable benchmark identified above is hard to implement in practice. The domestic private sector benchmark is associated with serious conceptual problems from an economic point of view, suggesting a weakness in either the text of the *SCM Agreement* or possibly the Panel's interpretation thereof. And foreign sector benchmarks are virtually non-informative. Only under highly special circumstances would one expect input prices to be the same among trading partners, even absent "protectionist" policies. The Panel was thus right not to accept the US methodology in this respect.

4.3.3   Does the degree of vertical integration matter for the benefit conferred on Canadian lumber producers?

The Panel report discussed the pass-through from harvesters to Canadian lumber producers, in particular the importance of the degree of vertical integration for such pass-through. The US had argued that no pass-through analysis was necessary, partly because Canadian harvesters and lumber producers were not at arm's length, since most lumber producers also harvest timber. Indeed, according to the US,

...the laws and regulations of each Canadian province (with the partial exception of Ontario) generally require that tenure holders be sawmills.

(p. A-13, para. 1)

Canada, on the other hand, maintained that a significant proportion of harvesting is done by firms at arm's-length relationships to lumber producers. For instance, more than 30 percent of the timber harvested on Crown land in British Columbia is said to be harvested by entities not owning sawmills. The essence of the arguments thus seemed to be that while the US claimed that the vast majority of Canadian lumber producers are vertically integrated with harvesters, Canada argued that a significant proportion of logging is still done by independent harvesters. The general impression we derive from this exchange is that while some stumpage contracts are open to larger foreign firms, a variety of provisions hinder this in other contracts. But determining the prevalence of such hindrances is hard, since here "the devil is in the details" to a very high degree.

The Panel viewed the main issue before it to be whether the USDOC conducted a pass-through analysis in those cases where this was legally required. In the opinion of the Panel (and also the parties), the extent of analysis required depended on the vertical relationships in the industry. In cases of vertically integrated operations, such an analysis was not necessary, according to the Panel:

> ...It is clear that in such circumstances of complete identity between the tenure holder/logger and the lumber producer, no pass-through analysis is required....

(7.72)

On the other hand,

> ...in such cases, where a downstream producer of subject merchandise is unrelated to the alleged subsidized upstream producer of the input, an authority is not allowed to simply assume that a benefit has passed through....

(7.74)

Hence, in cases of arm's-length vertical relationships,

> ...the investigating authority should examine whether and to what extent the subsidies bestowed on the upstream producers benefited the downstream producers....

(7.71)

The Panel pointed to the fact that the records before the USDOC at the time of its determination showed that *some* Canadian lumber producers had an arm's-length relationship with harvesters, and that the USDOC did not investigate whether these lumber producers benefited from the stumpage programs in these cases. The Panel thus concluded that the US acted inconsistently with the *SCM Agreement* in these cases. The Panel also found that the US should have performed pass-through analysis in cases where sawmills bought logs from unrelated sawmills, and where remanufacturers purchased lumber from unrelated sawmills.

As can be seen, the Panel drew a sharp distinction between cases of arm's-length relationships and vertical integration. The importance of this distinction is not obvious, however. As argued by the Panel, in the case of vertical integration it is indeed likely that a subsidy inducing more harvesting of logs also increases Canadian lumber production. But the presumption that similar effects would arise also with arm's-length relationships is almost as strong: the increase in the supply of logs is highly likely to depress the price of logs, which will stimulate lumber production. If a pass-though analysis is deemed unnecessary in the case of vertically integrated firms, it should not be necessary with arm's-length relationships either. Hence, whether the industry is vertically integrated or at arm's length seems largely immaterial to the question of whether Canadian lumber production benefits from the measure.

5   Do benefits to Canadian lumber producers cause injury to US competitors?

The discussion in this dispute concerning pass-through largely focused on the issue dealt with above – whether or not the Canadian lumber industry benefited from the subsidy. However, to the extent that the purpose of the WTO Agreement is to help countries get out of a Prisoners' Dilemma-like situation, the US should not be allowed to countervail unless there is injury to the US lumber industry.[20] The Panel did not have to address the issue of injury, finding that the USDOC had not shown the existence of a subsidy.

To see why the existence of injury is not a foregone conclusion, consider the impact on US lumber producers of increased Canadian log

[20] The method advocated by the Panel, whereby the subsidy is calculated as the ratio between the total subsidy payments and total sales, is conceptually flawed from this point of view, since it does not measure the harm to US producers.

harvesting. Assume first that Canadian logs are *not internationally tradable* to any significant degree.[21] Lumber producers located in Canada must then absorb the increased supply of logs, and these should mainly be Canadian firms. Hence, this would be a case in which a Canadian upstream subsidy would benefit Canadian lumber producers at the expense of their US competitors, which is the situation the US has claimed is the situation in this dispute. Note, however, that the negative effect on US producers of the subsidy is likely to arise regardless of whether harvesters and lumber producers are vertically integrated.[22]

Now turn to the case in which logs are fully tradable internationally. If the harvesters are at arm's length from lumber producers, any price-depressing effect of Canadian logs will spill over and depress the prices of US logs as well. Therefore, to the extent that there is a pass-through of a subsidy to Canadian lumber producers, it *benefits US producers to the same extent*. Hence, in the case of arm's length relationships, the extent to which logs are tradable is of crucial importance for the impact of an increased supply of logs. This confirms the Panel's view that a pass-through analysis is necessary in this case.

The impact of the increased supply of logs is less clear in the case where Canadian logs are not tradable internationally, but where the Canadian industry is vertically integrated. Suppose for simplicity that all Canadian harvesters are integrated with Canadian lumber producers. These firms can by assumption either use the logs for their own lumber production or sell logs to US firms. What will they prefer to do? This question of whether *foreclosure* is feasible and profitable for Canadian harvesters-cum-lumber producers does not seem to have attracted sufficient interest in the dispute.

A simple example can illustrate the basic incentive for foreclosure. Suppose two firms, one Canadian and one American, compete in the

---

[21] It is immaterial to this example whether logs from other countries are tradable.

[22] This should be the case regardless of whether the harvester uses a standard constant price contract (a "linear" price), where the payment to a log producer is strictly proportional to the volume that is bought, or a non-linear contract. For instance, a simple form of the latter would be one with a fixed franchise fee, and a linear component. In this latter case, the market would function exactly as if firms were vertically integrated. The linear component would be set equal to the marginal costs of harvesting. If the latter were reduced through a subsidy, the input price of logs for lumber producers would fall. Similarly, if the price of logs were determined through bargaining between the harvester and the lumber producer, a reduction in the marginal costs of producing logs should increase the output of lumber.

market for lumber. The Canadian firm owns the supply of a type of logs particularly suited for the production of this type of lumber. Would it be in the interest of the Canadian firm to sell such logs to its US competitor? There is a basic reason why it might not want to do this: by providing the US firm with some but not all of this input, the Canadian firm increases the competitiveness of the US firm. The firms will become more alike in terms of costs, and the increased competition will tend to destroy industry profits. The best option may therefore be not to sell to the US firm, thus partly foreclosing it from the lumber market.[23] The force of this incentive depends on a number of things, including the type of contracts the two firms can sign, and the degree of overlap between the firms' markets.

The outcome in this example is consistent with the view that in the case of vertical integration, a subsidy to Canadian harvesting will harm US lumber producers; this is here "shown" to hold, even taking into account the possibility for the Canadian firm of selling logs to its US counterpart. But the case rests on very special assumptions. Suppose, for instance, that the US lumber producer has access to better marketing channels, so that logs are more valuable when processed by this firm. There will now be an incentive to sell the logs to the US firm. But if the US firm can indeed purchase logs, it will benefit rather than lose from a subsidy to Canadian harvesting. The story will also be more complicated once additional Canadian and US firms are introduced into the picture.

The conclusion is thus that an economically satisfactory injury analysis would be a rather daunting exercise in this case. It would need to take into account the interaction between the contested measures and other government measures, such as export restriction on logs. In particular, a pass-through analysis should be required both in the case of vertical integration and of arm's-length relationships in order to establish a link between the subsidization and the injury to import-competing firms.

6   Concluding discussion

The main conclusions from the discussion above are the following:

1. Canadian provincial governments supply timber, and stumpage contracts specify the "prices" at which these goods are traded. These

---

[23] The possibility that the Canadian lumber producer would leave it to the US firm to monopolize the market is disregarded, since this would probably not be in the Canadian firm's longer-run interest.

"prices" include not only stumpage fees but also the other obligations stipulated by the contracts.

2. For stumpage programs to subsidize lumber production, they must increase the total volume of logging relative to a no-subsidy benchmark situation. There are two basic ways in which this may occur: more intensive logging per acre and increased harvested acreage. The focus in the dispute is on whether the design of the existing stumpage programs is such as to reduce the price of logs. But the question of whether the stumpage programs are part of a policy to increase or reduce the acreage being harvested seems not to have been addressed.

3. A no-subsidy benchmark cannot be identified in *US – Softwood Lumber* by simply revoking government measures, since the no-subsidy benchmark must still sensibly involve private harvesting of government land (and such an approach would in any event involve conceptual problems).

4. Economic theory would suggest that the basic undertaking of WTO Members is to avoid behaving in a beggar-thy-neighbor fashion. The no-subsidy benchmark should therefore be defined as the situation in which the design and supply of stumpage contracts are chosen by provincial governments, taking into account legitimate policy objectives, but without any protectionist motives. But this conceptually attractive benchmark would be very hard to identify in practice, even if the contested contracts only specified stumpage fees. For instance, it would require a determination of what are those legitimate policy concerns. The complexity of stumpage programs adds to these conceptual problems and makes the evaluation of the degree of subsidization exceedingly difficult.

5. The private sector no-subsidy benchmark imposed by the *SCM Agreement* is conceptually problematic; first, since it does not take into consideration whether differences between the private sector benchmark and actual government policy reflect the pursuit of *legitimate government policies*. Second, the interpretation of the private sector benchmark as referring to prices *in existence in the importing country* disregards the possibility that the benchmark may be significantly affected by any subsidization. Third, the solution to use *foreign market prices* as benchmarks is also fraught with problems. There are a number of reasons other than beggar-thy-neighbor behavior why foreign prices may differ from those in the allegedly subsidizing country.

6. It is not a foregone conclusion that subsidization of Canadian lumber production causes injury to US lumber production, even though this may seem likely to be the case. Other government measures in the context of the timber and lumber industry, such as export restrictions on Canadian logs, may interact in important ways with the terms of stumpage.
7. The Panel's determination that the USDOC did not convincingly demonstrate that stumpage contracts subsidize harvesters, or that all Canadian lumber producers hit by the preliminary measures were subsidized, seems correct from an economic perspective.

Finally, it does not seem implausible that Canadian provincial governments supply *more* standing timber than they would if they disregarded, for instance, regional employment effects in the domestic lumber industry. It does not seem implausible that they supply *less* standing timber than would private owners of these forests (regulation permitting) either. This case illustrates some of the conceptual difficulties in defining what a subsidy is.

References

Bagwell, Kyle and Robert W. Staiger. 2002. *The Economics of the World Trading System.* Cambridge, MA: MIT Press.

Grossman, Gene M. and Petros C. Mavroidis. 2003. United States – Imposition of Countervailing Duties on Certain Hot-Rolled Lead and Bismuth Carbon Steel Products Originating in the United Kingdom (WTO Doc. WT/DS138/AB/R): Here Today, Gone Tomorrow? In Henrik Horn and Petros C. Mavroidis, *Principles of World Trade Law: The World Trade Organization. The Case Law of 2001.* Cambridge: The American Law Institute and Cambridge University Press.

Janow, Merit and Robert W. Staiger. 2003. United States – The Treatment of Export Restraints as Subsidies Under the Subsidies Agreement of the WTO. In Henrik Horn and Petros C. Mavroidis, *Principles of World Trade Law: The World Trade Organization. The Case Law of 2001.* Cambridge: The American Law Institute and Cambridge University Press.

Leamer, Edward. 2001. Do Log Export Restrictions in British Columbia Confer A Competitive Advantage on its Softwood Lumber Producers? Submission prepared for the British Columbia Trade Council and the Province of British Columbia.

Nordhaus, William D. 2001. An Economic Analysis of Whether Long-Term Tenure Systems in British Columbian Provincial Forests Provide Countervailable Subsidies to Softwood Lumber Imported into the United States. July 20.

Submission prepared for the British Columbia Trade Council and the Province of British Columbia.

Sykes, Alan O. 2003. The Economics of WTO Rules on Subsidies and Countervailing Measures. John M. Olin Program in Law & Economics Working Papers, No. 186: University of Chicago.

12

European Communities – Trade Description of Sardines: Textualism and its Discontent*

BY

HENRIK HORN

Institute for International Economic Studies, Stockholm University
Centre for Economic Research Policy, London

AND

JOSEPH H. H. WEILER

Jean Monnet Center for International Economic Law & Justice
New York University School of Law

1 Introduction

The facts of *EC – Sardines* are simple enough. A European Communities (EC) regulation stipulated that the designation Sardines could be used on preserved fish only for the genus *Sardina pilchardus*. The broad rationale claimed for this measure was to prevent consumer confusion. Allegedly European consumers associated the appellation "Sardines" with the *pilchardus* genus. Subsequently the *Codex Alimentarius Commission* set an international standard which effectively would allow other types of fish e.g. the genus *Sardinops sagax*, to use the word Sardine as part of its packaging designation. Peru, which exports *Sardinops* to Europe could not, under the Community regulation, use the designation Sardines in any shape or manner even though this prohibition would be contrary to the international standard set by the Codex Commission. Obviously, this

---

* This study discusses the WTO Dispute Settlement dispute *European Communities – Trade Descriptions of Sardines* (WT/DS231/R, 29 May 2002 and WT/DS231/AB/R, 26 November 2002). We are grateful for helpful discussions with Gene Grossman and Petros C. Mavroidis and the other Reporters in the project, as well as for the many useful comments provided by participants in the ALI Invitational Conference in February 2004.

would have adverse effects on the marketability of Peruvian sardines. Peru challenged the Community regulation claiming it violated Art. 2.1, 2.2, and 2.4 of the *Agreement on Technical Barrier to Trade* (TBT) as well as Art. III.4 of the *General Agreement on Tariffs and Trade* (GATT). The Panel exercised judicial economy and decided the case entirely on the basis of Art. 2.4 TBT, which provides as follows:

> Where technical regulations are required and relevant international standards exist or their completion is imminent, Members shall use them, or the relevant parts of them, as a basis for their technical regulations except when such international standards or relevant parts would be an ineffective or inappropriate means for the fulfilment of the legitimate objectives pursued, for instance because of fundamental climatic or geographical factors or fundamental technological problems.

The Panel's general finding was that the EC measure was in fact inconsistent with that provision.

The Panel determination was appealed by the EC. In the language of the AB, the following issues were on appeal:

(a) whether the appeal is inadmissible as a result of the conditional withdrawal of the Notice of Appeal filed on 25 June 2002, and the filing of a new Notice of Appeal on 28 June 2002;

(b) whether the *amicus curiae* briefs submitted by the Kingdom of Morocco and a private individual are admissible, and, if so, whether they assist us in this appeal;

(c) whether the Panel erred by finding that Council Regulation (EEC) 2136/89 (the "EC Regulation") is a "technical regulation" within the meaning of Annex 1.1 of the *Agreement on Technical Barriers to Trade* (the "*TBT Agreement*");

(d) whether the Panel erred by finding that Art. 2.4 of the *TBT Agreement* applies to existing measures, such as the EC Regulation;

(e) whether the Panel erred by finding that CODEX STAN 94–1981, Rev.1–1995 ("Codex Stan 94") is a "relevant international standard" within the meaning of Art. 2.4 of the *TBT Agreement*;

(f) whether the Panel erred by finding that Codex Stan 94 was not used "as a basis for" the EC Regulation within the meaning of Art. 2.4 of the *TBT Agreement*; whether the Panel correctly interpreted and applied the second part of Art. 2.4 of the *TBT Agreement*, which allows Members not to use international standards "as a basis for" their technical regulations "when such international standards or relevant parts would be an ineffective or inappropriate means for the fulfilment of the legitimate objectives pursued";

(g) whether the Panel properly discharged its duty under Art. 11 of the *Understanding on Rules and Procedures Governing the Settlement of Disputes* (the "DSU") to make "an objective assessment of the facts of the case";

(h) whether the Panel has made a determination that the EC Regulation is trade-restrictive, and, if so, whether the Panel erred in making such a determination;

(i) and whether we should complete the analysis under Art. 2.2 of the *TBT Agreement*, Art. 2.1 of the *TBT Agreement*, or Art. III:4 of the *General Agreement on Tariffs and Trade 1994* (the "GATT 1994"), in the event that we find that the EC Regulation is consistent with Art. 2.4 of the *TBT Agreement*.

The Panel decision was in substance largely upheld by the AB with reversals of certain methodological points. The main point where the AB took a radically different position than the Panel concerned the distribution of the burden of proof.

In this analysis of the AB decision we do not intend to cover all the issues on appeal, nor take direct issue with any of the substantive outcomes – though we will raise serious doubts as regards some of them. We will instead concentrate on two main themes. The first is the method of interpretation exemplified in this decision with its rhetorical emphasis on "textual" interpretation. We say rhetorical since we believe that in its actual practice, even in this case in the very way Article 2.4 itself is construed, the AB does not always practice what it preaches and that many of its holdings which masquerade as textual are in fact driven by other hermeneutic bases. This textualist leaning of the adjudicating bodies will be discussed in the next Section.

The second main theme to be discussed is the question of how to allocate the burden of proof in the context of Art. 2.4 TBT disputes. The Panel claimed it was for the EC to establish that the international standard is inefficient and/or inappropriate to fulfill its legitimate regulatory objectives, but the AB instead put the burden on the complainant, Peru.

To our mind, both the textualist approach and the unsatisfactory analysis of the burden of proof issue, result from the unwillingness of the AB to analyze the more general role of the TBT. There is a focus on details, but there is no overarching vision of the agreement that guides the AB in its determinations concerning the details or at the least, no such vision is made explicit. As a consequence, there is a risk of a "tyranny of the incremental steps," whereby the cumulative effect of the often reasonable incremental decisions is to substantially restrict WTO Members' regulatory sovereignty without such an outcome ever being explicitly analyzed by the AB.

2 The AB's textualist approach to legal interpretation

The TBT (alongside the *Agreement on Sanitary and Phytosanitary Measures* (SPS)) represents as big a paradigm shift to international economic law as, say, the prohibition on the use of force and the introduction of the Security Council with binding resolution and police powers represented within the classical world of international law. A central facet of this shift is the move towards an internationally determined normativity – the central issue in *EC – Sardines* – whereby international standards achieve a prominent role as a basis for Members' individual technical regulations. What is critical is that an unjustified deviation from an international standard could constitute a violation even if it were not discriminatory, i.e. even if it were not such as to afford protection to domestic production. In *EC – Hormones,* the EC was held in violation not because its measure gave less favorable treatment to imported beef and afforded protection to competing domestic products.[1] The EC measure was found to violate the Agreement because it did not conform to SPS normativity independently of the question of discrimination. The same type of legal logic informs the TBT.

The paradigm shift is so profound that it should call into reexamination many of the hermeneutic presumptions which were formed, developed and consolidated either in an epoch of international economic law in which national administrations were accorded not only normative but full procedural autonomy, or in the context of the GATT, where the main constraint on regulatory autonomy came through Art. III.

The single biggest failing of *EC – Sardines* is not related to the actual decisions adopted by the AB which, perhaps with the exception of the issue of burden of proof, are (as far as outcome is concerned) at least defensible if not always compelling. The failing lies in the pedestrian way in which such an important paradigm shift – *EC – Sardines* being the first major TBT case – was treated or not treated as a background to its hermeneutic choices.

---

[1] *EC Measures Concerning Meat and Meat Products (Hormones) – Report of the Appellate Body* (WT/DS26/AB/R and T/DS48/AB/R, January 16, 1998).

AB hermeneutics is, of course, not made of one cloth. The composition of the AB is ever changing, introducing different sensibilities and different emphasis practiced by different Divisions in different time. But there is one strand which is present in a considerable number of cases: the strand which privileges in its rhetoric a certain type of textualism. This strand is driven by an understandable concern for the legitimacy of the AB and is based on the premise that a pretense to determine the legal meaning of a text based on the ordinary meaning of words somehow bestows greater hermeneutic propriety on the resultant interpretation. Any critical reading of the case law will show that when it appears fit the AB is no less teleological, contextual, or systematic than any other tribunal of similar standing. The difference lies in the level of its pretense, in its often obsessive use of dictionaries, and in its repeated claims about self-evident textual propositions which, at times, as for example in the LAN case, are evident to the AB alone to the exclusion of Panel, Parties and Secretariat of the WTO.[2] *EC – Sardines* is a striking example of this strand but unfortunately in a dispute where the stakes are unusually high, being the first TBT case.

Art. 31 of the Vienna Convention, often referred to by the AB to motivate its textualist mode of interpretation, provides that words have to be interpreted in their context and in the light of the object and purpose of the instrument in question. Clearly the paradigm shift from local discretion to an internationally determined standard and, even more importantly from a regime of discrimination to one of non-justified obstacles is the most germane factor establishing the object and purpose and the context of the TBT (and SPS) and should cast a hermeneutic shadow and/or light over any interpretation of its specific terms.

It may (or should) for example, influence hermeneutic choices and tests. In the domestic law of many jurisdictions there is a different standard of judicial review of public measures depending on the norm which they allegedly violate. A public measure allegedly compromising a constitutional principle such as, say, a fundamental human right or the principle of non discrimination will receive very strict scrutiny requiring the public authority to give compelling reasons in justification. A lower level of scrutiny, requiring simply that the measure not be unreasonable

---

[2] *European Communities – Customs Classification of Certain Computer Equipment – Report of the Appellate Body* (WT/DS62/AB/R, WT/DS67/AB/R and WT/DS68/AB/R, May 6, 1998).

may be applied in other circumstances such as judicial review of an administrative regulatory measure. Greater deference is given the public authority in the latter case than the former. To the extent that TBT and SPS may involve disputes which do not involve protectionism and discrimination, but a dispute about the reasonableness of a non-discriminatory measure in achieving a certain public policy, one might expect also a hermeneutic shift by AB or at least a discussion of the yardstick against which alleged violations would be judged. This cannot be found in the *EC – Sardines* decision. This, in our view, is regrettable.

It is not self-evident that a narrow textualist approach necessarily bestows greater legitimacy on the decisor and that a broader approach will inevitably appear more "activist" and hence less legitimate. There is an appreciable difference in the legitimacy of a decision where the decisor is seen to have recognized fully the context (understood here in its broad sense) of the text under interpretation and which is seen to inform its decision whatever the outcome, and a decision in which the decisor seems oblivious to the context of its decision. Likewise, and no less importantly, there is a difference between a decision which is seen to be aware of its consequences, and is seen to have made its hermeneutic choices in full awareness of such consequences. When the Vienna Convention speaks of interpretation in the light of object and purpose it simply invites a consequentialist approach. Jurists' prudence is usually a recipe for good jurisprudence, but it is not to be confused with narrow textualism.

Textualism is now threatening to become more than a hermeneutic curiosity, becoming counterproductive to the very legitimating purposes for which it is employed. It actually affects the credibility of the AB to be, *de facto* at least, the World Trade Court. There is beginning to emerge a wide gap between the jurisprudence of the World Court and that of the World Trade Court. The former is no less skilled or sophisticated in its hermeneutics – without, however, a reductionist textualism. But what distinguishes even more the approaches between the two Courts is *the unwillingness of the AB to situate its legal analyses within a framework which firmly articulates both the normative and policy considerations and consequences of its decisions.* The willingness of the World Court to go much further in this respect is noticeable in major decisions such as *Nicaragua* and *Nuclear Weapons*, but is typical of most of its cases in the last twenty years.

We will in the next subsections illustrate this textualist approach to legal interpretation by the adjudicating bodies, as it was applied to two principal issues which came up on appeal.

2.1   The legitimacy of international standards

The EC argued that only standards that had been adopted by an international body *by consensus* should constitute a relevant international standard for the purposes of Art. 2.4 TBT.

In the explanatory note to the definition of standard in Annex 1.2 of the TBT, we find the following:

> ... Standards prepared by the international standardization community are based on the consensus. This Agreement covers also documents which are not based on consensus.

The hermeneutic choice presented itself as follows: according to the EC the last sentence refers to documents prepared by bodies which are not part of the international standardization community. According to Peru (and the Panel) the last sentence refers to documents prepared by international bodies which were not based on consensus.

Which is the better argument? The treatment of this issue by the AB is the most telling in the entire decision. The AB goes through a minute analysis of the text – comparing the word "document" in the explanatory note to the word "document" in the principal text. Much turns, in the AB view, on the word "also" in the last sentence. And it refers to the chapeau of Annex 1 to find further textual support for the Panel view. Logic is also at play:

> The definition of "Standard" in the ISO/IEC Guide expressly includes a consensus requirement. Therefore, the logical conclusion, in our view, is that the *omission* of a consensus requirement in the definition of "standard" in Annex 1.2 of the *TBT Agreement* was a deliberate choice on the part of the drafters of the *TBT Agreement*, and that the last two phrases of the Explanatory note were included to give effect to this choice.
>
> (225, emphasis in original)

This logic is compelling only if you have already decided that the last phrase refers to the said international bodies whose decision must form the basis for decision by a Member. Some would say that the reasoning of the AB is a *non sequitur*. But it is not the conclusion we wish to fault but the striking absence of any consideration beyond the textual of the stakes involved in this decision.

There are profound issues of democracy and legitimacy both in the relationship between domestic decision making and its international counterpart and in the legitimacy and efficiency of international decision making itself. In effect, the decision of the Panel, upheld by the AB, would accord "bindingness" to non-consensual international decisions in circumstances where those very bodies, composed of largely the same Members, do not ascribe the same bindingness to their own decisions. Absurdity and unreasonableness are grounds to depart from the standard interpretative rules according to Art. 32 of the Vienna Convention. Is this outcome plausible? It might be, but it would at least require some explanation. There are, as it is, serious problems with the accountability and representativeness (and hence legitimacy) of decisions by bodies like the Codex even when adopted by consensus. These problems are aggravated by ascribing bindingness to non-consensual decisions.

Other issues are involved too: the AB in an off the cuff remark states that its interpretative decision on consensus is of no legal relevance to the international bodies themselves which have to follow their own rules. But this is naïve at best, disingenuous at worst. One of the most important ways the international standard achieves legal teeth (rather than being a voluntary enterprise) is through the legal obligations, presumptions and consequences accorded to it in the TBT and SPS. Surely a decision by the AB which holds that outcomes of the decisional process within, say, the Codex will have the same legal consequence within the TBT or SPS, whether or not adopted by consensus, is going to impact the decisional dynamics in those institutions. There is something startling to see this problem being resolved by an argumentation which is focused almost exclusively on the existence or otherwise of a word such as "also."

It is important to emphasize, at this point, what we are not arguing. We do not, of course, advocate disregard for words or language. Nor are we arguing that policy argumentation should replace legal reasoning. We are arguing in the first place that legal hermeneutics is a discourse which is far richer than the thin gruel served up by the AB in this decision; we further argue that since the AB itself often departs from its textual strictures it would be better to abandon the posture and rhetoric since they seem to have the corrosive effect of blinding it to the richer contextual matrix of its decisions.

We do not want to suggest that the broader context and a deeper examination of object and purpose should always be decisive and trump clear meaning of text. But we do argue that an acknowledgement and discussion of these broader contexts is important not only to the correct outcome of cases, but also to the dialog which should exist between a court and a legislator. A court may find that its hands are tied by the regnant cannon of interpretation. But its hands should not be tied in the dialectical relationship with other constitutional actors.

It could be objected that the AB is in some ways the prisoner of the parties and lawyers before it, and that the fault for the textually reductionist judicial reasoning falls on the shoulders of those who argue before the AB. This, we think, can only be partially true. Litigators are in the business of winning cases and they adapt their vocabulary to follow the signals which issue from the courts before which they argue. In the WTO, the Panels are being conditioned into the same hermeneutic mindset. Panels are in the business of deciding cases, but they are also in the business of not being overturned on appeal and browbeaten by a disrespectful AB. The results are progressively seen in the Panel Reports that come out.

In conclusion, the decision of the AB on the requirement of consensus may or may not be correct in terms of substance. But the hermeneutics behind this outcome does not give credibility to the outcome.

2.2   The meaning of "... as a basis for ..."

The first part of Art. 2.4 TBT does not oblige Members to use international standards, but to use international standards "*as a basis for*" their regulations, analogously to the SPS. This is clearly a weaker requirement, but in what sense?

In our view there are at least two possible approaches to this issue: a procedural approach and a substantive approach. Indeed, these two approaches can explain some of the most interesting differences in the jurisprudence of the Panel and the AB in *EC – Hormones*. What is the "procedural" approach? An example will best illustrate. In the EU it is said that the Commission proposes and the Council disposes: for most legislation the Commission of the EU has an exclusive right of initiative meaning that all legislation adopted by the Council and Parliament must start with a proposal submitted by the Commission. Strictly speaking, all legislation *is based on* a Commission proposal. This means that the Commission proposal is in fact the "basis" for the process. But in that process, amendments can be proposed, even radical amendments which *frequently* contradict the original Commission process. These amendments will be discussed, deliberated and either accepted or rejected according to the decisional rules. Procedurally the Commission proposal serves "as a basis for"*all* Union legislation whatever the ultimate content, even content which, *pace* the AB, contradicts the original Commission proposal.

A substantive approach, on the other hand, is not concerned with the process but with the end outcome. It might define the concept of "as a basis for" by considering the degree to which the resulting legislation is in conformity with the international standard, even if in the process of adoption it did not have in mind at all the international standard.

There can be much merit in either approach or in a combination of both approaches to defining the term "as a basis for." A procedural approach (if we return to the European example we gave) allows the Commission proposal to set the terms of the debate, and to condition a yardstick or benchmark against which amendments could be made, but gives the decisor ultimate freedom to decide the content. The substantive approach, in its extreme form, would not even interest itself whether the decisor had the original proposal before its eyes, but would only ensure that the outcome fell on the right point between conformity and loose influence.

In our view, a correct hermeneutic enquiry for the terms "as a basis for" (or "based on" in the SPS) should have articulated the two approaches, and tried to decide which (or what combination of the two) was signified by these words in the TBT (and SPS). A great deal turns on this. Is the idea of the TBT, for example, that in setting their regulatory standards, as a matter of process (like in the EU) the national decisor will have the international standard in front of them and use it as a basis for their deliberation – notably conditioned by the second phrase of Art. 2.4, namely the need, internally, to articulate reasons why the national regulation should depart from the international standard based on appropriateness and effectiveness? This approach would force the national regulator to articulate objectives, to assess means, and to rationalize results – a significant improvement in the process of regulatory decision making in many jurisdictions – but being less concerned with the eventual substantive compliance. One can see huge advantages for the overall purposes of the WTO, and the TBT in particular, for this approach and one could not *a priori* exclude that this was the idea. Or, is the idea of the TBT instead to provide a yardstick for *post hoc* substantive analysis of content? In addressing this issue as a hermeneutic matter, international law offers the decisor a wide range of interpretative approaches – especially if, as is often the case, the drafters of the Treaty may not have addressed their mind to this issue directly, but drafted with inchoate unarticulated notions, or if, as is also often the case, different negotiators had different conceptions in mind and the text represents a compromise.

And how do the adjudicating bodies address this *hugely* consequential issue? True to their belief in a textualist method of interpretation, out come the dictionaries! The Panel comes armed with Webster. The AB fields its favorite Oxford Shorter. And we let the learned wordsmiths whose dictionary definitions are the most extreme example of understanding language independently of context, and with no reference to object and purpose (i.e. the exact opposite approach to meaning of words which a legal interpreter of international texts should adopt), decide for the WTO the relationship between international standard setting and national administrative procedures.

It may or may not be that in this case the EU did use the international standard "as a basis for" its regulation; we are not objecting to the AB's bottom line. But we find the arid reasoning on which this decision was based inappropriate to address one of the most fundamental problems of the WTO: how to draw the line between national sovereignty and international commitments regarding domestic regulations.

2.3   Seemingly innocuous discrete determinations may have significant cumulative consequences

The AB Decision reads as a point by point analysis of the various issues on appeal. But, in our view, these issues are not discrete, as the AB would have it, and to treat them as such is another unsatisfactory dimension of the hermeneutics of this Decision. It is their aggregate effect which will define the contours of the new paradigm which TBT (and SPS) represent. Seeing all issues as part of a whole is essential to the individual determination of each of them. Consider the following selection of determinations made by the AB in *EC – Sardines*:

– a new standard applies to pre-existing measures;
– a standard must serve as a basis even if adopted without consensus; and
– "as a basis for" may not introduce a requirement of conformity, but does mean a lot more than "relates to" and certainly is not to be upheld if the national regulation contradicts the international standard.

Viewed one by one these are defensible if not compelling arguments. But note the inevitable legal connections between them: if you decide (in a teleological manner masquerading as textual!) that the new international standard applies to pre-existing measures, you will inevitably have to adopt the substantive rather than procedural approach to "based on." After all, there could not have been a procedural reliance on an international standard which had not come into existence. But seeing the interconnection between these two arguments, should they not have been discussed in conjunction with each other? Should the fact that a determination on the intertemporal effect of the international standard impacts the question of "based on" not have been part of the considerations to be taken into account in reflecting on intertemporality? Note, too, how the cumulative effect of these determinations is to cut significantly into the discretion of the Member States to apply even non-discriminatory measures. And yet this cumulative effect of the discrete determinations is neither discussed nor acknowledged. The point is that one cannot let a series of discrete determinations of individual points determine the TBT's overall regulatory contours. The individual determinations must be guided by a more general vision of the appropriate scope of the Agreement, but we cannot detect such a vision in the AB report.

2.4   Naming and labeling

The European Community argued for a distinction to be drawn between labeling requirements and naming. For its part, the Panel

> ...fail[ed] to see the basis on which a distinction can be drawn between a requirement to "name" and a requirement to "label" a product for the purposes of the TBT Agreement.
>
> (7.40)

and the AB instructs us that

> ...a 'means of identification' *is* a product characteristic. A name clearly identifies a product...
>
> (191, emphasis in original, footnote omitted)

Ergo a name is a product characteristic.

There is something ironic that a Panel and a Division of the AB so deeply concerned with textuality and language did not develop the potentially important principle implicit in the EC argument. For the Panel and the AB language is merely instrumental, a means of communication, and has no independent cultural value. Therefore it is not useful to distinguish between naming and labeling. But is this so?

Imagine the following hypothetical: A national regulation, say in Italy, stipulates that no product may be marketed as "Vinegar" if it is not made of wine. In Britain, there is a vinegar which is made of something, but certainly not of wine, which is referred to as "Malt Vinegar". Imagine a (non consensual) international standard which defined a standard for labeling vinegars and stipulated "X Vinegar" where X could stand for the content of the vinegar as in "Wine Vinegar" or "Malt Vinegar."

The approach of the Panel, approved by the AB, would focus on the means of identification test, based on a notion of language as an instrument of communication. But the interesting point about the distinction between naming and labeling is that there is a question of language integrity as a cultural asset. The objection to allowing non-wine vinegars to appropriate the name "Vinegar" and be labeled accordingly is because in the Italian language (as in Spanish), Vinegar means a product made of wine. The issue is not only consumer protection but language protection. To allow other products to take that name will not compromise the market place but a cultural asset. Whether or not this would be the case in the dispute over *EC – Sardines* is doubtful. But the categorical dismissal of the differentiation between labeling and naming would seem to deny in other more deserving cases the possibility to argue on the basis of cultural and linguistic integrity.

3   *EC – Sardines* and the evidentiary rules in the TBT

Art. 2.4 TBT only contains one sentence, but this sentence comprises two parts with very different implications. The first stipulates that Members shall use international standards. The second part specifies conditions under which international standards need not be adhered to. A crucial question is whether a country that is not following an international standard has to be able to prove that the second part of the sentence is applicable, or whether it is for a complaining country to prove that the standard would suffice to reach the respondent's policy targets? This issue is discussed in *EC – Sardines* under the heading of "burden of proof."

In the dispute the Panel argues that the EC has the burden to motivate the use of a regulation which differed from the international Codex Stan 94, and that the EC had not managed to do this convincingly. Reaching this conclusion, the Panel took the view that the default position of Art. 2.4 of the TBT is that where technical regulations are required and relevant international standards exist, Members should use them as a basis for their technical regulations. It would, thus, suffice for the complainant state to make the *prima facie* case that the defendant's regulation was not so based. Since Art. 2.4 provides justification for not using international standards, namely

> . . . *except* when such international standards would be an ineffective or inappropriate means for the fulfillment of the legitimate objectives pursued . . .
>
> (Art. 2.4 TBT, emphasis added)

the Panel took the view that if the defendant then wished to use this "exception" in explaining why it did not base its regulation on the international standard, it would carry the burden of *prima facie* proof of showing that the international standard is ineffective or inappropriate to achieve the legitimate objectives pursued. This Principal–Exception structure would be similar to the relationship in GATT between, say, Art. III and Art. XX (where the *prima facie* burden is on the party relying on the exception ex Art. XX). As will be discussed later, the Panel also took into account the difficulties for the claimant to spell out the legitimate objectives pursued by the defending Member.

The AB, basing itself on its earlier jurisprudence on this issue in *EC – Hormones*, and notably Art. 3.1 and 3.3 of the SPS (which are structurally similar, but not identical, to 2.4 TBT) dismissed this reasoning and insisted that the claimant, in this case Peru, had the burden to make the *prima facie* case as regards both parts of 2.4 TBT. It found, however, that Peru had fulfilled its task in this respect. While reasoning differently, the Panel and the AB thus both found the EC measure illegal. But the burden of proof is not a mere technical issue. On its face, the AB and the Panel produced fundamentally different views on the role of international standards in the TBT, and on the resulting appropriate allocation of the burden of proof.

In what follows we will argue that the analysis of the AB as regards allocation of the burden of proof is wanting.

3.1   What yardstick to use when evaluating evidentiary rules for the DS system?

The literature on evidentiary rules distinguishes between legal presumptions and burden of proof. The former concept refers to the adjudicating bodies' assessment of the probability that a party is guilty of an unlawful act, absent certain evidence. The burden of proof has two aspects. The first is the level of confidence required by the adjudicating body to change the initial presumption. This is "the burden of persuasion" (or the "level of confidence", or the "quantum of proof," or the "standard of proof") and may be expressed in terms of rules such as "preponderance of evidence" or "beyond reasonable doubt." The second aspect is the question of who has the responsibility to bring the evidence before the adjudicating bodies or else risk losing the case – "the burden of proof", or the "burden of production" or, sometimes, the "onus of proof." While these different aspects of evidentiary evidence often are hard to separate, it is useful to treat them separately as far as possible. In *EC – Sardines*, the discussion under the heading "burden of proof" seems to primarily concern the burden of production which may change during the proceeding, and less the weight of evidence of proof necessary to discharge the burden of production.

In order to determine the appropriate design of rules for the burden of proof, there are at least two issues that need to be addressed. First, one has to specify the *objective* of the dispute settlement system in the WTO, since it should be the extent to which the various possible rules achieve this objective that determines which rules to choose. As far as we can tell, there is no discussion at all of this in *EC – Sardines*.

Second, one needs to determine the "mechanics" of how different rules affect the outcome of the agreement. This is a highly complex issue, and we cannot here describe in any detail how current rules and interpretations thereof influence the working of the WTO. But it may anyway be of value to point to some of the channels through which the distribution of the burden of proof affects the outcome. It deserves to be emphasized that while the discussion is very general and "theoretical," the effects pointed at are often highly relevant in practice.

It is clear that within a given dispute, the distribution of burden of proof will *ceteris paribus* affect the probability that the different parties win, by making it harder for the party who is assigned this burden to prevail. It is customary to distinguish between two types of errors that the allocation of burden of proof should seek to minimize. The first is to strike down a measure that should be viewed as legal (Type I), the second is to allow a measure that should be declared illegal (Type II). When determining the allocation of the burden of proof, one has to take into account the costs associated with both of these kinds of mistake.

The *ceteris paribus* assumption is obviously only an analytical simplification. It is highly likely that the rules on evidentiary evidence will affect Members' behavior in a number of ways. To start with, it will affect the incentives of the parties to spend resources on the proceeding, and thus indirectly affect the outcome. But by affecting the balance between the parties, the allocation of the burden of proof will also affect the probability that the parties will actually end up in such a dispute, since it will influence decisions made by Members at earlier stages of the interaction. It may importantly influence the parties' incentives to settle issues before they are brought to the WTO, or to reach mutually agreed solutions. These effects will in turn affect the incentives for countries to search for illegalities to bring up with trading partners, and to possibly complain about. And if the propensity by which trading partners detect and complain about illegalities is affected, so will their incentives to search for illegalities. All of this will affect the incentives for Members to adopt illegal measures. Taking a step further back, changes in the extent to which the Agreement is adhered to, will feed into Members' incentives to make concessions in trade rounds. The problem is further significantly compounded by the fact that Members also interact in the setting of international standards in organizations outside the WTO. A complete analysis should take into account how the two processes are interrelated. For instance, countries' incentives to participate actively in the setting (or not setting) of international standards may increase significantly if a presumption is created that countries should adhere to standards.

A decision on the burden of proof will for the above-mentioned types of reasons inevitably have fundamental effects on the working of the dispute settlement system. The task before the adjudicating bodies, whether they like it or not, is therefore to weigh all these consequences, as well as the administrative costs of the system, both those directly connected with litigation, as well as those stemming from the supervision of trading partners' adherence to the agreement, taking into account the possibility for committing the Type I or Type II errors mentioned above. Needless to say, such a balancing act cannot be made with any degree of precision.

But the AB has hardly addressed these aspects at all. This is understandable, given their complexity. The AB may (and perhaps rightly so) have felt that nothing useful would come out of such an exercise. What it means however, is that *when discussing appropriate rules for the burden of proof, the AB has neither specified the yardstick by which to measure the usefulness of different rules, nor has it in any more systematic manner analyzed how the rules may affect the outcome.*

It should be noted that the effects mentioned in the discussion above may be very significant when it comes to the issues at stake in *EC – Sardines*. For instance, it is likely to make a significant difference to Members' willingness to make concessions in rounds, and to agree on international standards in other contexts, if these standards are seen as norms, and it is up to countries not following these standards to prove why the standards are inadequate, compared to the situation where complaining countries have to prove that the standards are adequate.

3.2   Who bears the "burden of proof"?

In *EC – Sardines* the AB discusses or at least touches upon at least four possible directions in which to allocate the burden of proof (we henceforth use this term as is done by the AB in the dispute):

(i)   to the informed party;
(ii) to the party who asserts the affirmative;
(iii) to the complainant; and
(iv) to the party claiming an exception.

These different rules are not all mutually exclusive, of course. For instance, a complainant can be interpreted as asserting the affirmative, and a complaining country may be better informed. In what follows, we will briefly discuss more principled aspects of these rules, and how they are dealt with in *EC – Sardines*.

3.2.1   Allocating the burden of proof to the more informed party

Although it is hard to point to a well-defined body of papers, economic contract theory, as well as the Law and Economics literature, suggest that in a choice between laying the burden of proof on the better or on the worse informed party, it is normally better to put it on the more informed party. The AB completely rejects such a notion, however:

> There is nothing in the WTO dispute settlement system to support the notion that the allocation of the burden of proof should be decided on the basis of a comparison between the respective difficulties that may possibly be encountered by the complainant and the respondent in collecting information to prove a case.
>
> (281)

An immediate question here is of course whether there is anything in the WTO dispute settlement system that would *prevent* the AB from using information asymmetries as a motive for a particular allocation of the burden of proof.

More importantly, the AB seems to argue that exporting Members' lack of knowledge of the reasons why importing Members choose not to adhere to international standards is not a serious problem for the enforcement of the TBT. The AB asserts that the TBT affords every Member adequate opportunities to obtain information on the objectives which inform other Members' TBT measures – either under Art. 2.5 or at the "enquiry point" ex Art. 10.1. But the AB itself realizes that these mechanisms may afford insufficient information for the purpose of legal assessment. And, as argued by Peru, although one should assume the good faith of Members, one cannot exclude the possibility of a Member being less than forthcoming in the context of these two procedures. Thus, the AB itself further explains:

> ... [T]he dispute settlement process itself also provides opportunities for the complainant to obtain the necessary information to build a case. Information can be exchanged during the consultation phase and additional information may well become available during the panel phase itself.
>
> (280)

But would not the very ruling of the AB on burden of proof provide an incentive to the defendant state to be extremely circumspect in providing such information? If the burden on the less informed complainant is not simply to establish a *prima facie* case that the national measure was not based on the international standard, but also that the international standard was not inappropriate or ineffective in pursuing the legitimate objective of the defendant, could the defendant not simply insist that the complainant make this *prima facie* case before it even has the duty to respond? How could the complainant then assert the appropriateness or effectiveness of the measure in respect of objectives which it would have to guess? Also, is there not something odd in saying that the complainant will receive the information which would enable it to build a case during the case that it has presumably built in order to be successful in discharging its *prima facie* duty? And how systematically should this source of information be used? Should a dispute be initiated every time a Member uses a measure that does not correspond to an international standard, in order to determine its legality?

Furthermore, the AB states that:

> A complainant could collect information before and during the early stages of the panel proceedings and, on the basis of that information, develop arguments relating to the objectives or to the appropriateness that maybe put forward during subsequent phases of the proceedings.
>
> (280)

Does this mean that Members are meant to bring cases without having any pronounced suspicion concerning the extent to which the challenged measures are illegal? And at what scale should they be able to do this?

3.2.2 Allocating the burden of proof to the party claiming an exception

As mentioned above, the Panel interpreted Art. 2.4 TBT as defining a hierarchical relationship, where the second part is an *exception* to the first. Employing the rule that the party using an exception should demonstrate that the required conditions are fulfilled, the Panel determined that the EC should prove that the international standard was ineffective or inappropriate. But referring to its decision in *EC – Hormones*, the AB points out that

> ... characterizing a treaty provision as an "exception" does not, by itself, *place the burden of proof on the respondent Member.*
>
> (271, emphasis added)

The AB also makes this point by quoting its decision in *EC – Hormones*, where it stated:

> The general rule in a dispute settlement proceeding requiring a complaining party to establish a *prima facie* case of inconsistency with a provision of the *SPS Agreement* before the burden of showing consistency is taken on by the defending party, is *not* avoided by simply describing that same provision as an "exception".
>
> (272, original emphasis)

Note that the AB in these two recitals discusses whether exceptions *as a rule* should be treated differently than other provisions, stating that they should not. Hence, even if there were a Rule–Exception relationship, this should not matter to the burden of proof issue.

In the next two recitals (273 and 274) the AB explains why the Panel is wrong to view the reasoning in *EC – Hormones* as "not having a direct bearing" on *EC – Sardines*, arguing that there are strong similarities between Art. 3.1 and 3.3 SPS, on the one hand, and Art. 2.4 TBT on the other.

In recital 275 the AB then draws the conclusion concerning the role of exceptions that the Panel should have drawn, had it relied on the AB's findings concerning Art. 3.1 and 3.3 SPS in *EC – Hormones*. But the conclusion it draws is now of a different nature than the conclusion drawn in recital 271–272: it here concludes that there *does not exist* a Rule-Exception relationship in Art. 2.4 TBT. But why does the AB address this issue of whether there is a Rule–Exception relationship in Art. 2.4 TBT, when it has already in recitals 271–272 determined that the existence of such a relationship is irrelevant for the allocation of the burden of proof?

The reason why the AB does not see a Rule–Exception relationship, as we understand it, is that in the AB's view, the first part of Art. 2.4 TBT refers to certain circumstances, and the second part refers to *other* circumstances. The right to take a certain measure in the latter case is therefore not due to an *exception* to the former situation – it might be an exceptional event in a probabilistic sense, but not as a matter of hierarchy.

At a more superficial level, and using the textual "normal meaning of the word" approach to interpretation, the term "except" in 2.4 TBT that links the two parts of the sentence, strongly suggests that the second part should be seen as an exception. The AB here takes a step away from its usual textualism, but in the wrong direction, as we see it. In fact, we cannot exclude the possibility that the AB was more concerned to impose its authority on the Panel by insisting that it follow its ruling in *EC – Hormones* than by the actual rational allocation of the burden of proof.

But the more important question is whether and how the existence of a Rules–Exception relationship matters to the distribution of the burden of proof. To clarify the structure of the issue, suppose that a country may find itself either in circumstance A or in circumstance B. Circumstance A may for instance be thought of as situations where either consumers do not care about the distinction between the two types of fish, or where they would not be confused by the label "Peruvian Sardines". B would be the case where they both care about the distinction, and would be confused by the label.

Let us now compare two alternative interpretations of Art. 2.4 in this context. Assume that the intention is to allow for the possibility not to use the international standard if and only if the circumstances are B.

The AB's interpretation would then seem to be the following:

"AB's interpretation":
(i)   Use the international standard if A;
(ii) use any standard you wish if B.

This would then mean that the two parts are treated symmetrically, and there is no "general rule–exception" relationship between them. If there would be a hierarchy between them, the interpretation of the provision might take the form:

"Panel's interpretation":
(i)   Use the international standard *regardless* of the circumstances,
(ii) but use any standard you wish if B.

The sense in which this seems to capture the notion of an exception is that the possibility offered in part (ii) applies to circumstances for which part (i) requires that something else should be done; that is, part (ii) introduces a change to what part (i) just stated.

The AB seems to argue that it follows from its interpretation of the lack of hierarchy between the two parts of Art. 2.4 TBT, that the burden of proof to show that a country should have used an international standard when it didn't, rests with the complainant and not the respondent. The only underlying reason we can see for this would be that the respondent is not to a larger degree asserting particular facts when abstaining from using the international standard than when using it; in one case it is implicitly asserting that circumstances are B and in the other that they are A. Since it should not be required of countries to prove that the particular circumstances are in place that allow them to use international standards, it should not be requested of them to do this when circumstances are B, if A and B are just viewed as two alternative possible sets of circumstances, with no particular relationship.

However, as far as we can see, A and B are not symmetric in this sense. For instance, the implications for a trading partner are very different (given the partner's limited information concerning whether it truly is A or B). The costs of falsely determining that it is A when it is B (Type I error), and conversely, are also likely to differ. Speculating, it seems as if in the context of TBT (or SPS – as in the *EC – Asbestos*) cases, the cost of a false positive finding – which would force the respondent to revoke the measure – is often larger than of a false negative finding – which would permit a measure that should not be permitted. This would suggest a rather high burden of persuasion for a complainant, from a *within* dispute perspective. But there will of course also be systemic effects to take into account. For instance, a high burden of persuasion is likely to invite the abuse of regulations for protectionist purposes. But given the often politically very sensitive nature of decisions under TBT, this may be necessary in order to induce Members to liberalize. However, these are just speculations to indicate what type of considerations a more satisfactory analysis has to take into account.

One possible difference between the two interpretations made above, and one which would partly speak in favor of the AB's interpretation, is that the lack of a Rule–Exception relationship implies that the importing country is not asserting the affirmative.

3.2.3 Allocating the burden of proof to the complainant or to the party making an affirmative assertion

In *EC – Sardines* the AB seems to use two somewhat different standards that happen to give the same outcome in this particular dispute. The first is that it is the party that makes an assertion who carries the burden of proof. The AB quotes its report in *US – Blouses from India*,[3] where it stated that

---

[3] *United States – Measures Affecting Imports of Woven Wool Shirts and Blouses from India – Report of the Appellate Body* (WT/DS33/AB/R, April 25, 1997).

...the burden of proof rests upon the party, whether complaining or defending, who *asserts the affirmative* of a particular claim or defence.

(270, emphasis added)

The second principle is that the *complainant* has the burden of proof. The AB refers to its determination in *EC – Hormones* where it said that

The general rule in a dispute settlement proceeding requiring a complaining party to establish a *prima facie* case . . .

(272)

In *EC – Hormones* (109) the AB also stated that

. . . the Panel should have begun the analysis by examining whether [the complainants] had presented evidence and legal arguments sufficient to demonstrate that the [respondents'] measures were inconsistent with . . . the SPS Agreement . . . Only after such a *prima facie* determination may the onus be shifted to the [respondent] to bring forward evidence and arguments to disprove the complaining party's claim.

(footnote omitted)

It is clear that there is an overlap between the two notions: a complaint is an assertion about an illegality. But they are not identical. For instance, the principle that the party who makes a claim should bear the burden to show it is correct according to the AB also applies to the respondent. It seems to us that while both these notions have intuitive appeal, they are at a slightly closer look not self-evident.

First, this argument, together with the above-mentioned interpretation that there is no Rule–Exception relationship, could be taken to show that a Member asserting the affirmative when using an international standard is in the same position when not using it. But this argument would not suffice to explain why the complainant is asserting the affirmative to any higher degree than the respondent, and thus should bear the burden of proof: the complainant makes an assertion – the measure is illegal. But the respondent also makes a claim by asserting that the measure is legal. The principle that the party who makes a claim carries the burden of proof implies that *both* should prove their positions. The principle thus does not have enough "bite" to put the burden solely on the complainant.

There is indeed nothing self-evident about letting the complainant bear the burden of proof. For instance, the "principle of good faith" that the AB refers to, suggests that the reason why the respondent chooses not to use the international standard is that the respondent has information concerning the ineffectiveness and/or inappropriateness of the international standard. Otherwise it would not be acting in good faith. Since the information is already at the disposal of the respondent, the burden of proof should weigh relatively lightly, and it would save on transaction costs to let the respondent bear the burden of proof.

Put differently, consider a case where at the end of the proceedings, when the parties have made their claims and counterclaims, it turns out that nothing has been learnt from their arguments. The AB would presumably rule in favor of the respondent since the complainant did not make a *prima facie* case for the illegality of the measure. But why should this be the presumption? After all, the situation is (by construction) such that nothing is known about who is right and who is wrong. It might equally well be argued that if there were any legitimate reason for the contested measure, the respondent, having access to information on why it is pursued, should be able to bring this information to the adjudicating bodies, regardless of whether the accusation is substantiated or not. If this is not done, it signals that there is no such defense for the measure, so the burden of proof should rest on the respondent, being the more informed party.

Of course, if one were to allocate the burden of proof to the respondent, this might have significant implications for the incentives to complain. If Members could with just a few words force other countries to motivate each and every policy, the DS system might be swamped by complaints. In addition, the respondents would have to spend enormous resources defending all their policies. This strongly speaks against allocating the burden of proof to the respondent.

Again, the point here is not to argue that any particular distribution of the burden of proof is necessarily right, but to suggest that there are a number of considerations to take into account when determining the rules for the burden of proof. These issues seem particularly important when there is a potential conflict between domestic regulations and trade agreements. We are simply not sure why the AB chose a particular path.

3.3   How convincing should proofs be?

The discussion above concerned the assignment of the burden of production. Of equal importance at least is the question of the appropriate burden of persuasion, the quantum of proof necessary for a party to discharge its burden of production. As we will argue, there are two important issues raised in *EC – Sardines* in this respect: first, the level of evidence that suffices for the complainant to discharge its burden of persuasion; and second, how the determination of evidentiary standards may determine what are legitimate (professed) regulatory objectives.

3.3.1 The limited burden of persuasion that suffices for a complainant to show that an international standard is effective and appropriate

The stated objectives of the EC Regulation are consumer protection, market transparency and fair competition. Since the parties agreed that these were legitimate objectives, the adjudicating bodies did not have to pronounce on their legitimacy in the context of Art. 2.4 TBT. But a central issue was still whether Codex Stan 94 is an appropriate and effective means to reach these objectives.

The Panel summarizes its findings as follows:

> We therefore conclude that it has not been demonstrated that Codex Stan 94 would be an ineffective or inappropriate means for the fulfilment of the legitimate objectives pursued by the EC Regulation, i.e., consumer protection, market transparency and fair competition. We conclude that Peru has adduced sufficient evidence and legal arguments to demonstrate that Codex Stan 94 is not ineffective or inappropriate to fulfil the legitimate objectives pursued by the EC Regulation.
>
> (7.138)

The AB, while allocating the burden of proof differently than the Panel, agrees:

> We note that the Panel concluded that "Peru has adduced sufficient evidence and legal arguments to demonstrate that Codex Stan 94 is not ineffective or inappropriate to fulfil the legitimate objectives pursued by the EC Regulation." We have examined the analysis which led the Panel to this conclusion. We note, in particular, that the Panel made the factual finding that "it has not been established that consumers in most member States of the European Communities have always associated the common name 'sardines' exclusively with *Sardina pilchardus*". We also note that the Panel gave consideration to the contentions of Peru that, under Codex Stan 94, fish from the species *Sardinops sagax* bear a denomination that is distinct from that of *Sardina pilchardus*, and that "the very purpose of the labelling regulations set out in Codex Stan 94 for sardines of species other than *Sardina pilchardus* is to ensure market transparency". We agree with the analysis made by the Panel. Accordingly, we see no reason to interfere with the Panel's finding that Peru has adduced sufficient evidence and legal arguments to demonstrate that Codex Stan 94 meets the legal requirements of effectiveness and appropriateness set out in Art. 2.4 of the *TBT Agreement*.
>
> (290, emphasis in original, footnotes omitted)

The AB thus first notes that the Panel had determined that Peru had fulfilled its burden of proof establishing the positive fact the Codex is not inefficient or inappropriate (which presumably implies that it is effective and appropriate). However, examining the analysis which led the Panel to this conclusion, the AB points to the negative finding that it had *not* been established that EC consumers associated "sardines" with fish of the species *Sardina pilchardus* only. It also notes that the purpose of Codex Stan 94 is the same as that of the EC Regulation, and that it stipulates different names for the two species of fish. On this basis the AB determines that it had been established that the Codex *is* effective and appropriate.

The ruling is important since it determines what constitutes a *sufficient* amount of evidence in order to prove the positive statement that an *international standard is efficient and appropriate*. In the dispute Peru submitted evidence suggesting that "sardines" by itself, or combined with the name of a country or region, is a common name for *Sardinops sagax* in the EC. Peru here referred to three dictionaries/publications, two of which were produced in cooperation with, or with support by, the European Commission, and one prepared by the OECD. But it should be noted that this evidence does not directly show that consumers would not confuse *Sarinops sagax*, if labeled as "Peruvian Sardines", with *Sardina pilchardus*. On the contrary, it might perhaps be argued that the existence of these lexica suggests that the classification of fish is not a simple matter, and that consequently there are reasons to suspect that consumers might be confused about the different species of fish. Hence, it is strictly speaking not clear what these publications say about consumer perceptions.

It is also established that "sardine-type" products have been sold in several EC Member states prior to the adoption of the EC Resolution under names such as "Canadian sardines." Again, this does not actually show that consumers have not been misled, it could instead be argued that it is exactly because of this practice that the Regulation is necessary.

The point here is not to argue that the evidence points one way or the other, but to highlight the rather *limited evidentiary weight that is put on the complainant*. This is more of a marginal observation in the context of the Panel report, since the Panel would strictly speaking not need any positive evidence of this form. It puts the burden on the EC to show that the standard is ineffective and/or inappropriate, and the EC has failed to do so. It is more noteworthy with regard to the AB decision, however, since the complainant has the burden of proof according to the AB.

According to the AB one does not have to bring any direct evidence on consumer perceptions in order to determine whether consumers would be confused by a certain type of labeling. It also seems as if, in the final analysis and without admitting it, the AB accepts the Panel's approach which puts the burden of proof on the EC. It could be argued that the burden is placed on the EC only because Peru had satisfied its *prima facie* burden. But, as indicated above, if this is the case, the evidentiary weight required to discharge the burden of proof is so flimsy as to nullify de facto the significance of the reversal of burden from Panel to AB.

The important consequence of setting the burden of persuasion this low in *EC – Sardines* is thus to effectively put the evidentiary burden of production on the Member that wants to deviate from international standards, to show the ineffectiveness and/or inappropriateness of these standards, despite their questionable legitimacy.

3.3.2   Do evidentiary standards in the TBT effectively restrain regulatory autonomy?

It is a premise of TBT and of *EC – Sardines* that the TBT discipline does not compromise the autonomy of the Member to determine the degree of risk acceptable and used as a basis for its regulatory regime. The duty in Art. 2.4 to base a decision on the international standard can be set aside if such standard is inappropriate or ineffective. A key factual finding by the AB in *EC – Sardines* is that Peru had indeed discharged its duty to demonstrate that the international standard met the legal requirements of effectiveness and appropriateness:

> We note, in particular, that the Panel made the factual finding that "it has not been established that consumers in *most* member States of the European Communities have always associated the common name 'sardines' exclusively with *Sardina pilchardus*.
>
> (290, emphasis added)

First, and questions of burden of proof apart, the AB imposes the requirement that consumers in *most* Member States should be adversely affected for the EC measure to be legal. Can it be denied that at least *some* consumers in *some* Member States of the European Communities have always associated the common name "sardines" exclusively with *Sardina pilchardus*? Is it not self-evident that they will assume that, say, Peru Sardines means *Sardina pilchardus* coming from Peru and not *Sardinops sagax* coming from Peru? Should it not be left to the EC to decide the balance between the interests of various consumer groups in the EC?

More generally, is this perhaps an inevitable feature of the TBT, that when determining the evidentiary weight necessary to establish that a national regulation that deviates from an international standard violates the TBT, the adjudicating body also indirectly puts a ceiling on how far a Member can go to eliminate risk, and how to weigh the welfare of different consumer groups? This is not the first place where the AB seemed to have made inroads into the regulatory autonomy of States through requirements for evidentiary burden. In *Korea – Beef*, the AB indicated the vitality of the interest protected (in that case too this interest was consumer protection) will determine what will be acceptable as necessary to enforce a national measure.[4] We would not necessarily argue against the line taken by the AB. After all, almost any regulatory measure can be defended as protecting the interests of at least some consumers. This ambiguity in TBT is clearly not easily resolved. But we would have liked to see at least a discussion of these crucial issues in *EC – Sardines*.

4 Concluding remarks

As regards the substance of the decision, a problematic aspect is the holding that since "it has not been established that consumers in *most* member States of the European Communities have always associated the common name 'sardines' exclusively with *Sardina pilchardus*," the EC regulation could not be justified. As we said, this could be seen as an encroachment of the AB into the autonomy of the Member State to determine its own level of risk, or its own balance of the interest of different consumer groups. While this argument is not unproblematic, it cannot be discarded without analysis.

On the burden of proof, we believe that the only way the AB can sustain its position that the complainant bears the burden to prove both a deviation from the international standard and the non-justifiability of the reasons for such deviation, is by stipulating an extremely low evidentiary weight required to discharge such burden. The AB has thus through its determination on the burden of proof effectively underscored the legitimacy of international standards.

We have not taken a firm stance on whether the outcome of the dispute – the declared illegality of the EC measure – is correct or not.

---

[4] *Korea – Measures Affecting Imports of Fresh, Chilled and Frozen Beef – Report of the Appellate Body* (WT/DS161/AB/R and WT/DS169/AB/R, November 12, 2000).

Instead, the brunt of our analysis has been to question the explanatory apparatus used by the AB. Both on issues of substance and on procedure, it helps neither the legitimacy of the AB nor the legitimacy of the WTO as a whole to decide issues such as the relevance of consensus decision making, the cultural integrity of a language, or the presumptions on burden of proof, without any meaningful analysis or even indication of an awareness of the deeper policy issues and consequences that are at stake. That is not, in our view, the correct way to apply the rules of interpretation of the Vienna Convention.

INDEX

Note: Cases are indexed under short forms; Agreements are indexed under abbreviations (eg SGA for the Agreement on Safeguards, TRIMs for Agreement on Trade-Related Investment Measures).

accountability 255
activism, judicial 129, 130
actori incumbit probatio maxim 29
adjudicating bodies, task of 29, 72, 263
adjustment, promotion of 112–114, 122
administrative review 14
adverse effects 47, 48, 49, 54, 56, 86
adverse selection 183, 184, 187
agricultural products 134, 154
Agriculture Agreement 133, 138–139,
   140–141, 146–148, 153, 157
aircraft, subsidization of sales of 88–98
aliens, protection of 188, 190, 192, 210
American Law Institute 3, 8
   Principles of Trade Law project 1, 2, 36
   Reporters' Studies 2–3, 4–11
Anti-Dumping Agreement 28, 119
antidumping duties 4, 12, 17, 28, 76
Appellate Body 10, 93, 123, 129, 275
   analysis of the Agriculture Agreement
      143–145
   Article 21.5 panels 91, 92
   burden of proof 263, 272
   causation 105, 106
   consequences of decisions 253, 258
   EC – Sardines 249, 250, 251
   evidentiary standards 5, 9
   interpretation of "benefit" 85
   interpretation of "injury" 104, 107
   interpretation of "similarity" 148
   interpretation of Paris Convention
      194, 196, 197
   interpretation of TBT Agreement 267

   interpretation of the GATT 108, 125,
      145–146, 148
   interpretation of the Safeguards
      Agreement 106
   interpretation of TRIPs 198–199,
      201, 203–204
   judicial economy 196, 199
   legitimacy of 252, 253, 275
   most favoured nation 206–208
   mutual recognition 208–219
   national treatment 206–208, 208–219
   non-attribution 120
   ownership of trademarks 203
   Paris Convention Article 8 204–206
   textualism 248–275
   and WIPO 200
Argentina 133–157
Argentina – Footwear 103, 105
arm's length operations 5, 241, 242,
   243, 244
automotive sector, India 158–178
autonomy, procedural 251
autonomy, regulatory 191, 194, 250,
   251, 274

Bagwell, Kyle 4, 7–8, 12–35, 133–157,
   158–178, 233
balance of payments defense, India
   165, 167
Beebe, B. 187
benchmark
   legal 15–17, 19–20, 23
   no-subsidy 9, 222, 229, 231–234, 245